WITHDRAWN

HARVARD LIBRARY

WITHDRAWN

On The Threshold Of The Closed Empire:
MID-19TH CENTURY MISSIONS IN OKINAWA

Edward E. Bollinger

William Carey Library

PASADENA, CALIFORNIA

BV
3450
.O4
B65
1991

Copyright 1991 by Edward E. Bollinger
All Rights Reserved

No part of this book may be used or reproduced in any manner whatsoever without written permission, except in the case of brief quotations embedded in critical articles and reviews.

Published by
William Carey Library
1705 N. Sierra Bonita Ave.
Pasadena, California 91104
818-798-0819

Library of Congress Catalog Card Number: 91-73083
ISBN 0-87808-230-1

Cover design by Beth Bollinger Glaze

Dedication

On the occasion of the One-Hundredth Anniversary of Baptist witness in Okinawa this book is gratefully and prayerfully dedicated to the pastors, evangelists and teachers of the Okinawa Baptist Convention, past and present, who have dedicated themselves to making our Lord Jesus Christ known, loved and served in the Ryukyu Islands and in all the world.

The Author

Contents

DEDICATION iii
ACKNOWLEDGEMENTS vii
PREFACE ix
INTRODUCTION (Edward E. Bollinger) xii
   The Objective of the Missionaries: Ryukyu or Japan?, xiii
   The Support of the Missionaries, xiii
   The Methods and Purposes of the Missionaries, xv
   The Fear of Proscribed Religion, xvi
   Protestant-Catholic Relations, xvii
   Overt Opposition to the Missionaries, xviii
   Bettelheim and Commodore Perry's Visit, xix
   The Second Landing of the Catholics, xx
   The Patience and Persistence of the Missionaries, xxii
PREPARATORY EPISTLE (William Leonard Schwartz) . . xxiii
MAPS xxvii

I. THE FIRST CATHOLIC MISSIONARY TO JAPAN OF THE NINETEENTH CENTURY (Msgr. Theodore-Augustine Forcade)
   Introduction 3
     Early Life and Education (Marbot), 3
     Forcade's Goal not Loo Choo, 4
     Character of Augustin Ko, 5
     The Political Situation, 6
     Forcade's Journal and Its Value, 7
   Chapter I: At Anchor in Naha. 8
   Chapter II: The First Mass. Dedication of the Mission. 19
   Chapter III: The Corvette Sails: Forcade's Reception. 30
     Appendix to Chapter III., 42
   Chapter IV: An English Schooner. The Bettelheims. 50
   Chapter V: The "Victorieuse" and the "Cleopatra" Arrive. 72

Chapter VI: Leturdu Writes of the Mandarin's Council. . . . 96

Chapter VII: The Admiral Will Report the Loochooan's Refusal. 113

Chapter VIII: (Extracts from) Departure. 127

II. THE CATHOLIC MISSIONARIES IN LOO CHOO: THE RELIGION OF JESUS CHRIST REVIVED IN JAPAN. (by Fr. Marnas)

I. From the Departure of Forcade (1846) to the First Abandonment (1848). 133

II. The Second Residence in Loo Choo, 1855 to 1862. . . . 149

III. THE PROTESTANT PIONEER: DR. BERNARD J. BETTELHEIM. (Edward E. Bollinger)

A. Introduction., 189

B. The British Seaman's Mission., 190

C. Bettelheim's Early Life and Preparation., 193

D. Landing in Okinawa., 197

E. Beginning His Ministry., 200

F. Growing Opposition., 203

G. Perseverence in Persecution., 206

H. Improved Opportunities, Persistent Opposition., 214

I. Bettelheim's Medical Practice., 218

J. Translations and Linguistic Studies., 222

K. Bettelheim and Commodore Perry., 224

L. Evaluation., 230

M. Postscript., 233

IV. CONCLUSION.

A. The Catholic Witness. 237

B. The Protestant Witness. 239

NOTES 241

BIBLIOGRAPHY 248

ABOUT THE AUTHOR 251

Acknowledgements

The author gratefully acknowledges the generous permission of Dr. and Mrs. Paul E. Mueller to use the handwritten translations and comments of Mrs. Mueller's father, Dr. William L. Schwartz, on the mid-19th Century Roman Catholic activity in Ryukyu. This material was inherited by Mrs. Virginia Mueller from her grandfather, Dr. Henry B. Schwartz, Methodist Missionary to Okinawa from the year 1906.

The cover design is the work of Beth Bollinger Glaze, who with her parents spent most of her years of childhood and youth in Okinawa, and to whom the Shurei no Mon (Gate of Courtesy) depicted on the cover of this work was a familiar sight.

The encouragement, assistance and loving patience of the author's wife, Margaret, who read proof, corrected many mistakes, and without whose help the work could not have been completed are thankfully recognized.

The author also wishes to acknowledge the invaluable assistance and patient efforts of a good friend, Charles Jenkins, in teaching him about word processors and helping put the whole manuscript into form for the publisher.

Edward E. Bollinger

Preface

Some years ago my book on the Christian message in Okinawa was published under the title, *The Cross and the Floating Dragon: The Gospel in Ryukyu*.[1] At that time I had no detailed record of the first Catholic fathers to serve in Okinawa in the mid-19th Century. With the help of the excellent doctoral thesis of Professor Yoshihiko Teruya, written for his Ph.D. degree at the University of Colorado,[2] I was able to write a chapter about the ministry of the first Protestant missionary to Ryukyu, Dr. Bernard J. Bettelheim.

After returning to the United States for retirement from missionary service, I was introduced by an Okinawan friend to Dr. and Mrs. Paul E. C. Mueller of Sacramento, California. Their deep interest in Okinawa stems from the fact that Mrs. Virginia Mueller is the granddaughter of the Rev. Henry B. Schwartz, the first Methodist missionary from the United States to reside on Okinawa and supervise the work of establishing Methodist churches there. His ministry began in Okinawa, after some years in Japan, in the year 1906.

Among the many books inherited by the Muellers from Mrs. Mueller's grandfather is a handwritten ledger in which Mrs. Mueller's father, Professor William Leonard Schwartz, had translated into English a 19th Century work in French by Mgr. Theodore-Augustin Forcade, with notes by Fr. E. Marbot, and part of a later work by Fr. Marnas, both of which deal with the mid-19th Century Catholic mission to Ryukyu.[3]

The early Catholic records set forth many details of which I was not aware when writing earlier about Bettelheim. It was very informative for me to read the Catholic record, and then compare and contrast the experience of the priests with that of Bettelheim, as recounted in my previous book. These two records together form the earliest account of Christian missionaries residing in what is now Japan in the 19th

Century, their trials and frustrations, and their respective accomplishments.

I have sought to make brief comparisons and contrasts between the ministries of these early missionaries, as well as noting the nature of the contacts they had with one another. It is obvious that the French clergy were very much hindered, in the long run, by the official support of the French naval commanders at various stages of their effort. The English missionary did not enjoy the same degree of support from the British ships, and he was much more bold and importune in his attempts to evangelize. His abilities as a medical doctor and as a linguist enabled him to make some lasting contributions to the people of Okinawa.

Portions of a further work concerning the Catholic mission on Okinawa, translated from the French by William L. Schwartz, is also herein included.[4] It deals with the time from the departure of Mgr. Forcade from Okinawa in 1846 to the first abandonment of the mission in 1848, and it recounts the second residence of Catholic missionaries in Okinawa from 1855 to 1862. Dr. William Leonard Schwartz, Professor of Romance Languages at Stanford University, translated the portions of this record which seemed to him most significant.

The large captions marking sections of the Catholic record are not a part of the original books, but are headings to the notebook translations from the French made by Dr. Schwartz.

I confess that I do not have the ability in French to check the accuracy of Prof. Schwartz' translations, but I have every confidence in the thoroughness of his work and in his careful choice of words in presenting the real thought of the original authors.

I have taken the liberty of adding some punctuation where it seemed to me to be necessary and of revising some phrases without changing the meaning in any way, but to add clarity to the text. Prof. Schwartz says in his *Prefatory Epistle* which follows: "In regard to linguistic errors, I am sure every page is marred with unidiomatic English and bad grammar, especially by many unmarked inversions of adverbial phrases and some misspellings, and to my attempt to be faithful to the French texts."

What liberties I have taken with Prof. Schwartz' translation, in the very few minor changes which have been made, I am confident make no changes at all in the meaning of his work.

This copier takes full responsibility for having accurately set forth Dr. Schwartz' translation.

The last major section of this work is a reproduction of my chapter on the work of Dr. Bernard J. Bettelheim in the book above-mentioned. While this is not Bettelheim's own record of his work, as are the Catholic missionaries' accounts of theirs, it presents a view of his life and work which allows one to compare and contrast the approaches of the Catholic and Protestant missions. And it contains many of Bettelheim's own comments, observations and interpretations. The *Introduction* is entirely my commentary on the Catholic and Protestant approaches to the Ryukyu Kingdom in the mid-19th Century.

Edward E. Bollinger

Introduction

There was intense interest in the Ryukyu Islands in the mid-19th Century on the part of western nations. The interest was occasioned because of the strategic location of the islands approximately three hundred miles off the coast of China and some eight hundred fifty miles southwest of Edo, the capital of the closed empire of Japan. Western powers were intent upon concluding treaties of friendship and commerce with China, and also with other smaller nations in the Western Pacific. They were especially concerned with normalizing relations with Japan, which had been all but closed to trade with the west since the beginning of the 17th Century.

Among the ships from western nations which had put in at Naha early in the century were the "Alceste" and the "Lyra," ships of the British Royal Navy. The visit of these ships to Okinawa was greeted by Okinawan fishermen in their sea canoes offering provisions of fresh water and food to the British. The way in which this visit led to the formation of the British Seamans Mission and the sending of the first Protestant missionary to Okinawa in 1846 is related below. It is obvious from the account that the goal of the British Seamans Mission was the evangelization of the Ryukyu Islands.

The entrance of the Roman Catholic Missionaries from France into the Ryukyu Islands in 1844 was quite a different story. As the record shows, Msgr. Forcade, the first head of the Catholic mission to Okinawa, spent the year 1842 in special training for his task as a missionary priest and set sail for Macao in 1843. Japan was his goal, but being barred from entry into that country he was taken to Okinawa through a special arrangement with the French naval forces. It was agreed from the beginning that Forcade should land in Ryukyu to learn the language of the country, at that time thought to be Japanese, and to serve as an interpreter for the French in concluding a treaty of friendship and commerce with the King of Okinawa. It was thought that this would create an opening to enter the "impenetrable Japanese Empire" for the French missionary priests.

Because of the initial role of the French priests as interpreters for the French navy and because of their stated goal to eventually reach the main islands of Japan in their mission endeavors, it has been said of them, "These men behaved themselves with patient restraint and made no overt attempts to win converts to Christianity."[1] Their approach to the people of Ryukyu was, indeed, far different from that of the British Protestant, but the record shows a patient and persistent effort on the part of both Catholic and Protestant missionaries to win Okinawans to the Christian faith. There were, of course, reasons why their methods varied, but their goals were very similar in the matter of evangelizing Ryukyu.

The Objective of the Missionaries: Ryukus or Japan?

The following record of the Catholic missionary priests indicates clearly that their objective in landing in the Ryukyu Islands was to find an opportunity to reach the main islands of Japan. Their excuse for remaining in Ryukyu, already stated, was to learn the language and act as interpreters. The record shows, however, that every occasion and opportunity was used to propagate the Christian faith among the people of Ryukyu.

On the other hand, the goal of the British Protestant was to communicate to the people of Ryukyu the Christian message. As his ministry progressed, it became his desire to reach the main Japanese islands, also, particularly with his translations of portions of the New Testament. He did not sufficiently realize at first that the dialect of Okinawa into which he had made the translations was not comprehended in the main islands of Japan.

The Support of the Missionaries

The head of the Catholic mission to Ryukyu, Father Forcade, having spent time in the *Seminaire of the Societe des Missions Etrangeres* and having joined this society of secular priests, was supported by that society. But he was also backed in his journey to and landing in Ryukyu by the French navy. The French admiral, in turn, received important advice from the missionaries, such as that which led to the removal of the French warships from Naha to Unten, where negotiations took place. (This move was extremely inconvenient for the Ryukyu Royal Party negotiating with the French, and it added to the display of French arrogance so evident throughout the discussions). There the French were very condescending in their treatment of the Okinawans. They made threats of force by displaying their power and sought to pry the doors to the kingdom open by using the treaty concluded with the Chinese following the Opium War.

In the negotiations with the Okinawans, it was clearly stated by the admiral that the priests were necessary as interpreters for France, and he requested teachers for them that they might learn the language. The admiral obtained all the requested benefits for the priests, though some of the agreed-upon liberties were neglected after the warships left the islands.

The Protestant missionary, Dr. Bernard J. Bettelheim, may have also benefited somewhat from the presence of the French warships. The record shows that his limited liberty to preach openly was in part due to the regular arrival of French men of war. He stated they had a deep moral effect on the entire country, including the rulers.

The British, on the other hand, were sometimes less than helpful. The British Admiral Cochrane was a decided hindrance, rather than a help. He accused Bettelheim, the missionary of the British Seamans Mission, a definitely private mission society, of misrepresenting his relationship with the British government to the officials of Ryukyu and recommended that his naturalization papers be cancelled. The missionary was forced to reply that the Okinawans had never been led to regard him as a British official. This was very evident, he said, in their failure to respond to his various requests. The British admiral made it plain that the missionary had come privately to the island to engage in a good work, but that the British government was not supporting him, nor did it have the authority to remove him.

In the year 1850, however, relations between the British missionary and the government of Okinawa were improved by a request made by the British government through Captain Craycroft of the H.M.S. "Reynard" that the Okinawan officials avoid any attempt to force the missionary out or persecute him in any way. This request by the British captain did indeed improve the situation for the missionary, as the record indicates.

The Methods and Purposes of the Missionaries

As previously stated, the Catholic mission in Okinawa was thought of by the missionary priests as a preparation for entering the main islands of Japan. But this did not hinder them in requesting permission to preach and teach the Christian faith. As they summarized their situation in writing, they stated that they sought diligently for the words in which to express their faith and longed for opportunities to share it with the people.

The Catholic missionaries were on occasion given hope by indications they received of the existence of secret believers and did their best to follow up the contacts which came their way.

The head of the Catholic mission, Msgr. Forcade, on a visit to the southern part of Okinawa saw the ruins of Tamagusuku Castle and expressed the thought that it would be an ideal site for a seminary and church, if only the government would allow them possession of the ruin for that purpose.

As far as the record shows, the Catholics were able to instruct only one convert to the Christian faith, that being in the second period of their presence in Okinawa, beginning in 1855.

The principal work of the Catholics was, indeed, to study the language and to use the opportunities afforded them in working with their interpreters and guards to propagate the faith. They state frankly that they had never preached in public like the Protestant, but admit that they had often done so in private whenever the opportunity afforded itself.

The Protestant, on the other hand, came to Okinawa with the support of a mission founded to propagate the Christian message to the people of Ryukyu. For this purpose he stated that from the beginning he intended to be their physician, their teacher of western learning, teaching European arts and sciences, and their evangelist.

There is an account in the following record of the measure of his success in these endeavors. His influence as a medical doctor, as a channel of western learning and as a source of technical information from the west to the Lords of Satsuma through the Kingdom of Ryukyu is well documented. He produced portions of the New Testament in the dialect of Ryukyu, and also a "Grammar and Dictionary of the Loochooan Language," a monumental piece of work which went unpublished and wound up in the British Museum.

All of his activities were aimed at the dissemination of the Christian message, but so far as is known, his eight years of activity in Ryukyu resulted in only five baptisms and an unknown number of inquirers. He is remembered today far more for his success in linguistic studies, for his translation of portions of the New Testament, and for his introduction of western medicine and technology to Okinawa and Japan than for his success as an evangelist, though his influence led indirectly to the sending of the first Protestant minister to begin lasting Christian work in Okinawa to that island in 1891.

The Fear of Proscribed Religion

The missionaries, both Catholic and Protestant, failed to appreciate the political situation of Okinawa as a country dominated by the Satsuma clan of Japan when they first arrived in mid-19th Century.

Christianity had been proscribed by Satsuma in the early 17th Century, and the early Catholic converts of Yaeyama had been tried and executed on New Year's Day, 1635, by the Ryukyu Kingdom under orders from Satsuma.[2] The prohibition of the Christian faith was announced by edict boards erected throughout the islands by Satsuma and by the *fumie* (crucifix to be tread upon in proof that one was not a Christian; found implanted in each port area) noted by the missionaries upon their arrival.

But with the arrival of the first Catholic missionaries in Ryukyu, the Senior Minister of the Japanese Government, following the advice of Satsuma, decided on a combined policy of leniency and severity, depending upon the occasion. It was determined that a measure of communication and trade with foreign powers would be beneficial to Japan, but the spreading of the Christian faith was not to be tolerated.[3]

Forcade noted very early after his arrival that there seemed to be no fear of the sailors from the French ships, and there was little fear of the missionaries, either, when officials were not present. But for those who had been informed of the reason why the missionaries came, when they knew of the proscription, and when they noted that the missionaries could use a bit of their language, there was real fear of communicating with them.

In the response of the officials to the requests of the French for a treaty of friendship, allowing for trade and commerce, the reply was that they were forbidden to trade with any nation but China. And they further declared, quite frankly, that their fear of Satsuma was the reason why no pact could be negotiated.

As for the Protestant, there appears to have been little understanding of the relation between the Ryukyu Kingdom and the Satsuma Clan, in the early phases of his ministry, at least. During most of his time in Ryukyu, he was cut off from the kind of contact with the people which would allow him to do the work he longed to do. After 1850, the visit of certain British ships carried messages from the British Government which caused a relaxation of surveillance on the part of the government of Okinawa, but the fear of the foreigner's religion still prevented the kind of contact for which the missionary longed. The fear of the Christian faith and the government's continued control of the missionary's activities strictly limited his effectiveness in accomplishing his mission, though his contributions to Okinawan society were varied and very significant.

Protestant-Catholic Relations

It should be noted that very early after their meeting, Bettelheim invited the Catholics to dine with him on Sunday, an invitation which was refused. He further attempted to share his scripture translations with them. The reply was that they would like a personal copy, including a Chinese translation, if that were available. It was their desire to check its accuracy with the Latin Vulgate. What came of this exchange, the record does not state. But the response was typical of the times in Protestant-Catholic relations, and we may assume that the translations, though carefully prepared, had little distribution anywhere at the time.

At the same time, Bettelheim requested that the priests share with him information on the subject of the Ten Lost Tribes of Israel, a matter on which he was collecting data. Mrs. Bettelheim sent a cake to Fr. Leturdu in return for some wine the Catholics had sent to Bettelheim on request, and in addition the Bettelheims sent twelve copies of the Gospel of John and a dissertation on the Ten Tribes.

At this point all desire for discussion between them appears to have been on the side of Bettelheim. The Catholic account indicates that they were definite in considering him an agent of heresy, an enemy of the mission of Mary, and one for whose conversion they should pray.

Leturdu's subsequent message to Bettelheim suggesting that they come together to frankly discuss their respective faiths was quite open to the possibility of different conclusions as to the truth. Indeed, he stated in his letter to Bettelheim that he believed they were thrown together in Okinawa by Divine Providence that they might consider the truth together.

The response of Bettelheim was to accept the challenge, but what came of the proposal is not clear. Bettelheim, on his part, stated that he believed that both of them had the doctrine of Christ, and that because they differed on major points did not mean that one of them was on the road to perdition. He was convinced that both of them were Christians.

Overt Opposition to the Missionaries

The event which marked the close of Bettleheim's public preaching ministry and put an end to the more public efforts of the Catholic fathers to visit house to house, particularly in Shuri, and disseminate their tracts occurred on October 31, 1847, the day set for the funeral of King Sho Ho. The priests had invited Bettelheim to accompany them to Shuri to pay respects to the king. This he did, and on the way they were attacked by a group of Okinawans. Bettelheim went to the defense of Adnet, one of the priests, protesting that they were simply on their way to pay respects to the king. The crowd calmed down, and the party returned unmolested. A more complete account of this event appears hereinafter, but it appears that Bettelheim was invited to go along with the priests because they had been warned to stay away from Shuri.

The French had been pelted with stones and threatened to be beaten in December, 1846. Their efforts at calling in homes had been concentrated in Shuri. Bettelheim reported the matter in his journal of December 26.[4]

This event probably made it more difficult for all the missionaries to engage in direct evangelistic efforts, but there is no evidence that they ceased their efforts. Indeed, Bettelheim's efforts led to more severe persecutions and even beatings.

The injuries he suffered from the beatings he received, on occasion for entering homes of noblemen uninvited, and on occasion for gathering produce from the marketplace in a way which angered the people, caused Bettelheim to appeal to the British government for protection.

It appears that the overt opposition to Bettelheim increased after the departure of the French missionaries in 1848, and he was stoned and left in the street after an altercation over a farmer's produce, which he had commandeered, in January, 1849.

Bettelheim's position was somewhat improved later in 1850, as previously stated. He complained to the British legation in China, and as a result, an angry reply and threat from the British Foreign Secretary was sent which sought better treatment for the missionary.

Bettelheim and Commodore Perry's Visit

Details of the influence of Bettelheim's perspectives on the situation in Ryukyu on Commodore Perry and his approach to the islands is hereinafter related. And also, the influence of the visit of the American ships to Ryukyu on the treatment of the missionary is noted. But by this time, the missionary was intent upon leaving. Although missionary help was on the way, Bettelheim was tired and not in very good health. There was some alienation from the leadership of the British Naval Mission, and Bettelheim decided to leave without the consent of the mission organization.

Bettelheim's influence, however, went beyond that which he was able to experience directly. The sharing of medical knowledge in Ryukyu with Okinawan doctors influenced their practice far beyond the missionary's stay in the island, and his sharing of European publications containing European technical and scientific knowledge with the Okinawa Regents were passed on to Nariakira, Lord of Satsuma, where the knowledge thus shared is said to have greatly influenced the period of the Meiji Restoration through Satsuma's role in it.

In addition to the contributions heretofore mentioned, Bettelheim aroused the interest of the people of Ryukyu with the words, "All men, including the king and the noble, are equal before God."[5] The time was not ripe for such revolutionary doctrine to make any great impress, but it was understood later as one of the great contributions of Christian faith to the society of Ryukyu.

The Second Landing of the Catholics

After four years in Ryukyu, Leturdu left for good on August 27, 1848. The second landing of priests took place on February 26, 1855. For their second entry into Ryukyu, the priests planned to attempt to avoid any appearance of government sponsorship, and in order to do so sought to be transported to Ryukyu by an American ship. This plan did not materialize, and they finally arrived on a French merchantman, the "Lion," and Captain Bonet of that ship sought to negotiate a place for them to stay and permission for them to remain. The permission which was eventually granted was only for two or three months, but they considered this a victory for their mission. They were quite sure that once settled in Ryukyu they would be able somehow to remain indefinitely.

Again, their real goal was the main islands of Japan, though they made every attempt to achieve meaningful contact with the people of Okinawa and do missionary work among them, their opportunities were very few, indeed.

By this time they understood that the Ryukyu dialect was not Japanese. It was for this reason that Bishop Forcade had previously elected to remain in Hongkong and study there with a Japanese convert to the Catholic faith. Finally, quite discouraged and in ill-health, he sent a letter to his superiors saying that he was weary of waiting for the opening of Japan, that he found his physical strength, as well as his moral and intellectual powers waning, and he requested to be landed on the shores of Japan without waiting for its opening to the western powers.[6] But he suffered ill health, and finally left China for good on

January 27th, 1852, three years before the second effort in the Ryukyus began.

The three missionaries who began the second mission to Ryukyu were Fathers Girard, Furet and Mermet, later joined by Fr. Mounicou, who had been assigned to Japan, but was unable to land there. They moved to the old temple site which the Catholics had previously occupied, but later succeeded in building a house in the center of the city of Naha. But they immediately found that they were effectively isolated from contact with any neighbors and were no more able to do the work for which they had come than previously.

During this second period of Catholic missions in Ryukyu, though they were able to study the Japanese language to a limited degree, they experienced only one conversion among the teachers with whom they had contact. The story of the persecution meted out by this man's family and his subsequent disappearance are related in the narrative of "The Second Residence."

They were effectively isolated from the community, and they reported, "a conversation with us entails capital punishment." M. Mermet wrote: "It is like living in a desert. This was formerly one of the busiest streets; now it is overgrown with grass and thorns." There were various changes in mission personnel, but the mission was not abandoned until 1862. Some of the missionaries were able to find their way to Japan. M. Girard arrived in Yedo, September 6, 1859, where he was present at the formal ratification of the French treaty with Japan. He was recognized as interpreter for the French Consul-General.[7]

M. Mermet reached Hakodate in November, 1859, where he gave lessons in French and English. He had a house built at the cost of $100, and a month later began work on a chapel. There he experienced both Buddhist curiosity and Buddhist opposition.[8]

M. Monicou left Okinawa in 1861, and M. Petitjean removed to Nagasaki in 1862, having spent two years in Ryukyu. It was he who made contact with the "Old Catholics" remaining true to their faith after the proscription of Christianity at the beginning of the Tokugawa Shogunate in the 17th Century.[9]

In 1866, M. Furet reached Nagasaki, having left Ryukyu in 1862.

It was the French ship "Dupleix" which carried the word to Ryukyu that the missionaries were to be removed. The Okinawans were overjoyed at the news. They reimbursed the French for the building of the mission residence and a wall enclosure.

The mixture of relief and sadness at leaving Ryukyu is reflected in the words of Furet written to Libois about the final departure: "It was a heart-break for me. May we at least do a little more in Japan!"

As the following document shows, eighteen years had elapsed from the beginning of the Catholic mission to Loo Choo under Msgr. Forcade and the termination of the effort as Fr. Furet left the islands in 1862, no exact date being given.

The Patience and Persistence of the Missionaries

The whole account of both Catholics and Protestants shows clearly their deep devotion to their mission, the extreme pathos of the situation in which they were placed, the unremitting opposition of the authorities, the great patience with which they pursued their goals, and the inevitable irony of the confrontation between the missionaries and the officials of Ryukyu.

Edward E. Bollinger

Preparatory Epistle

To my Dear Father: Merry Christmas and a Happy New Year!

In offering you this compilation from French sources of materials relating to Loo Choo, and more particularly to the work of the Catholic missionaries there, a few words of introduction are urgently needed. This MS has been a growth, as my original purpose was only to translate Archbishop Forcade's Journal, supplementing the same with notes from the biography by Marbot, as my title page indicates clearly enough. I then began to prepare a list of foreigners connected with Loo Choo based on Papinot's dictionary, which you will find on pp. 122-4; and as I took down "Togo's Country" to get the name of Moreton, I was reminded that I had not yet discovered the piquant incident relating to Bettleheim's preaching, as told by Leturdu on page 129. I therefore at once took down the book by Marnas, whose existence I had completely forgotten, and in three days I transcribed the 70 pages giving us an account of the last years of the Catholic missionaries, and on the fourth day, I felt obliged to search in Pages for those facts relating to Loo Choo and the activity of the missionaries there in the 17th Century (pp. 175-178). This may account for some of the many blemishes in this work, for which I must ask your indulgence.

In the matter of bibliographical notes, I have transcribed the title pages of each work consulted, and these will be found at the commencement of the citations. In giving the dates of letters, I have often embodied the author's note in the text, but I have not failed to give these whenever they were to be quoted. In all cases the errata have been untouched, though often marked with a 'sic', and every utterance given in direct quotation has been quoted in full. Nor has one single mention of Loo Choo been omitted, nor any speech of the missionaries. Occasionally a word has been inserted in order to complete the meaning of a phrase, and dates have been added often for convenience. Of course I have been helpless in the face of omissions, marked...., to be found in my originals. Great divergence is to be found in the spelling of proper names. Marnas and Pages and Papinot each use different uniform spellings, while Forcade usually follows the Chinese pronunciation. I have made no attempt at uniformity in this matter. As the headings of each page have been added rather hastily, it may be that some of them will not seem very apt. For this, I must again ask your indulgence.

I can fairly say that there are no errors of transcription in this work. In regard to linguistic errors, I am sure every page is marred with unidiomatic English and bad grammar, especially by many unmarked inversions of adverbial phrases and some misspellings. These are all due to my haste, and to my attempt to be faithful to the French texts. Here, too, certain inconsistencies are to be noted. Capital letters have been applied to the Deity and to sacred things in accordance with French usage. The title of Monsieur has sometimes been deleted. Lastly, I must mention the words: *gardes* (Eng. guards or keepers), *bonnets* (caps or hats or bonnets), *confrere* (the word used by the missionaries about each other: brothers, companion, co-worker, co-laborer, colleague, confrere), *bonzerie* (a neologism applied to Buddhist temples or monasteries) and *mission* (meaning mission or field of labor), in which my renderings are apt to vary greatly and may often be wrong. For this I ask once more for your indulgence.

In facilitating the use of this book, I have added a few cross-references, but not half as many as are really needed. The page-headings may also facilitate your consultation of the book. The list of foreigners, though unfortunately badly out of order, has been verified by reference to all sources at my command, the Encyclopedia, etc. It was a great convenience to me in my work to have all biographical material concentrated for the purpose of ready reference, and I also flatter myself on the discovery of some new facts and books about Loo Choo. I am sorry to say that there exist certain lacunae which I am quite unable to remedy. The most curious of these is the fact that the exact day of the abandonment of Loo Choo in 1862 is not stated anywhere in my books.

As for the value and utility of this work, it is a mine of judgments and descriptions by clever writers, many of which hold good today.

Take for instance, the naive declaration of Bonnet, the French merchant captain about the people of Loo Choo, on (page 148), or Father Mermet's paragraph detailing the qualifications needed for a missionary in Loo Choo (p. 158). Such quotations add spice and interest to any narrative.

> I remain, very respectfully,
> Your affectionate son,
> William Leonard Schwartz
> Kagoshima, Dec. 19, 1911

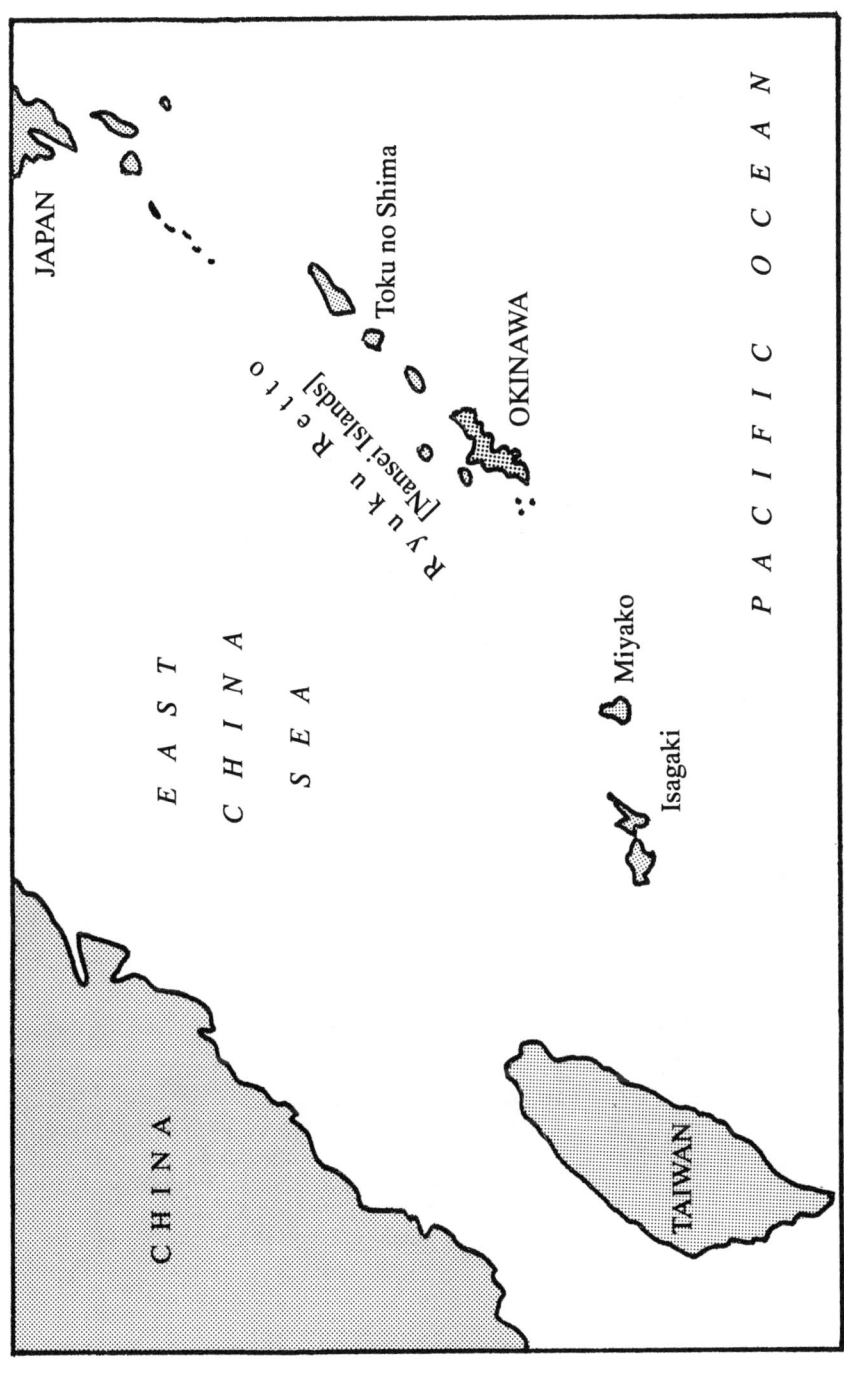

Selected portions of:

LE PREMIER MISSIONAIRE CATHOLIQUE DU JAPON AU XIXme SIECLE

par

Mgr. Theodore-Augustin Forcade,
Archeveque d'Aix

Lyon, 1885

Bureaux des Missions Catholiques

Avec des notes tirees de "la Vie de Mgr. Forcade"
par le chanoine E. Marbot
Aix: Achille Makaire, Editeur. 1886.

Note: Translated from the original French to English by William. L. Schwartz, December, 1911. Verbatim translation of pp. 1-138. Also, extracts from chapters VII and IX.

Introduction

Early Life and Education (Marbot)

Theodore Augustine Forcade was born March 2, 1816, at Versailles; the son of an employee of the prefecture Seine-et-Oise, who later received a collectorship in the village of Epone. At the age of nine, Forcade's education began at the Petite Seminaire of the larger town of Mantes, where the rough and simple ways of the school tempered a rather turbulent and impetuous temperament, and also laid the foundations of a most vigorous constitution. In 1824 he removed to the Petit Seminaire of the city of Versailles, a school of 800 pupils, not all of whom were destined for the priesthood. In 1830 this school was broken up on account of the Revolution of Paris, but his secondary education was continued and completed at Mantes.

In 1834 he entered the Grand Seminaire at Versailles, and completing his course in theology in 1838, he became for a short time professor in the reestablished Petit Seminaire. March 16, 1834, he was ordained a priest, aged 23 years and 14 days. The next year he was made vicar and administrator of the difficult parish of Sucy, whose incumbent had been judged incapable of guiding his flock, who could not be removed. After one year of barren labor, he was appointed professor of philosophy in the Grand Seminaire, where he was not in the least successful.

He had already turned his thoughts toward the Orient, and after spending the year 1842 in the *Seminaire of the Societe des Missions Etrangeres,* joined this society of secular priests, and set sail for Macao, January 20th, 1843.

Arrival at Macao. Forcade's Plans. Note on His Journal

He fought against seasickness by following the advice of a sailor. "Strive to keep from lying down, and fill the stomach every time it empties itself." Four days sufficed to effect a complete cure, and after a voyage of 7 months, Macao was reached on the 23rd of August.

Macao was the financial base of the missions in China. This station was in the hands of Father Libois. As he was entitled to choose an assistant, and as he liked Forcade, the latter was made a member of his household, but failed to please. Japan was his goal, but Forcade felt barred from this country by the impious *ju-sumi* (*yefumi*,* mistake due to the gothic letters jefumi of the letters from the Jesuits). It was now 1844, and the Opium War had obtained the opening of several ports to Bristish commerce. The French Ambassador, Lagrenee, now planned to obtain the same privileges from the neighboring states, and an agreement was made with the French naval forces that Forcade should be transported to Japanese soil, or at least, to the Lieou-Kieou Islands. (Marbot notes that this spelling variation was from an abstract of a fuller diary, unfortunately lost, the abstract being made at Manila in 1846). Here it would be given out that Forcade was sent by the admiral to learn the language of the country and to serve as an interpreter in the following negotiations.

Forcade's Goal Not Loo Choo. Note on Admiral Cecille

After having thus created an opening in the impenetrable Japanese Empire, he would see a suitable occasion later to push his steps further. This was the plan. Its execution must be marked by a consecrated boldness. Forcade was ready, and Cecille** the French admiral, was no less prepared.

---

* *Yefumi* — the crucifix upon which all must tread to prove rejection or non-affiliation with Christianity.

**Rear-Admiral Cecille, whose name is so often mentioned in these pages, was born of a family of working people who lived at Rouen. As a child, he showed his vocation for the sea by sailing around his father's flooded cellar in a washtub. Later he ran away from home, travelling on foot from Rouen to Havre and shipped as a cabin-boy on a merchant vessel. For this action, he asked and received his father's forgiveness, and he was then "pressed" into the Navy by the First Empire. Here he was assigned to the post of cook, but he succeeded another sailor, who had been killed, as wardroom steward and attracted the attention of the officers, one of whom taught him to read, and when peace was signed, he was able to enlist as a volunteer cadet, thus opening the road to promotion. Later he became vice-admiral, ambassador at London, Senator of the Empire, and, by the request of Forcade, he was made a count by Pope Pius IX. He was the life-long friend of Forcade.

A note by Marbot says: "Let us notice an act of the admiral's, touching in its simplicity. At the time when Forcade served with the admiral, he noticed that out of a very fine silver service, a certain worn knife and fork had the preference of the admiral, who always used it himself. His intimacy allowed him to put a question to the admiral, and the latter told him that when he became an officer his mother,

The admiral himself was detained in China by the ambassador. However, he detached the corvette "Alcmene" from his fleet to conduct the so-named future interpreter of the French navy to his destination, and he gave orders to Captain Duplan, commander of the vessel, that on no account should he allow himself to be carried away by his feelings and interfere with the missionary.

The "Alcmene" then prepared for departure and set sail on April 3rd, 1844, reaching Nafa on the 28th of the same month.

Character of Augustin Ko

Forcade did not go on board alone. Of course, a catechist was a necessity, and there was at this time a tested Christian at Macao. Professor of the faith, he had spent two years in the prisons of Canton, pinioned, sleeping on straw, and devoured by vermin, but refusing firmly to buy his liberty by betraying his conscience. Ad. Cecille himself was the person who had obtained his freedom. He was named Augustin Ko.*

He was indeed the man who was needed at the side of the one who was to become the first missionary to Japan in the XIXth century. Forcade did not fail to recognize in him the providential companion of his apostleship. "And having chosen this new Silas, he departed,

---

gathering together all her savings, had made him a present of these articles. Even at that time they were no longer things of value, for they bore the monograms of two successive owners. These initials were effaced in a way that they could still be seen, and, proud of her child, the poor mother had "M. Cecille" inscribed on the handles. At the summit of his honors the admiral desired no other silverware for his own use. One day, nevertheless, with a poorly concealed excess of emotion, he said to Msgr. Forcade: 'My dear lord, you will live much longer than I: I may die at sea, or anywhere, and I would be inconsolable if this set were lost. Here, take these, and keep them to remember me by; they are the only things by which I set any store.' When he visited the bishop at his see of Nevers, he always used the gift of his mother."

* Note by Marbot: "Augustin Ko owed his imprisonment to his loyalty to his religion. He was arrested at the moment when he was guiding a missionary into the interior of China. After having been the companion of Mgr. Forcade, he was recalled to the province of Yunnan, his home. Very intelligent, a very good latinist, and above all, very virtuous, he has been raised since then to the priesthood." (The above is an abstract of pp. 1-55 of Marbot's book).

surrendered by his brothers to the inspiration of the grace of God: *Paulus vero, electo Sila, profectus est, traditus gratiae Dei a fratribus."*

The Political Situation

The time is 1844. England had just humiliated the Celestial Empire, and her victorious arms had compelled the Son of Heaven to open several of his ports to her and to recognize her right to import opium and with it the depravity and ruin of which the baleful narcotic is the source. The circumstances were favorable to assure to France the liberty of her commerce and her beliefs. The government of Louis Phillipe charged Monsieur de Lagrende, its minister plenipotentiary, with this mission; and Admiral Cecille had the order to assist the negotiations by making a demonstration with his fleet which, according to his orders, should not be other than peaceful.

While M. de Lagrende negotiated with the Chinese government and obtained from it a treaty favorable at the same time both to our commerce and to our holy religion, Ad. Cecille profited by the favorable opportunity, and tried to enter into relations with Annam, Korea, Japan, and the kingdom of Lieou-Kieou, and, if it was possible, to conclude treaties with them, which would, according to his idea, open these countries to the commerce and civilization of France.

With this purpose, the admiral resolved to visit these various countries, but he could not execute his project at once. Kept himself in China during the negotiations of M. de Lagrende, he detached the corvette "Alcmene" from his squadron, commanded by Captain Fornier-Duplan, and sent her to reconoitre the Loo Choo Islands. At the request which he made to the Procurer General of the *Missions Etrangeres,* a young missionary, newly arrived from Europe, and a Chinese catechist, Augustine Ko, whom the admiral had just rescued from the prisons of Canton, where he had been detained for his faith, took passage on board in the capacity of interpreters. Their purpose was to establish themselves in the Loo Choo Islands if circumstances allowed. It was this missionary and this catechist who had the glory of being the first to commence the grand work of the resurrection of the Church of Japan.

Forcade's Journal and Its Value

The "Alcmene" set sail April 3, and after 25 days of navigation, safely arrived in sight of the Loo Choo Islands. We reproduce the most interesting portion of the journal of Forcade, where we find, noted day by day, the details of his sojourn in these isles, and the first relations of France with the Japanese.

Nothing is better able to give us an idea of the prejudices which existed then among this people and their aversion for foreigners, with, at the same time, a glimpse of their manners and customs. Whoever only knows the Japanese by what he sees of them today, and who would judge the past by the present, would fall into strange error. In a few years this nation has advanced with gigantic strides in what is usually called modern progress, and her present infatuation for European civilization is only equalled by the horror she had of it in the past. From this point of view, the journal of Forcade is doubly interesting. It is a page of history, and it is, so to speak, the story of the archaeology of a people who no longer exist.

Chapter I
At Anchor In Naha

Visitors

April 28, 1844. Feast of the Patronage of St. Joseph. The weather has turned fair, the brilliant sun arises, we are favored by the breeze. As soon as it was dawn, we began to move toward the bay of Napa. While sailing along, we frequently noticed some of the islanders who observe us from the coast, we also met fishing boats, passing close to them, but none of them came along side.

At last, at exactly nine o'clock, we were in the harbor, and we let the anchor drop. The sails were not completely furled before a boat came to the ship's side. It brought out to us the famous Aniah, with whom Dumont d' Urville had already made us acquainted, and another mandarin who took precedency over him, though they both wore the same kind of cap and costume. Four lesser officers accompanied them, two of whom, interpreters no doubt, somehow manage to murder a little English. These six persons wore clothes which only differ slightly from those of the Japanese; they spoke and understood Mandarin Chinese very well, though amongst themselves they made use of another language which seemed very agreeable to our ears.

The commander received them in his apartments, and, with Augustin, I was the only one who assisted at the interview. It is useless to give here the answers to the questions, "From where have you come? Who are you?" and the like. We in turn asked their names and titles, and when they said merely that they were officers of the governor, Capt. Duplan requested an audience with that high personage in order to himself inform him of the goal of his voyage. The envoys then manifested the desire to have in writing the names and titles of the commander, your servant and Augustin; the name of the ship, its dimensions, the number of guns and other insignificant matters. All this was written out by Augustin. The interview closed itself with a collation which the captain had served to them, and to which they did justice. Then, after having conversation in a friendly manner with us during almost an hour, our visitors, who had the best faces one could possibly imagine, regained their craft, and returned to their city.

Let us note, however, that under the good-nature, they showed themselves extremely reserved on all that which concerned their country. I asked them several times what was the language which they spoke among themselves; whether it was a tongue peculiar to their islands, or whether it was Japanese, and I was never able to get any answer. Sometimes they pretended not to understand, sometimes they gave an answer which did not agree in any way with my question. Augustin, on his side, asked them where their king dwelt. They all appeared taken aback, and having taken council together in an uneasy manner, they ended by making no answer.

Between 5 and 6 p.m., the inferior officers came back with three boats, and they brought water, wood, poultry, saki (the fermented liquor of the country), eggs and other provisions, together with a letter from the governor to the captain.

Prostrate at the feet of the excellent Fornier-Duplan, they offered him all that we have just enumerated, and would grant him the desired audience on the morrow. When dawn broke, a pilot would put out to the corvette to steer her to a better mooring than the one where we are at present, and after this, the solemn audience would take place.

While the provisions they brought are being unloaded, the boatmen moved freely through the ship; they showed themselves to be gay and delightfully amicable, and generally they had an intelligent air. The mandarins descended to the wardroom where the officers feasted them, and Augustin followed them there to make them chatter. These gentlemen only withdrew at nightfall.

Preparations for the Interview with the Governor of Nafa

I add nothing about the view of Nafa or the rather numerous junks at the anchorage. I wish to see them better and to inform myself more fully before I speak of them.

Upon going on deck to say my prayers, I noticed one thing which was rather strange, and for the present, I cannot imagine any explanation for it. While one village, situated at the northern tongue (perhaps: at the tongue of land to the north) of the bay appears illuminated like the *rue de Rivoli* at Paris, we do not see even a stump of a candle burning in Nafa.

April 29th. In the morning, as they had promised, two pilots conducted by petty officials came on board. We changed our anchorage and we are placed in a more sheltered position in the bay, but at the same time we have been guided as far as possible from the town, and brought nearer to the village which was so brilliantly illuminated last night. They presumed to make us take this place for the capital. Our interview today with the governor of the city is also to take place in this village. Aided by pencilled notes taken during the meeting itself, I am going to try to give an account of it, and I hope to be able to do so with the most minute exactness.

Toward the appointed hour of 1 p.m., two of our boats, fully manned, conducted us on shore. The captain was accompanied by his second in command, the surgeon-major, and several other officers, all in field uniform, as well as Augustin and myself. We wore our best European clothes without any other distinguishing marks. Three mandarins with yellow caps and several other officers of lower rank awaited us on the shore. About them were crowded a numerous throng which appeared to be generally composed of men of the lowest class.

Scene of the Negotiations. The Governor.

Hardly had we taken a few steps on the beach before we had already reached the place for the interview. A man dressed in bluish silk, covered with a purple cap, dressed in good style, but without any mark of luxury, at once appeared there to receive us. He seemed to have a respectable countenance and to be about 60 years old. The others told us that he was the governor.

Now, imagine if you will, in a fairly large enclosure, badly tended and surrounded with poor walls, a kind of wooden hovel; the floor covered with mere matting, the walls decorated with two or three grotesque figures painted on blue paper, and you will have a fair idea of the palace in which we entered. Moreover, it is evidently intentional that we are to be received in this miserable spot. The people of Loo Choo attempt above everything to pass for a poor, indeed, a very poor nation in the eyes of foreigners.

However this may be, we attempted to begin our business. The captain, placing me on his right, and having a lieutenant on his left, seated himself at the end of the room, before the opening of a kind of alcove on a plank raised about half a foot above the ground. The French officers, the mandarins and the governor himself, squatted on the ground, and the diplomatic seance began.

Before speaking the captain pointed out the mandarin with the purple cap who had gone to seat himself at the other end of the room, so that the two men could not converse together directly.

"Is this mandarin the governor of Nafa?" asked the captain. "Would the governor deign to come closer to me so that I may communicate more easily with him?"

"In a moment," was the reply.

Nevertheless, tea, tobacco and pipes are passed by sturdy fellows, wearing red caps, but who appear to be only hangers on or domestics. There are at least a dozen of them. At last their work is over, and they retired.

The Interview. Captain Duplan Speaks
The French Emporer's Message Delivered

The captain spoke. "Now could the mandarin come closer?"

"The governor does not understand the Chinese language; you cannot communicate directly with him," they said.

"But there are interpreters here who know Chinese, and who no doubt speak the language of their own country. We can converse by means of them. Why has the governor disturbed himself for us? We could have gone to meet him at his own house at Nafa," said the captain.

"You are in the city of Nafa, in the governor's house," they said.

"But no, we are not there. The city is not here. It is yonder." said the captain.

"And yet, this is the governor's house," they replied.

"Certainly this is not his habitual residence. I ask why he has taken the trouble to move?" said the captain.

"It was to do you more honor," they answered.

"You are very kind," answered the Captain, with the air of a man who was not convinced of the fact.

He continued: "For 200 years the Emperors of France and China having always been friends, our Emperor (Louis Phillipe was not such, but the title was assumed to give him equity with Oriental potentates) has always sent some warships to China, but the intercourse between the two empires having increased, he now sends many more ships. He has given orders to the commanders of these vessels to visit the neighboring countries to see if their kings do not wish to form alliances with him and open commercial relations. He has declared, moreover, that it is nowise his intention to disturb these other countries in any way whatsoever, and that, on the contrary he would be always ready to support the laws of justice and equity, and that he would even lend help to the weak against the strong, if justice willed it thus... This is why I, Fornier-Duplan, Post Captain, have put in at your island, and I have no other purpose than to offer your King the friendship of our Emperor."

In reply it was said: "We are already friends of your Emperor. You see that we receive you kindly, and we ask nothing better than to supply you with whatever you may need. Concerning commerce, our country is small, it is poor, and we have nothing to exchange for your European articles, which are all like to many precious stones." This answer was made by an interpreter. This man appeared very honest. We had seen him two or three times on board, and on account of his manners, we agreed in considering him some great personage in disguise. He made answer for himself without saying a word to the governor.

The captain went on: "It is not your answer that we seek, but that of the governor. Translate, therefore, to him what we have told you, and give us his answer, and not yours."

"The governor does not understand Chinese," they said.

"Well, you understand it, and you certainly also can speak the language of your country, so do communicate our words to him," the captain requested.

"The governor does not speak Chinese, but he can read it; you must therefore make your requests in writing, and after that he will make answer. As for me, I fear lest I should misunderstand your words," said the interpreter.

"Well, as it appears to me that you cannot give us an answer without previous reflection, and as on the other hand we are only to remain here a few days, I shall warn you that a larger ship will come in one month, bringing the commander-in-chief of all the French ships in these seas. You will have to give your answer to this high dignitary," the captain warned.

"Please, then write all of that," the interpreter requested.

The announcement of the near arrival of the Cleopatre, Ad. Cecill's flag ship, seemed, moreover, to please them very slightly. In the meantime, the red-capped officers arrived for the second time carrying some pretty little tables loaded with delicacies. Farewell to politics!

"But I have not finished!" exclaimed the Captain. "I have still more to say!"

No answer. But the impassive governor came and placed himself before the captain's table, while the yellow-capped mandarins shared the other tables with our staff. We ate their pastries and stews with the aid of Chinese chop-sticks, and found them very nicely served and not in the least disagreeable.

The Captain, after a proper lapse of time, again spoke: "This is enough. I have other things to tell you. The Commander-in-Chief having need, as I do, of interpreters among your people, has given me the order of leaving in your island the Chief Imperial Interpreter, named Forcade, and another interpreter of lower rank. I beg you to take the greatest care of them and to furnish them with all the necessaries of life. They will pay you, moreover, for all their expenses and will submit themselves to the laws of your kingdom."

Forcade, Chief Imperial Interpreter.
The Question of Payment.

A profound sensation is produced; emotion is painted on every face.

"Do not say such things in public," they cautioned.

"Before my officers it makes no difference; if you have people who embarrass you, you are quite free to send them away!" said the captain.

In fact, a fairly good number of curious on-lookers gathered around the wide-open hall were sent away. This operation performed, they repeated again and again: "Do write this. Write this!"

Nevertheless, the excitement seemed to be continually growing among the mandarins. Conquered by fear, they did not dare to say no, but in their hearts they surely desired to refuse.

"According to your request," continued the captain, "tomorrow we will give you all this in writing; then you may answer at leisure. I thank the governor for his generosity to me yesterday, but as I will need a much larger quantity of fresh provisions, I beg him to tell me of an honest man who can furnish meat at a fair price with water, beef, sheep, pigs, etc. My intention is to pay for everything. It is the custom of the French to deal thus with all foreign nations."

In reply they said: "We will give you whatever you need, but what you ask is of too little value for us to accept your silver; our kingdom, though poor, can make you a present of it."

The captain: "I have a crew of 140 men. One ox a day would hardly be enough, and we cannot impose on you such a heavy burden as that of feeding us. If we should not pay, we would be much embarrassed, and from our scruples, we would not be able to ask for things that we need of you."

They answered: "Do not fear to ask; these things are of little value."

The captain replied, "I insist absolutely on paying; once again, our customs demand it."

The answer: "And our customs forbid us from taking your money. At any rate, accept these things now; write out your request, and we shall see about it later."

The captain: "A puff of wind having broken a spar of our ship, we desire to buy another!"

The answer: "We can easily furnish you a suitable stick of timber, and you will not need to pay for it."

The Captain: "We wish to pay for it."

The response: "Well, we give it to you, and will discuss payment later; but you must show us the French unit of measure."

Minor Privileges Requested.
The Captain Takes a Walk.

I presented them with a metre. It was passed from hand to hand and seemed to command general admiration.

"Could we have a drawing of the timber needed?" they asked.

The captain sketched it in pencil, and the drawing was given thereon. This business was more simple for them than the rest.

"I ask for all my officers," added the captain, "The permission to go walking in the country, and even in the town of Naha."

"They may go for walks along the coast in the part of the island where we now are, but they must on no account enter the town," they replied.

"Why may they not go into the town?" inquired the captain.

"It is more pleasant to walk in the country," they replied.

Though this was a poor answer, the captain did not think it wise to insist on this matter.

"Tomorrow is the birthday of our Emperor. Now it is the custom on such a day to dress ship and fire 21 guns at noon, but loaded only with powder, and I forewarn the governor of this custom. If he foresees that the noises of the cannon might frighten the populace we will abstain from this, notwithstanding. I also invite the governor and the mandarin next in rank to him to dinner at 4 o'clock," said the captain.

"You may fire the salute. We even wish to hear it. The governor accepts your invitation to dinner with thanks," they replied.

"When the officers go ashore, may they hunt?" the captain inquired.

"Yes, provided they do not use firearms," they replied.

"Why not? With what are they going to hunt, then?" asked the captain.

"The noise of the muskets might frighten the people. Also, someone might be killed," they said.

"The sound of a cannon pleases you, and you are afraid of the report of a musket? Do not be uneasy. No one will be killed. To whom should the document you have requested be submitted?" inquired the captain.

"We will send out to your ship for it," they said. It was about 3 p.m. when the audience was terminated.

Police and Populace

Our first care upon quitting the audience was to move about in the enclosure where we found ourselves. It appeared melancholy and badly kept. At one extremity opposite the gate was a little edifice on piles, somewhat dilapidated and of shabby appearance. It was closed, and we did not ask to have it opened for us, but we were told it was a temple of the kami. The governor was still there when we left. He had waited, we were told, in order to show us respect. The captain wishing to take a little walk with us, we first turned to the left, following the shore of the sea. The crowd which we had seen at the moment of our disembarkment preceded and followed us, surrounding us in every direction, but their attitude was respectful, and they kept such a profound silence that we were astonished. If sometimes a few of the bolder ones allowed themselves to approach too close to us, the members of the police fell upon them with severe blows from their bamboos, and the poor fellows, without saying a word, withdrew at once with truly admirable docility.

Everything went smoothly up to this point, but when, soon after, withdrawing a few steps from the shore, we wished to enter a short distance into the interior, endless objections and supplications began.

"Don't go yonder. Our wives and children are there. They are afraid; go over there; follow this path," they pleaded.

In brief, these annoying officials, after making us pass through a little grove, had skill enough to bring us back in a few minutes exactly to the point whence we had started. Wearied and annoyed, the captain judged that the best thing for us was to return to our boats, and at ten minutes of four we were on board.

The above is a faithful account of the first interview. I have read it to the captain and to Augustin, and both of them found it perfectly exact.

April 30. In the morning several of our officers went ashore again, going in different directions with the intention of employing no violence, but of going wherever they might wish, making no exception of the town of Nafa. In order not to compromise my future ministry, I left them to make this useful but delicate experiment, and I remained on board, waiting for the results. It was hardly 3 o'clock when two or three of the adventurers came back. As yesterday, the petty mandarins wished to prevent them from leaving the shore. But without disturbing themselves over the prayers, protestations and prostrations, they none the less peaceably continued their walk. The simple people, far from having a timid or hostile air, appeared, on the contrary, to be delighted to see them. They tried every means of approaching and showing politeness to our officers, and nothing but horrible blows were able to drive them away.

Toward noon, three of the petty mandarins from the town came on board. Among them was the little interpreter named *Ikaridziki*, who we meet everywhere, and who decides all questions alone. They represented themselves as sent by the governor to seek the document promised yesterday, and also to enquire what we wished in the way of provisions; but their true purpose evidently to complain of the officers ashore who had taken the liberty of advancing into the interior of the country and the town. They were given the letter with a memorandum about the provisions, and answer was made to the principal item of their request that it was unreasonable and impossible to compel the officers to only walk in the sunshine of the beach. Therefore, they would go wherever they wished, as long as they did no harm, and without the captain making any objection.

Sailors Kindly Treated Ashore; The Mandarins Surprised

"But the people are not used to seeing strangers, and they are afraid," they said.

"It is not true. Yesterday we noted just the opposite. The people welcomed us most cordially," we replied.

"Well, then, the women and children," they said.

"If they are afraid of us, then let them stay at home. Once more, we repeat that we do not desire and will not do you any harm, but we cannot submit to any of your demands that are out of place. We will go wherever we please, with the exception of houses, into which we have not the least intention of entering," we replied.

While this conversation took place on the ship, an officer embarked in a boat with the intention of ascending the course of a river which passes through the town. He was able to read satisfaction there on every face, but he had none the less to put up with the protests of the petty mandarins who vainly begged him not to continue his excursion. On his return, he was much astonished to find his boat filled with cakes, sweetmeats and provisions of every kind. The men of the people, unknown to the mandarins off on the scent of the officer tourist, had plunged into the water to take the sailors on their shoulders, and carry them to shore. Not being able to succeed as fully as desired, they brought them delicacies for themselves and their companions.

In the afternoon, a little before nightfall, Ikaradziki and an old fellow brought us an ox, some pigs, goats and a magnificent piece of timber. These men were brought down into the officer's quarters, and as they professed to have never seen any Frenchmen, they seemed to have much difficulty in distinguishing us from the English. Maps of France and England only threw a very dim light on the difficulty, but what caused them veritable stupefaction was a tolerably exact view of Nafa which they were shown in the voyage of Dumont d'Urville.* They were more and more astonished in recognizing, in three or four other lithographs, their costumes, and even the features of old friends. When finally they were told the adventures of Aniah with the Europeans, and when it was affirmed that all their history was written in that book, they could not disguise their profound uneasiness.

---

* French vice-admiral. Three trips around the world. Rescued La Perouse. d. 1842.

Chapter II
The First Mass

Dedication of the Mission: The Vow

May 1st. Since my departure from Macao I have been unable to once offer the holy sacrifice of the mass. Today, feast of the Apostles Peter and James, and the first day of the dear month of Mary, I wished absolutely to procure myself of this consolation. I took measures in this direction, therefore, and at 5 o'clock in the morning I celebrated it in the sick-bay of the corvette. After the celebration, in fulfillment of a vow previously made, I placed my mission under the special protection of the Sacred Heart of Mary, promising that if Christianity were ever established during my lifetime in Lieou-Kieou, I would do everything to obtain from the Holy See the placing of these islands under the patronage of this Immaculate Heart.*

---

* Note from Marbot: "From respect for this document we give it as it is: 'O most holy heart of Mary, heart the most rich, the most pure, the most noble of hearts, heart which is a perennial source of bounty, mansuetude, pity and love, admirable sanctuary and most pleasing model of all the virtues, heart inferior only to the divine heart of Jesus, I offer thee, present, dedicate and consecrate to thee now as fully as I may, and so it is fitting for me to do, these islands of Lieu-Kieu, the first evangelization of which is confided to me despite my great unworthiness, moreover binding myself, as soon as a few at least of these islands have turned from the vain worship of idols to Christianity, as soon as the smallest sanctuary shall be built and the mission truly commenced and established, to do without delay all that I can do to obtain that the Holy See shall openly and authentically place this whole kingdom under the same special patronage. O most pious heart, most powerful over the divine heart of Jesus, heart that no prayer has ever invoked in vain, do not disdain my most humble supplication, render better my wretched heart, enlighten my intelligence so clouded by the shades which envelope it, deign to gain for us the spirit of humility, prudence, wisdom and strength amidst so many difficulties and dangers, that by your mediation, Omnipotent God, Father, Son and Holy Spirit, you will not disdain to use this vile instrument to confound the strong and destroy what exists; and that this people for centuries seated in darkness and in the shadow of death may be at last converted, directed and guided to the light of the Holy Gospel and eternal life. Amen.'

"The vow of the missionary was fulfilled in 1862, when Girard, one of his successors in Lieu-Kieu and the superior of the Japan mission, obtained authority to celebrate the Feast of the Immaculate Heart of Mary, double first-class with an octave. The vow was written on a mere scrap of paper."

Forcade Takes a Policeman for a Walk

The holy mass concluded, I felt a very natural desire to go and visit a little these latitudes to which I had just given, in as far as it was in me, such a good and powerful patron. The experiences of yesterday had, moreover, sufficiently reassured me of the possibility and opportuneness of such an enterprise. I left Augustin on board where he was needed to serve as interpreter for all visitors, and accompanied by an officer, the surgeon major, and an ensign, I directed myself toward Nafa.

In ascending the river we noticed at least 15 large junks at the anchorage; they were all, judging by the sailors' hair, Japanese, and there was no shadow of a Chinese. We passed before a shipyard where many hands were working at a junk already well nigh completed. At last, after having moved at leisure over the surface of the river, agreeably distracted by the sight of various people who had run to the two shores to watch us; and by the pursuit of a little boat with mandarin, which was never able to catch up with us, we peacefully disembarked at the quay and sent our boat back to the ship.

We had exactly the same experience as the officer of last evening: a similar reception on the part of the people, similar embarrassment for the police, as much coolness and assurance on our side. As for me, I literally fell into the arms of one good fellow. Hardly had I taken two steps before he said to me, offering his arms, "You cannot walk! You cannot walk here!"

I replied, "I can walk," and taking his arm, I set out. At every instant and at every turn in the road, the catchword was repeated, and I, none the less, invariably answered, "I can walk."

For three hours I walked him around, arm in arm, in the town and in the fields, by every street and road, and, note this last, the rain pouring on our backs, without his losing patience for a moment. Though always repeating his refrain, he constantly showed himself full of regards and attentions toward me.

At the moment when he quitted me, I wished, in order to repay him for his trouble, and also to see what he would do with it, to present him with the gift of my umbrella, which he had admired and carried. I was quite unable to make him accept it. Desiring, nevertheless, to prove to him in some way that I was pleased with his services, I commended him to a mandarin who seemed to be his superior, saying merely, "This man is a good fellow, and he has taken great care of me." This most natural compliment seemed to embarrass the unhappy wretch. I seemed to have compromised him in some way.

The Latin Cross.
Nafa.

At the close of this stroll, I made a discovery there, without thinking of the matter, and as if by chance, which perhaps has no meaning, but may also have some importance. While I was standing waiting for the boat, what was my stupefaction to notice a Latin cross, perfectly formed, on a fairly large paving stone at the extremity of a jetty which advances into the bay and which serves as a landing platform. I looked at it more than once, believing I was dreaming, but it was impossible that I should be mistaken. I pointed the thing out to the doctor, who, like myself, was unable to see that it differed from a cross.*

" What is this sign?" I asked two or three mandarins who accompanied us, and who spoke Chinese. They appeared confused and did not answer. Only one of them passed his foot lightly over the stone, following the outline of the cross and stammered out, "I do not know. This has no meaning." I added, "Isn't this the character *che*?" (This Chinese character, which means ten, has the form of a cross). They appeared delighted with the interpretation, and, showing me their ten fingers, they assured me with earnestness that I had guessed well. I thought it was wise to seem to put faith in this explanation; but, weighing everything carefully, it seemed to me that this could well be a trace of the usage which existed in Japan, that of trampling the cross under foot. One of the mandarins said to Augustin, though against all probability, that no one in Loo Choo had ever heard of the religion of the Europeans. However this may be, when the doctor proposed, after returning on board, to go and remove or efface this cross, I thought I ought to oppose him for many reasons. I thought that it was best to see

---

* The *Jesumi*, cross to be tread upon.

nothing in it but the character for a numeral, as they said concerning it, and to pay no attention to it.*

But let us return to our walk. Naha seemed to me to be a rather large town. Two forts defended the mouth of the river, and they would perhaps be redoubtable if they were not completely disarmed. The wharfs are fairly well built, the streets were generally clean and quite straight, but the houses, almost all one-storied and built of wood, had a most shabby appearance. The only thing which gives them some charm is the little garden which ordinarily surrounds them. I could not say what they are like on the inside. We were unable to enter any of them, except the wretched cabin of some very poor people. There exists a rather considerable species of lacquer. But thanks to the government, which wishes us to believe that there is no trade here, all the shops were hermetically sealed. Though the pagodas have a little better appearance, nevertheless, there is no important building in Nafa. Leaving Nafa, we pursued a fairly fine paved road for about half a league which led us to the village where we had held our first interview with the governor. We had really seen nothing there the first time; but the houses, without being magnificent, are generally better built there than in the town. They appeared, almost all of them, to be dwellings of the opulent and aristocratic.

The Dinner to the Governor. Augustin's Instructions

We finally returned to the scene of our diplomacy of last Monday. Today this has become the headquarters of the factotum interpreter, whom we shall call henceforth the Messenger of the Court, for according to all appearances, this is the title which best suits him. He had at his order there, not to count the men, twelve saddled and bridled horses. We received a welcome from him which I could not call very gracious, but which was assuredly very prompt. Pipes, tea, and cakes were offered us. After a few minutes rest we went to the beach to wait for our boat.

At about 2 p.m., the governor, three mandarins with yellow caps

---

* Marbot writes, "Our readers have divined that the missionary was not mistaken. He was indeed confronted by the *Jesumi*, but prudence told him to pay no attention to it, since the authorities did not."

and the court messenger, who as usual was in charge of everything, came on board. These illustrious persons were saluted with seven guns. They were taken for a walk in the gun-room. Their ears were agreeably flattered by the sounds of an old grind-organ. They were stuffed willy-nilly with European dishes until, at the end of the second course, they surrendered and broke up their camp. In vain we told them that it was not finished. "This is enough, enough," they exclaimed and vanished hastily. At this banquet, at which all the staff officers assisted, good Capt. Duplan had the kindness to place me between the governor and the court messenger. The latter, whom the officers wished to render talkative for several reasons, was far from lending himself to our plan. In vain the toasts of our august emperor and his illustrious king, the health of the governor and everyone else, were called. He only appeared to drink, but did not. Moreover, he seemed to know how to employ his time well, apparently honoring Augustin with his confidence, expressing his fears, and asking his advice, etc. But he was trying, as we say in France, to "pump" him (like "to pull worms from his nose"). Augustin reported everything to me later.

May 2. It is impossible to transcribe here the whole of Augustin's conversation with the Loo Chooan diplomat. In concert with the captain, I had recommended my faithful servant to no longer hide his nationality, but to say that he had been entrusted to the French officers to serve as their interpreter; that the latter noticed with regret the suspicion of which they were the object; that they were animated by no evil purpose; that they wished to pay for all their purchases, as they ought in all justice; and that as other ships were soon to come, the Captain had the order to leave two interpreters in the country to perfect themselves in the study of the language, and that he was strictly obliged to carry out this order, etc., etc. The occasion for putting these instructions to good use soon came. The court messengers arrived in the morning and had a long conversation with Augustin at which, let it be clearly understood, I was not present. I had it from the witnesses of the scene that the two speakers appeared to be very animated and greatly preoccupied. My poor Augustin was so much moved that he was absolutely incapable of giving me the details of the interview. He must have time enough to grow calm. In any case, it appears that the Loo Chooan chiefs strongly oppose my residence in the island.

Though Opposed, Forcade Pleads to be Received

May 3rd. This morning I questioned Augustin about the conversation he had with the messenger of the court. Everything happened as I had foreseen it, and they wish absolutely to prevent me from living in the country. I learned, moreover, that there would be a great meeting of mandarins at the temple where we had our interview to settle the matter. It appears that they desire that I should attend, but without its seeming that I went there on purpose; for example, I ought to come in under the pretext of stopping for a moment's rest. After having consulted the captain on this subject, I decided to go with Augustin to the desired meeting, and both of us left after lunch. On the way, I thought of the Feast for the day, and having on me a reliquary of the true cross, I prayed with all my heart to Him who had died for us on this consecrated tree that He might deign to exalt it in the midst of these lands, where His image is only known that it may be trampled under foot.

The rain which fell at the moment when I stepped ashore furnished me with an excellent pretext for entering the bonzery. I found over one hundred persons gathered there, beside the mandarins. The messenger of the court received us and took us in hand, and he was not able to understand why I desired so much to remain there. My persistence in my plan appeared to disturb him. I might even say, to terrify him beyond all expression. The other mandarins shared the same apprehensions. I tried to persuade them by every means that they had nothing to fear from me. I tried every resource to make them inclined to keep me, and I ended by saying in a voice full of feeling, for I was indeed much affected:

"You do not know why I wish to remain with you. I do not come to ruin, but to save you. I hope to prove this later. Until you know, instead of seeking to send me away, you would beg me with greatest insistence not to leave you! What I tell you is very true, and I do not lie. I swear this to you before the God whom I serve!"

Gifts are Presented; Forcade Sings and the Loo Chooans Do Likewise. The Governor's Dispatch on Foreign Trade.

This appeared to make some impression on them, but I was none the less unable to obtain a definite answer. They only told me that the decision would be transmitted in writing that very evening, and that they would give it to me during the session if it were not a breach of propriety. The rest of the time passed in trifling conversation. While we were thus seated and talking of one thing or another, suddenly presents were offered to Augustin and to me. For each there were ten fans, two little rolls of print (cloth), a ream of paper, a pipe and tobacco pouch. At first I refused them, saying that since they would not take anything from us, I could not properly accept anything from them. But in sum, they insisted so often, they showed themselves so disheartened at this refusal, that I thought I ought to take what they offered, for it was not worth while to make so much fuss over such a trifle. I disposed of these articles in favor of the officers of the corvette in order to show them my gratitude for their kindness to me.

The first scene was followed by another which was still more solemn. The governor with his purple bonnet arrived, surrounded by his staff, and gave me, along with the answer, all sorts of little gifts for the captain. I must mention, however, that everything which was given us was more coarse than that which we saw everyday on the backs or in the hands of the people. This denoted more clearly the intention to prove to us that the country was very poor, that it had no special productions, and that it could not be profitable to settle there or to carry on any commerce. Nothing remained for me to do but to go back on board, but the boat being late in coming, the mandarins bethought themselves of asking me if I did not play the violin in order to charm their leisure and mine. (Without doubt, some European vessel must have left them that musical instrument). Upon my reply in the negative, they said, "But at least you know how to sing. Sing for us, then, some airs of your country."

I consented, though I am a sorry chorister, and in this house devoted to the fiend, I successively chanted the *Magnificat, Stabat,* etc., and I closed by the *Te Deum.* These poor people seemed to find these songs admirable; as soon as I stopped, they begged me to continue, and I was unable to stop until at the end of my strength. "That will be fine," they said. "It is indeed a pity that we are not able to understand it."

In turn, feeling that I ought to respond to their politeness, I begged them to let me also hear the songs of their country. This they did with the best grace in the world. I do not know what these songs amounted to. I know nothing about such things. They closed with a song in Chinese to which they begged us to pay particular attention. I did not catch a word of it, but according to what Augustin told me, this is about the meaning: "The voyage is difficult in coming to Loo Choo; it is still more difficult to live here. So why leave one's country when it is fair to go to a poor land, etc."

(In a following note, the translator, W. L. Schwartz, verifies the contents as follows:

Difficult is it to come to Loo Choo, Harder it is to remain;

"Why leave a home and a land that is fair?" We, poor Loo Chooans, complain).

No one could tell me, "Get out!" in a more kindly fashion.

Once back on shipboard we opened the wonderful dispatch, of which this is a translation:

"The orders of a great Empire are to be feared, and we beg that you will deign to receive the homage of a petty kingdom. We beg in consequence that we may be spared out of pity the establishment of commerce. According to the report of the Governor of Nafa, named Chang-Liang-Pi, a great French commander has ordered us to establish friendly relations, commerce, and to give an answer on this subject after much reflection. It is in complete conformity with reason that we inform you of the motives of our response.

"Now, humbly reflecting among ourselves upon your desire to carry on commerce with us, we consider that this is derived from no other source than a feeling of friendship. But our land is a country of very slight importance, our islands are barren! They produce nothing but a little rice, they have neither gold nor silver, nor copper nor iron. The whole population is barely able to obtain daily nourishment. Tools and utensils are generally scanty. Now, from antiquity, we have exchanged our rice and the other products of our kingdom with the neighboring islands, and it is thus that we have been able to satisfy our needs in some degree. But should drought or storms come upon us, then ensues a great dearth of all products, and we cannot carry on commerce with these lands as we would like to do. So now, if we should carry on trade with your kingdom, it is true that our kingdom would not be able to bear such a burden.

"On the other hand, our kingdom has always been invested with its royal dignity by the Chinese Empire, though the crown is hereditary, and it pays tribute to the reigning dynasty. Thus we never decide for ourselves anything of great importance. That is why we always gave this same answer in the years 1803, 1827, and 1832 when the kingdoms of *Mongiali* (?), *Iamilikami* (U.S.) and *Inigiti* (Great Britain) wished to establish commerce; and at the same time we begged them to excuse us from so doing. We therefore beg the great commander to examine our true motives with care, and to do us the signal favor of pitying us and releasing us from the alliance and commerce. We adjure him to kindly make himself our intercessor with his Emperor, when he returns to his own country, and to obtain for us our desires, and then all the mandarins and the great ones of the kingdom, lighting incense sticks, will worship him to eternity."

> In the reign of Tao-Kouan, 24th year, 16th day of the 3rd moon. (May 4, 1844).
> The Governor General of Chang-Lang, City of the First Class, Kingdom of Loo Choo.
> Hiang-Neng-Pao

The Governor's P.S.   Captain Duplan's Answer.

Post script added to the above dispatch:
"The great commander desires that the two interpreters may be left ashore. We have discussed this. Now, never before have men of a foreign country landed to dwell here. We fear that these two men, should they remain here, may contract some sickness on account of the bad temperature, for the climate is unhealthy. This is a great drawback. We pray that it may have your full attention."

The answer to the question which concerns me is neither a "yes" nor a "no" in its phrasing. I think, however, that they fully expect we should take it for a "yes". According to all appearances, it is from fear, perhaps of Japan, perhaps of China, that they have replied in these vague terms and have only mentioned the matter in a postscript.

We replied to the letter of yesterday in the following terms: (The letter was in Chinese).

May 4. Post-Captain Fornier-Duplan, etc.
"I have received your letter of recent date. I have read it carefully.

I have also received your presents, and for these things I thank you. You have correctly esteemed that our proposal to carry on commerce came from no other source than our friendship for you. Now, in order that commerce may be carried on between two nations there must be some profit for both the one and the other, and two of them must consent to it. This is in conformity with justice, and we do not wish to infringe her laws in any way. For this reason I shall inform our Emperor that you cannot carry on commerce with us, and I shall beg him to accept your excuses. I shall tell him also that you have received us very kindly, and that you have supplied our wants with a generosity beyond parallel, not being willing to accept any money for the expense we have caused. I am also certain that His Majesty will order the commanders of his ships to treat you with kindness and good will.

"I am happy that you have not refused to receive the two interpreters, for since I had received the order to leave them in your country, I should have been forced, nonetheless, to leave them in spite of your refusal, and I myself would have shared greatly in the trouble which I would have caused you. The observations which you make on the subject of the climate, and your fear lest the health of these two men might not be impaired attest your goodness of heart. But you must know that when the French have received an order, they execute it even at the risk of their lives. Thus I shall land these men tomorrow with their belongings, commending them again to your kind care. I shall sail day after tomorrow, if, as I hope, the weather will allow it."

Final Arrangements: In Case of Death.

The captain had the kindness to carry this letter himself to the house of the interview, and he permitted me to accompany him. On the way, we visited the inside of a junk. The reception which we received at *Po-tsung* (Tomari) was excellent. They are resigned to keeping the two of us and merely request us to leave them a testimonial in case that, in spite of the best treatment, we should happen to fall sick, or even die, in order that the French officers would not hold them accountable for our disappearance. The survivor, in case of the death of one, would do this on behalf of the dead man, and if he saw that he himself was attacked by sickness, he should hasten to fulfill this duty, in his own case, as soon as his disease began to take a serious turn. This we promised. Time did not allow me to enter into fuller details.

May 5th. The petty mandarins came on board to say their farewells. We were not able to make them accept the money for the provisions which they had furnished for the crew during the week. We even had much difficulty to make them accept a telescope and several other trifles which we wished to leave with them at all hazards. Finding themselves alone for a few minutes with Augustin and myself, they took Heaven for a witness that they would always treat us as brothers and as friends. They begged us in the most touching manner not to bear them ill will, and they conjured me in particular to protect their interests in my relations with the great French officials. It is useless to give my answer in this place, since it is not hard to guess. My landing takes place tomorrow morning.*

---

* Marbot says: "The diplomacy of the Loo Choo had displayed all the resources of its arsenal. We shall see it later persevere in the employ of these three weapons. (i.e., the poverty of the land, the refusal to accept cash payments, and the fear of the people). Forcade could well say with the Apostle: *'Vincula me manent.'* The goal was at last reached. The "interpreters" could remain in Loo Choo. Nevertheless, good Captain Duplan was only half assured of their safety. As he himself said to him who here retraces this struggle between human nature and God's grace, he had tried to dissuade M. Forcade from his dangerous enterprise. He saw dangers of all kinds in it, and his faith as an old seaman did not go so far as to understand that so much boldness was justified by the desire to save souls, the more so that these were absolutely opposed to the first advances made to them. The priest thanked the captain for his friendly interest, tried to calm his fears and remained firmly disposed to suffer imprisonment and death for the name of the Lord Jesus. Nevertheless, Duplan made the authorities responsible for the life of Forcade. This ultimatum may not have been a vain threat. Some time later, the Japanese Government demanded the head of this intruder who had domiciled himself on their soil in spite of the existing laws. But the fear of the French guns restrained the Loo Chooan king, while on his side the Dutch Resident at Decima (Japan), by a feeling of brotherhood as another European, calmed the angers of Yedo, which reflects much honor on him. For it is to this double circumstance that Forcade owed the fortune of saving his life in the peril which the love of souls had placed him."

Note of translator, Schwartz: *No authority is given for the above statement. Yet it was made by the governor of Batavia to Adm. Cecille. (See, p. 118 for a curious confirmation of the same).*

Chapter III
The Corvette Sails

Forcade's Reception Ashore.

On the morning of May 6, Msg. Forcade and Augustin bade farewell to the captain and his staff and went ashore. A great crowd awaited them on the beach. The officer who had accompanied the missionary could not avoid being moved when they had to part from their compatriot, a man whose qualities and virtues they had tested, and whom they were going to leave, defenseless and alone, in a strange land. Though affected himself, Msg. Forcade was sustained by the hope of saving some of these souls which were already so dear to him, and that of soon seeing one or more confreres come to share his labors and sufferings. This double hope was not realized. The missionary was unable to work for the salvation of his people in any other way than by his tears and his prayers, and because of a chain of unexpected circumstances, he had to live for two years alone with his beloved Augustin, whose virtue and devotion never failed him. We take from a letter* of Msg. Forcade, dated August 12, 1845, some details about his life in Loo

---

* Annals of the Propagation of the Faith, year 1846:"At the moment of our landing in this island,** we were led at once to the bonzery of *Tumai* (real name of Po-tsung). This was the dwelling, or rather the honorable prison, which was destined for us. This we were unable to escape, and we still remain here today."

** From Marbot: "Hardly had the French corvette doubled the point of Naha harbour before the missionary was entangled in a living net of petty mandarins and their satellites. One of them spoke in the name of all, or rather in the name of the state, and thus hypocritically addressed him. 'The noble commander has declared that you are a distinguished man whose life is precious. The King of Loo Choo, wishing to render homage to your dignity, in spite of the poverty of the realm, has decided that you should be furnished with the guard of honor given to a dignitary.'

"'But I would gladly go without it,' exclaimed the missionary, who was not misled by so much officious attention.

"'No,' replied the mandarin. 'We owe this to you, and then, you see the people of this country are very ignorant and vulgar. They might lack in respect toward you, and we do not wish the noble commandant to have any reason to complain on his return.'

"By way of peroration, the orator made a sign, and all set out for the neighboring temple of *Amikou* (at Tomari Port)."

Choo, and the obstacles which were raised against the preaching of the Gospel.

Life in Grand Style
Relations with the Authorities

We found here, beside a large guard posted in every direction, (Marbot says 100 men, renewed a third at a time, and for whom barracks were raised as if by magic), a very good-sized circle of mandarins installed near us for the unique purpose, so we were told, of charming our leisure. And beside these, I don't know how many servants.

Attentions were not failing in the beginning, night or day. We could not blow our noses, cough or sneeze, without beholding ourselves assailed by a dozen people who, with distracted air, came to ask us if we had swooned. The table corresponded to this grand style of life. The country was supposed to have exhausted its products to support us, but we have clearly recognized since then that all that they gave us with so much display was very little compared with the natural resources. Poverty is not so great in Loo Choo as they would have us believe. I have said "us" because, though Capt. Duplin always represented Augustin as of a much lower rank than mine, and though he himself always kept at a fitting distance from me, they chose to treat us on a footing of absolute equality. Things have changed since then, and since sometime ago, my catechist and myself have taken the respective position which belonged to each of us in the eyes of all.

However this may be, it was the intention of the masters of this land that, dazzled by so much brilliance and swimming in the midst of abundance, I should have nothing left to desire in the world, and that thus laughing, eating, and above all, sleeping soundly, I would wait patiently until some one should come to take me from these shores. Great, then, was the stupefaction of my attendants when, appearing even more than indifferent to all this fuss (lit: "to these chimes"), I demanded an audience, after several days, not of the king (I would never have obtained it), but at least of the governor of the province. They did all that they could to parry the blow, but I remained firm, and they had to come around to this.

The interview took place in a house which I think was a school. I would have been better pleased if it had taken place at the capitol and in the palace of the governor, but this was refused. He who was presented to me as this personage was a tall, handsome man of about forty, rather richly dressed, and followed by a numerous suite. He was dignified and incredibly grave. During the two or three hours that the conference lasted, he sat stiff as a *Fotoque* (Buddhist idol) in his pagoda, and if he opened his mouth it was only to absorb the dishes of the indispensible diplomatic dinner. He accomplished this marvelous function wonderfully. An interpreter, accredited as Court Messenger, speaking, replying, and deciding everything in the way which seemed best to him, fulfilled all the other duties.

The Provincial Governor. A Struggle for Liberty.

My purpose in requesting this interview was merely to clear the ground and to put myself in relations with the authorities. This was not a hard result to reach, and I attained it at this time. Dating from this interview, which was followed by a second a month later, several letters have been sent on both sides, and many communications have been made orally.

That which I demanded above everything else was my liberty. Without it, what would I do? But at the beginning I did not enjoy even the shadow of independence. I was not in the least free inside my house, since night and day I had at my heels this crowd of mandarins and officious servants with whom I have already entertained you, and since I could not take a step without being followed or make a movement that was not observed. I was in no wise free out of doors, for I was barely allowed to take any exercise, even along the sand and mud beside the sea; and again, I could not go here alone. I was surrounded by the inevitable mandarins, preceded by attendants armed with bamboos to beat the poor populace and drive away the passers-by, a thing which would naturally make me odious enough to everyone. After many difficulties, they consented to devote the room in which I slept in the temple and a little garden attached to it to my sole use.

As for my excursions out of doors, here are the means, somewhat risky perhaps, but by which I finally obtained some improvement in my situations. Finding that I had not and would not gain anything through diplomatic channels, suddenly, without giving any heed to the clamors of my troop, I began to move about at my ease where I wished, but without ever leaving the public highways.

Arrested! Better Treatment Follows.

At first they contented themselves with shouting and putting into use all the little tricks employed in that land in such circumstances, but when they clearly saw that they wasted their time in doing this, they resolved to employ force. And on one fine day when, a quarter of a league away from my temple, I was advancing peacefully along the main road of Nafa, a mandarin seized me by both hands and prevented me from going further. I asked this man if he acted in the name of the sovereign authority, and on his reply in the affirmative, I retraced my steps and returned home. The next morning, however, I at once wrote to the governor, asking him to let me know for what offence or crime I had been arrested like an evil-doer. His Excellency replied that I had not been guilty of any offence or crime, but that a law of the nation forbade strangers and foreigners to walk about except on the sea shore, and he reminded me that the captain of the ship which had brought me had promised that I would submit to the laws of the kingdom.

I replied, among other things, that the captain, in promising obedience on my part to the laws of the kingdom, had meant to say that being on the same footing as other individuals, I would obey all the laws which governed them. But he had certainly not intended to speak of any arbitrary prohibition which would place me outside of the common law, a prohibition which he had very clearly proved that we would not recognize, since he himself had gone walking wherever he wished. I added finally that "until it is explained to me that I am in the wrong, the governor need not be astonished if, relying on my own conscience, I do not go back in any way on my former conduct."

No answer was made to this note, and since then I have been able to move about at my ease without being subject to more violence.

I still had to get rid of the mandarins and their satellites. In order to succeed here, this was the expedient to which I had recourse. The more numerous my suite, the more trouble they made, and the more they beat the poor plebs, the faster and farther I went. When they noticed this, the numbers of my escort were decreased little by little, and today I am not accompanied on my walks and ordinary excursions by more than one or two mandarins and a servant. I aim to talk with passers by as I walk along, and I am even sometimes invited to enter a temple or a private house to take tea, or to rest a moment. In a word, though I am far from being free, since I am never left alone, my slavery has become a little more tolerable, both for me and for the general public.

Permission to Adopt Native Costume or to Preach Refused.

You recommended me, my dear Mr. Libois, to assume the dress of the country as far as I was able. A faithful follower of your instructions, I did not delay to request from the natives the honor of wearing their costume. You may perhaps imagine that these good people, flattered by this request, hastened to satisfy my desire. Not in the least! In spite of all our urging, they have never permitted either Augustin or me to buy or make one of their garments. The most I have been able to adopt of the local garb has been the foot-gear, because it has sufficed for that if I put my bare feet inside a pair of sandals, which are about as difficult to describe as they are uncomfortable to wear.

The most important business has been to obtain the liberty of preaching our holy religion and of securing for the people of the country the liberty of embracing it. Unless this permission is authentically granted, and without this guarantee for the people, whom I believe to be much oppressed, it would be very difficult for us to enjoy any success; but were this concession once made, I have reason to hope that, by the grace of God, we would soon see conversions, and that these would even be fairly numerous. I did not begin with this question when treating with the mandarins, but I reached it at length, none the less, and after having broached it, I have pursued the subject with the greatest perseverance. My first demand was followed by a refusal,* but this was so feebly supported that I was able to come back to the attack. This time the answer of the mandarin, though negative, was better founded upon

---

* One day the governor said awkwardly that the people had no taste for the Christian religion. "How do you know this," said the missionary, "since this religion has not yet been preached in this kingdom? One has neither a taste nor aversion for things which are unknown." The governor was silent, but his silence spoke for him. (Marnus, op. cit., p. 126).

reason. It was based principally upon this motive, that if tolerance was granted to me, China would break off relations with the kingdom. And on the other hand, Japan, which alone does any trade here, would hold back her ships. This double misfortune would cause the ruin of the country.

Forcade Reasons In Vain. The Study of the "Japanese" Language

It was necessary to reduce these apprehensions to their true value. I replied, therefore, first, that I knew that kingdoms tributary to China, for example the kingdoms of Annam and Siam, had accorded the liberty of religion in epochs when our faith was proscribed in China, without that empire refusing their tribute or even raising any complaint, and secondly, that if it was a case of opening the port of Nafa to European trade, Japan, which might suffer from this, would no doubt have some reason for complaint. But concerning a simple affair of internal administration and of the police, I did not see in what way this concerned a neighboring state, of which they claimed to be entirely independent.

Another point about which, for reasons which I think are good, I made no formal demand to the authorities, but which has been from the very first the object of all my application, has been the study of the language of the country, or, if you prefer it, of the Japanese language. I do not think I am mistaken in saying that the same, or nearly the same, idiom is used by both countries. This tongue is the only one spoken here. Chinese is only understood by certain interpreters descended from former immigrants from Fukien, and even then, these do not use it in the ordinary commerce of life.

I cannot recount for you all that has been done to make the study of this tongue impossible for me. Not only have they never been willing to give me lessons or to procure any book for me, but they have even refused for a long time to inform me of the names of the most common things. Often they amused themselves by misleading me about the meaning of the expressions which I had picked up by chance, or again they intentionally taught me the words of the written language which are never employed in ordinary speech.

Nevertheless, by the special favor of God, our petty mandarins in the temple have, since about seven or eight months ago, suddenly changed their disposition in this particular. One of them especially, who seems to have taken a liking to me, has given me, and continues to give me, great help. He has even gone as far as to dictate to me some little dialogues which have been very useful to me, and will be no less useful to my fellow-workers some day. In brief, I have at present made for myself a dictionary of 10,000 words. I can understand almost everything and carry on any conversation without too much trouble. This morning I was asked several times to act as interpreter for the captain of an English ship which has just put in at Nafa, and I managed the business without any trouble.

The Situation Summarized. Hope for the Future.

Here are what have been my efforts on the most important questions. I have informed you as clearly as I can of what results they have produced. On the whole our situation is not bright. I summarize the state of affairs in three sentences. 1. I find myself *de facto* a prisoner, whether in the temple where no one may approach me without the consent and the supervision of the mandarins, or without my residence, from which I cannot stir a step without being followed. 2. I am face to face with the most formal opposition on the part of the authorities. If they do not persecute me openly because they do not dare to do so, they lose no opportunity to make me the prey of all the trifling vexations which they can imagine. 3. As a preacher of the Gospel, I do not find words corresponding to our dogmas in the native language, and I fear to imperil them by an attempt at translation which might disfigure them. In this difficulty, I must have recourse to you; try to find me some religious books, some good books which the Jesuit fathers must necessarily have written when they were in Japan. Hunt for them, I know not where, but find them, at least.

Yet should we feel discouraged? Oh no! God grant us that we may never lose our confidence. It is he who has sent me into these islands, who has preserved me here up until today, and who appears to wish to keep me here longer. I place all my hope in Him. He will never abandon me. Perhaps we will have to cast our nets throughout a long night, but when the hour of the Lord arrives, the miraculous draught will well repay us for the waiting. We would be all the more hopeful because the common people here are excellent. They ask nothing better than to see, speak and listen to me, for I have obtained the proof of this on more than one occasion.

Thus, last year, I had gone out for a walk with Augustin. My petty mandarins, who were annoyed by my long walk, found that I had indeed gone very far. But since their remonstrances were not heeded in the least, they had recourse to another means of procedure, a trick of their invention which was often used successfully. They assumed the air of wearied, exhausted people. They seemed not to have enough strength to put one foot in front of the other and followed me at a distance, stopping to sit down, at every moment persuaded that, according to my habit, I would wait for them, take pity on them, and finally turn back. But on this day, utterly tired of their acting, I suddenly doubled my pace, and soon a little hill cut off my catechist and myself from their sight.

Our escort no longer knew where we were, and for the first time we found ourselves all alone. Profiting by the opportunity, we advanced by all kinds of paths as far as the ruins of a city, which must have been the capital of the Southern Kingdom. Everywhere, on the roads and in the hamlets, the peasants saluted us and were polite.

Arriving at the end of our walk, while Augustin went still further by way of exploration, I remained seated on the summit of a little knoll. The villagers had no sooner perceived me than they left their fields and hastened to gather around me, some offering me their pipes, their tobacco, or going to fetch fire from one of the isolated houses! The others spoke to me and questioned me, and though I had much trouble in understanding their dialect, I carried on what conversation I could with them. This was the first time that they had seen me. They could have known nothing of me except the calumnies scattered everywhere against me, and, in all probability, no European had ever appeared among them. Nevertheless our first relations were those of mutual goodwill. I had sat there for some time, and all was going in the best fashion, when my eternal escort suddenly appeared. At the sight of these, my poor friends yielded the field and fled away in fear in every direction.

Peasant and Mandarin

Another time, on one of my walks, I met a good villager to whom I addressed some questions, and who amused me greatly by his answers, for he was innocence itself. I said to a petty mandarin who accompanied me, "Truly there is a fine fellow. His frankness is such that he cannot conceal anything. One may take him at his word."

But my supervisor judged that the occasion was a good one to teach me a lesson. "Isn't it true," he asked of this innocent, "that when the teacher walks about everywhere in your villages, you peasants are much frightened?"

The tone with which this question was put clearly dictated the sense of the proper answer. There was no reason to feel in doubt nor to meditate, nor did the peasant hesitate either.

"Yes," said he. "We are much afraid, but I will tell you that we do not fear at all the European teacher, for we know well that he will do us no harm; but it is on account of the attendants and the mandarins that we are terrified."

Even though this was not precisely the answer called for and expected, it was so true, so marked with good faith, and so naive in its expressions, that my young scholar could not restrain a burst of laughter.

Even these mandarins, though they are here, as elsewhere, men of the worst sort, they are not all bad. There are several of them who would be convinced if they were permitted to lend an ear to the preaching of the truth. In the very beginning of my residence in Loo Choo, one of those who are constantly about us, and who has always seemed to us, moreover, upright, capable and highly educated for so backward a country as Loo Choo, having provoked Augustin to it by his questions, had a little discussion with him upon the existence of a Creator God, upon the worship which we ought to give Him, etc. Hardly had he obtained a glimpse of our sacred truths, then, touched no doubt by grace and suddenly smitten with the sublimeness of a doctrine which he then heard for the first time, was unable to disguise his admiration. It did not satisfy him to express this in his own words. He went even so far as to improvise a pretty bit of Chinese poetry, in which he praised the learning of my catechist and expressed his desire to listen to him all the days of his life.

This beginning gave me the fairest hopes, but unfortunately our future neophyte was immediately taken from us, and we have never seen him again. Has he perhaps paid dearly for this frank expression of his noble sentiments? May the Lord in His mercy take into account this homage to the truth by disclosing to his eyes the divine truth of the faith whose first gleam had made so great an impression on his soul.

The Attitude of the Mandarins Toward Religion

Since this sad incident, my catechist has had no opportunity to speak of religion in his intercourse with the mandarins. Every time that in one way or another he has wished to bring the conversation around to this subject, he has seen every ear stopped and his auditors move away on various pretexts. They never discuss, they do not contest any points; they only refuse to hear anything. Do not believe, however, that they act in this way from indifference or apathy. I have no doubt that this conduct is dictated by the orders which come from *Choui* (the capital of the kingdom). However this may be, I flatter myself that I have among my mandarins, even today, at least one demi-proselyte. But I fear greatly that he is already suspected by the authorities. Out of prudence we are obliged to seem to be rather coldly disposed toward him. Oh! If we were free! Let us trust in God, and it will come to pass.*

M. Forcade, by the aid of several historical documents and his personal observations, says something of the preaching of the gospel in the archipelago, a fact which he considers very probable, and he hints of the possibility of finding living fruits of this evangelization.

I will close these observations by the following anecdote, which

---

* A brief parenthesis by Schwartz, the translator: After some details on the relations between the kingdom of Loo Choo and Japan, relations which the authorities of the country endeavor to hide from policy, but which the practical identity of language and costume betray, M. Forcade, by the aid of several historical documents and his personal observations, says something of the preaching of the gospel in the archipelago, a fact which he considers very probable, and he hints of the possibility of finding living fruits of this evangelization.

still remains an enigma to me, though I have many times racked my brain to solve it. At the commencement of our sojourn here, Augustin formed the habit of going every evening at nightfall to recite his rosary by the side of the sea which washes the walls of our garden. At this time, he would neither speak nor understand four words of the language, and since, thanks to the sentinels placed around us, he could not escape unnoticed, he was generally left alone.

A Mysterious Event and a Possible Explanation

Now on the second of October, on a very dull dark day, when everything was in an uproar because of the news of the death of the Crown Prince which had arrived in the morning, Augustin suddenly heard a sound like that of a man walking in the water. It was indeed a man; he appeared before him, an oar in his hand and speaking in a whisper. Pointing to the temple, he seemed to ask some information with much insistence. My surprised catechist, not knowing what was wanted of him, and fearing he had to do with some evil-doer, put himself in an attitude of defense. And then the stranger ran off to leave his oar somewhere, so that it would arouse no more fear, and then he came back with all haste and renewed his salutations, genuflexions and prayers (or requests).

This mysterious interview lasted for four or five minutes, and Augustin was still unable to make anything of it, when two young men of the watch, drawn there probably by the affected voices of the two speakers, ran up to the spot. The questioner no sooner perceived them than he disappeared in the direction of the sea even more quickly than he had come. A second person, whom Augustin had not noticed, but who was standing near there on watch, fled with the first, and jumping into a boat, they moved off with all the speed of their oars. Over this I have, and still continue to lose myself in, conjectures. Might not these men be descendants of former Christians?* Believe me, if we were free, we would perhaps discover many things which we do not hardly expect. Oh! Liberty! Ask God earnestly to grant us this blessed, holy liberty!

---

* Marbot says: "Some time later when they were on freer terms with their prisoner, the mandarins told him that there were men in Japan without any religion who were never seen inside temples. This remark, as well as the adventure which is described above, could only be fully understood later when Mgr. Petitjean, one of the successors of Msg. Forcade, discovered those thousands of Christians, who, in secret and with no priests, and with only the sacrament of baptism, had perpetuated their number from the time of the great persecutions right down to our own days."

APPENDIX TO CHAPTER III

Passive Resistance to Pay for his Food

Marbot reports that the first struggle of the missionary was an attempt to pay for his daily food. He reports this struggle in the following terms:

"It will be remembered that these diplomats who had bested the captain of the 'Alcmene' had refused to take any money for the provisions furnished to the corvette. In the same way they had desired to force Forcade to allow himself to be maintained at state expense, in the hope, no doubt, of being able to thus dampen his ardour. But the latter, suspecting the trap, and finding that his prestige would be injured by such conduct, and he declared he wished to pay for his food and that of his catechist. Though the Chinese language, written or spoken, was made to show both of them its most seductive reasoning, no picture of ease was able to shake the resolution of a man who seemed to raise this detail to the height of a state question. Yet the mandarins were deaf to all his protests. One day Forcade wished to settle the matter. Adopting in turn the weapon of passive resistance, which was so skillfully employed against himself, he declared at meal-time that he would not eat until he had paid for that which had been served up for him. The faces around him were lighted with a smile of incredulity. What a childish fit of sulking! They waited for night, hoping that he would be enlightened by a day of fasting. But when evening came, the missionary renewed his ultimatum, and again sent away the proffered dishes untouched. In the morning the same declaration greeted the mandarins, and the fast was continued. But this stubborn fellow will confess himself defeated in the evening, after passing forty-eight hours without food! Not so; at supper time he maintained the same attitude toward his stewards of the household. But these were then stupefied and turned pale. The mandarins were informed! An excited council held a short meeting. They decided that a man capable of such firmness was powerful and a person to be feared, and they agreed to consent to the bargain which he had imposed on them.

"In seeking an audience of the governor, Forcade had no thought of improving the standard of comfort in his house, and he continued to sleep on the ground with a French dictionary by Noel and Chapsal for his pillow."

The Arrival Of A Frigate, H.B.M. "Samarang"

"A year had passed from the day that the Alcemene had brought Forcade to Loo Choo. Adm. Cecille had expressed his intention of not allowing this time to elapse without himself coming to visit the exile and bringing him one or two co-laborers. June 19, 1846, a European sail appeared on the horizon, running with the wind and steering toward Naha. Any doubt was hardly possible. It must be a ship from the fleet, perhaps the 'Cleopatra' itself. Friends were near, and with the joy of hearing his own language and news from home, the missionary could obtain new strength for his work. The ship entered the bay and passed Tumai, but so far away that it was impossible to make out her flag with the naked eye. Truly it was a frigate, but it was soon known, alas, that she was English.

"Forcade demanded the next day that he should be taken on board this vessel, and though they made some objection, they ended by yielding, and so, with a guard trebled for the occasion, a boat took him on board the 'Samarang,' H.B.M. frigate, commanded by Sir Edmund Belcher. The latter was ashore at this moment. The surgeon-major received the visitor in the kindliest fashion, adding to the charm of his cordiality that of being able to speak French, which even on the lips of a foreigner seemed very sweet to the ear of the missionary.

"Considering that the boat which the missionary had used was not good enough, and leaving it to his suite, the officer had a boat manned and conducted Msg. Forcade to Naha, where they soon met the commander. Capt. Belcher had just learned of the residence of a French priest in the island from the governor, with whom he had an interview. Passing over all the formality of an introduction according to English etiquette, he saluted Forcade most graciously, and taking him to one side, he began to talk of all that might interest him. Unfortunately, having left Hongkong rather suddenly two months ago, he had no direct commissions for him. But the captain declared himself ready to do anything for the missionary when he should return to Naha in the middle of August in order to meet another English ship bringing him provisions.

"The fate of this Frenchman cast on this unknown shore greatly interested the commander and the officers of the 'Samarang.' Before leaving him, they delicately wished to be informed of his needs, and since his funds were exceedingly low, they generously put enough money at his disposition so that he could wait for the arrival of the division, which could not delay long. The 'Samarang' departed.

"On August 11th, the 'Royalist' arrived in turn.

The ship under the British flag which bore this name was the one which was to revictual the frigate. Her commander, Ogle, was soon in touch with the missionary, who, as he then possessed a sufficient knowledge of the language, served him as interpreter.

"Seven days later, Monday the first, the 'Samarang' again cast anchor in Naha. And three days later, after having overwhelmed him with kindness and consideration, they bade him farewell and left for Hongkong. They carried his letters, the principal of which was addressed to M. Libois, procurator of Macao (This letter forms the substance of Chapter III).

"Life in the temple returned to its habitual monotony, the time being divided between prayer and the difficult study of the language. On every propitious occasion a new attempt was made to obtain either some books and a teacher of grammar, or to obtain some liberty to preach. But alas, everything failed because of the ill-will of the government. The series of walks, too, continued to be the series of more or less forced exercises which the prisoner imposed on his guards. According to the weather, the fluctuations of politics perhaps, or the caprice of the mandarins, things changed, but most often in a way for which Forcade could not see any reason. The number of obligatory escort was doubled, trebled or decreased. One day when the missionary had a rather large escort, he decided to enter some paths where he had never set his feet before. Soon he noticed that a certain uneasiness painted itself on the features of his men. 'Don't go yonder,' they said to him. 'This is a dangerous road which leads to some precipices.' From these remarks he concluded that the road was good and would lead him to make some discovery. In fact, after several windings, he came out upon a magnificent road, large and spacious, the finest road he had ever seen in the land."

The Snakes on the Way to Shuri. Before the Gate of the Capitol

"He suspected at once that he was on the road to the capital, the existence of which they had never betrayed by a word. This supposition was not long in becoming a certainty, as his petty mandarins surrounding and entreating him murmured, 'Don't go along there, for there are many snakes.'

"'What! Snakes! We find none along the little path, and they swarm on this high road?' exclaimed Forcade.

"'Ah!' the mandarins answered, never at a loss for an answer, 'it is possible that in your country the serpents stay in the paths, but in Loo Choo they always keep to the high roads.'

"'Well, so much the worse for you. I am not afraid of them, for you surround me so closely that they must twine around your legs before they can reach me. Therefore, I shall go on!' replied Forcade.

"But in which direction? Forcade hardly knew, but he had barely asked himself this question before a horseman appeared. Immediately one of the petty mandarins detached himself from the escort, went to the new-comer, and spoke a word or two in his ear. The former then quickly turning back was off like an arrow. Then, the missionary conjectured, it is in this direction, and he himself took the same direction.

"The capital was not far distant. A triple gate gives access to it, and before it the space was empty. Within and beyond, the people seemed to be numerous. Forcade moved toward the central gate, but a mandarin stood before it. 'No admittance!' He presented himself before the other gates and the same thing was repeated.

"'But after all,' Forcade said, 'I do no one any harm, no law forbids me to enter the town. I certainly have the right to go where others do.'

"'No, you may not enter,' was the reply.

"'Then have you an order from the King? Do you speak to me in his name? Then arrest me!' said the missionary.

"The suite replied with a convinced expression. 'We do not have an order to arrest you, yet if you enter here we will be punished.' And they indicated with a gesture the anvil upon which the bamboo would fall.

"'As for that,' exclaimed the missionary, 'you have deserved it already, for you have played quite enough tricks on me!'

"But promptly restraining this impulse, which was not very apostolic, he added, 'What you have told me is, again, a lie, and at the same time you are failing in respect toward your king. At the top of this gate I read these words, 'To the King who preserved justice!' Your sovereign is therefore a just man, but you make him out to be a tyrant, since he will punish you, you say, for not observing an order which he never gave.'

"Then, all out of arguments, the highest of the petty mandarins of the escort put one knee on the ground, and said in a tearful voice, 'Great man, listen to the prayer of a little man: Do not pass these gates!'

"Periculum Est Hic." The Victory of the Umbrella.

"During this scene, and evidently on account of the alarm given by the above-mentioned horseman, a crowd had gathered in the street before the gate. A word of command had imposed the greatest silence upon them. They were silent, and no sentiment betrayed itself in their compact ranks save that of curiosity. Yet this silence was not very reassuring. Augustin, the catechist, who would hardly be called a coward, began to feel alarmed at this, and for some little time he had been repeating, *'Pater periculum est hic ... oportet abire.'* Forcade himself began to feel uneasy over this adventure, whose outcome he could not foresee. Nevertheless, this was indeed a case for him to call into play all the resources of his energy. 'For months,' he said to himself, 'I have obtained nothing except by my moral ascendency, and if I fall back now without doing something, my prestige will vanish and all will be lost.'

"It was then that the thought of the most bizarre stratagem came to his mind. Even the idea of it can only be understood by the high and peculiar opinions formed in the extreme orient about the little-known Europeans who were easily imagined to be in possession of occult powers. Augustin, standing correctly behind his master, carried under his arm a large umbrella from Paris which he owed to the generosity of M. Libois at the time of his departure from Macao. Forcade, who had not yet paid any notice to this detail, perceived it at the moment when the ranking mandarin, kneeling to earth, offered his supplication to the 'great man.' Answering to this invocation of his guardian with the words, 'When the desire of a small man contradicts that of a great man, does not the latter triumph? I go on!' And turning to Augustin, he added, *'Da nihi umbrellam!'* Seizing the umbrella from the hand of his catechist, he placed the handle on his chest, raised the point in the air, and took three steps forward.

Its Result. Hardships due to Lack of Money.

"Jupiter-Tonans armed with all his lightnings would not have obtained more success. The crowd recoiled from instinct, with a movement of fear, and opened its ranks.

"How could they believe that this unknown weapon with which the western barbarian was armed was harmless? Forcade passed the gate, and his prestige was unimpaired. But it was dangerous to enjoy too long the fruits of this victory of the will. It was necessary not to allow these good people to recover from their surprise. The missionary then turned to one side, went out of another gate, and again took the road toward Tumai (Tomari) to the great contentment of his escort.

(This day was most unusual, but the result produced was not to be disdained. Forcade's courage strongly impressed both authorities and people. Perhaps it was on account of this incident that he was able later to enter Choui (Shuri) with the naval officers without any difficulty. Nevertheless, he never repeated such expeditions, as they were of little direct value, and the life in the temple became more calm.)

"Perhaps the missionary also felt that his strength was decreasing and that he could no longer rely on the vigor which such acts of firmness demanded. The fact was that the money which the English had furnished him was decreasing, and no ship of the French navy had appeared. It was therefore necessary to economize upon a fare which already was very meagre, for after having so strongly insisted upon paying for his food, if he were subsequently obliged to accept gratuitous nourishment, his officers would see a fatal defeat in this, and everything would be compromised. This would be the end of his moral authority, the only power which supported him in his struggle. One morning he consequently gave a new order to Augustin that in the future he would only eat sweet potatoes, which cost but a trifle. His liquor could not be changed, for from the time of his landing, he drank nothing but water, flavored by a few grains of rice parched by his catechist. This diet had to be kept up for six months.

"Has the reader fully comprehended all the labor of this apparently sterile apostleship? To be a prisoner *de facto*, to be always kept under watch, not being able to move except when surrounded by attendants; to be only able to converse with his jailers with difficulty; to be most frequently lied to; and only to arrive at a knowledge of the language by sheer force of perseverance, and in spite of all the tricks invented to baffle his intelligence; to be unshod, or at least practically barefoot and to follow with an uneasy eye the ravages of time on his garments; to only have food which had to be parsimoniously measured, and for six months seek anything with which to satisfy his hunger; to sleep on the ground and wonder every night if he were not to be assassinated; and last of all, to fix anxious glances on the horizon, waiting long months for friends who had promised to return promptly; to even believe oneself abandoned! Such was the story of the two years which Forcade spent in Loo Choo, sketched in phrases that are in no wise exaggerated, but merely robbed of all poetry and enthusiasm.

The Celebration of Daily Mass

"And now does he wish to know when the missionary drew the strength to resist so many trials? Here is the secret. The morning after his incarceration in the temple at Tumai, Forcade wished to recite the holy mass. In his baggage he had a missionary's portable tabernacle, some irons with which to bake wafers, some wheat, some candles, and some bottles of wine which, if carefully portioned, might last a long time. Thus, at four o'clock in the morning, rising without any noise in the midst of his sleeping attendants, he dressed his altar with the aid of Augustine, and assumed his vestments. Hardly had he commenced the prayer, *"In nomine Patris,"* than the guard which was awakened with a start, lost themselves in wonder at this strange spectacle. Augustin, who had been warned before, then turned around gravely and said in Chinese to the mandarins, "The Master prays to his God. Woe be to you if you stir! Either leave at once or, if you remain here, go down on your knees!" On that day they knelt and remained. The next time, perhaps fearing some occult influence, they left, and from that day, the holy mass was daily celebrated at Tumai. This was an ever renewed source of strength and courage to M. Forcade; and it was no less satisfaction to think that as he occupied the most extreme outpost of the Far East, every dawn he might be the first priest in the world who ascended the altar."

(End of Marbot's appendix to chapter III).

Chapter IV
An English Schooner

The Bettelheim Family.

(Explanatory note, probably from Marbot: The ship which carried Forcade's letter to Hongkong was an English frigate, the "Samarang." She had appeared on sight on the 19th of June, 1845.....and left for Hongkong in company with the "Royalist" on August 30th. After the departure of the English vessel, Msg. Forcade continued his life of isolation under the surveillance of his amiable jailers. The fresh efforts which he made to get rid of his annoyances, to obtain a little liberty, to procure some books and teachers capable of guiding him in his language study had no better results than before. He had also asked the prime minister of the kingdom if he would be allowed to preach in the kingdom if China should grant the free exercise of our holy religion, since the fears alleged on that score would disappear. He was only answered by evasion, and the situation was not bettered. This state of affairs continued until April, 1846. Forcade's diary gives us the story of the events which followed).

April 30. An English schooner anchored in the Bay of Nafa, the first European ship which has appeared since the departure last year of the two frigates bearing my letters. I hastened to go on board, and I found there an individual named Bettleheim,* who has told me that he has been sent to Loo Choo by a philanthropic society to act in his capacity as a physician. He had with him, beside much baggage, his wife and two little children (the youngest only 5 or 6 months), an English nurse and a Chinese manservant. The so-called doctor (for it appears he is a Protestant minister) received me well, gave me some news of China and Europe, and in return

---

* Parallel account in Marbot: "A sail was noticed in the offing. Her modest size did not permit the illusion of the year before. So the missionary was not deceived upon seeing an English schooner. Alas, this vessel was even a carrier of the truth. Going on board, Forcade was greeted by a certain Bettelheim, who called himself a doctor sent out by a philanthropic society of some sort. This newcomer offered to be of any service to the man who had anticipated him in the islands and ended by confessing himself to be a Protestant minister, classically accompanied by a large household. We do not believe that the cause of free discussion has gained much by this expedition."

asked me a host of questions about the country, offered me his services, even as far as his purse, finally telling me that he was a Protestant, but that although our religious ideas were not quite the same, he hoped, nevertheless, that we would meet and live together on good terms.

The Power of the Devil in Heathen Lands is Illustrated

May 1st. (Second anniversary of the first mass of this mission and of its consecration to the Sacred Heart of Mary).

The doctor of yesterday landed with all his party. The authorities of the country, being unable to get rid of him, put them up in a temple near the entrance to Naha and guard him no less carefully than they do me. We are a good half league apart.

Leturdu Arrives on the "Sabine."   "Bishop!"

At the moment when this affair took place, a European sail appeared in the north,* and at noon, though I could not yet distinguish the

---

* Marbot says: "Early in the morning, Forcade had offered the holy sacrifice. He had just finished this act of grace when Augustin said to him with an embarrassed air, *'Pater, nihil audivit per missam?'*
'Nihil,' he answered. *'Quid dicit?'*
'Per totam missam cantabat avis navis venit, navis venit!' replied the catechist.
"Hereupon the missionary, taking up his catechist for a phrase so inconsistent, brought his thoughts back to the teachings of the faith contrary to such pagan superstitions. The sway which Satan exercises in heathen lands is really unbelievable. This infernal spirit succeeds in justifying by secondary causes the most irrational associations of ideas....and profits by coincidences which are of a nature to justify error. The fact is that, leaving the temple after this rebuke from the missionary, Augustin walked to the end of the garden, only to come back on a run a moment later, repeating with accents of irresistible conviction, *'Revera pater, navis venit, navis venit!'*
"Conquered by this insistence, Forcade climbed a mound which closed the yard on the side toward the sea and saw in fact a ship with tall masts far away on the horizon. How can we paint the anxiety with which he watched the slow movements of this vessel?"

flag, a salvo of artillery for the birthday of Louis-Phillipe told me, to my very great satisfaction, that she was indeed a French ship. The wind was contrary and weak, the movements of the ship desperately slow. It is probable she cannot enter today.

Nevertheless, I moved heaven and earth to procure a large boat and go to meet the corvette before she came into harbour, but they played with me for a good part of the day, and I could only set out quite late. It had been dark for some time, and no one saw me coming when at my cry of "France!" the ship was heaved to. I came alongside, scrambled on board, stood on the deck of the "Sabine" as a man fell on my neck and exclaimed, "An old pupil and now a fellow-worker!" It was my dear Leturdu.* I also received an excellent reception from the commander and the officers. My letters, for which I had waited so long, were here, etc., etc.**

"They descended to the wardroom, and a meal was served of which he had great need, but which was spoiled by his emotions. He was given news of all kinds in a word or two...and that night was sleepless. Yet a more sacred and profound emotion still was reserved for him. In the package of letters handed to him, the first envelope was from M. Libois. He opened it and found that the venerable procurator announced his promotion to the episcopacy. He was then thirty years old and had no other feelings than those of Saint Paul when he declared himself, in his humility *'minimus apostolorum.'* He was named 'Bishop *in partibus* of Samoa and Apostolic Vicar of Japan.'"

The "Sabine" in Harbour. Visits to the Governor and to Bettelheim.

It was two years since I had seen my collaborators, two long years living as if abandoned on this foreign shore. It is both useless and impossible to tell all that I then felt.

---

* Marbot quotes: "Was not the arrival of the disciple after the long solitude and suffering the consolation of God, given to comfort the meek?"

**Again: "We must renounce the attempt to describe the impression of this hour. Forcade was surrounded; all endeavored to shake his hand, congratulating him on being alive and on safely reaching the ship. He was then told that the Lagrenee Treaty had prevented the admiral, to his great regret, from coming earlier, but that the "Victorieuse" and the "Cleopatra" were to follow.

May 2nd. The "Sabine," which had anchored yesterday night after I came on board, set sail at dawn, entered the harbour, and cast anchor near the temple in which I live. A petty mandarin with a yellow bonnet soon came aboard and asked the usual questions in this country:

"From whence have you come? What is the size of the ship? How many men form the crew, etc?" They also offered some presents, but the captain did not take them, and he acted wisely. The regular policy of the country toward Europeans is to offer them, with much ceremony, a few presents of small value, first in order to assume toward the foreigner, to whom they seem to be offering the best that they have, a poverty which is far from being as great as they say; and secondly, in order to be able, without angering anyone, to refuse any useful or necessary articles, the only things for which ships come to their islands.

In the afternoon the captain went to pay his call on the governor of Nafa, and I accompanied him. They began to relate to him all the stories which they invented long ago for Europeans, but the worthy captain formally declared that his visit was not a matter of business, that he has no commission, and that he only came to announce the arrival of Adm. Cecille, who could discuss affairs.

This declaration seemed to be far from giving them any pleasure, and great was the fear of these folks! Fresh presents and fresh refusals. Capt. Guerin* obtained, without too much difficulty, that which no other captain had obtained before him, namely, the privilege of paying for his purchases.

In the evening the English doctor paid me a visit. I received him politely, but without making many advances toward him.

May 5th. I set out to return the call of Mr. Bettelheim, and I met him on my way. He was going to an interview with the governor-general, from whom he hoped to obtain a house. The people would not bring him their sick. He was very uncomfortable in the temple where he was "pocketed." And as a climax of misfortunes, his wife, left alone with her two babies, was in the greatest trouble, as the nurse whom he had with him did not dare to land. (You will have more, my poor man).

---

* The commander of the "Sabine," later becoming Rear-Admiral, he concluded a treaty with Loo Choo.

Forcade's House Evacuated.
Strange Adventures of the Governor

The other day, the whole temple in which I had lived in only one room for the last two years, was entirely given over to me. The petty mandarins quitted their post of observation within, and the bonze carried away his devils and all their paraphernalia. A good sign, and may they never come back! This result, thanks to the presence of the French flag, was not hard to obtain. I only observed to the government that my room was too small to suitably entertain there the French officers who came to visit me, and that I requested them consequently to kindly concede the whole house to me. They hastened to clear out of the place on my first demand.

May 6th. Today, as every day of late, the officers have been walking in every direction, even in the city and close to the royal palace. No one hinders them, no one speaks to them; the people rent or even lend their houses to them whenever they ask for some. Things did not go thus with the officers of the "Alcmene." Many things have changed in the last two years. This is due partly, if not altogether, to the recent news from China, I believe.

May 7th. At the moment when I finished my breakfast, the governor general of Choui (Shuri) arrived at the gate of my temple with a noisy and numerous escort. His Excellency did not come in, but he sent me, by two or three of his retainers, an invitation to dinner on that very day. They added that I would be honored by the commander of the corvette. Since the invitation had not been delivered to him, I answered that it was not proper that I should accept before he did and without knowing what he would do. I suggested that they should begin by inviting him, and when he had decided the matter, I would see what I myself would do. The governor then asked me to follow him on board to serve as his interpreter. Not finding it very advisable to join the suite of this strange personage and to follow among his scribes and satellites, I answered that it had been agreed by the commander that they would send a boat's crew to fetch me whenever I was needed, and that I would await the coming of this boat. The great mandarin then went to the landing, embarked in his boat and moved off to the "Sabine." The commander, who was not expecting him, had gone for a walk on shore, and the officer on watch, who was ignorant of the rank of the visitor and could not understand his fine words, did not show him much honor, so he and his party went away as they had come.

Guerin Invited to Dinner. Arrangements for Leturdu's Landing

Toward two o'clock Capt. Guerin, who knew nothing of this adventure, came toward my house wearing a white jacket with the simple design of paying me a visit and then going for a walk. He was much astonished to be escorted by mandarins in full dress, who seemed to be posted on shore to await and receive him. I explained matters to him, and as they insisted in order to make him accept the dinner, he answered that he could not decently present himself at the house of a great mandarin in his present costume, and moreover, that an invitation of this kind should be sent the day before if people do not wish to expose themselves to the disappointment such as they felt today. Hereupon the captain was asked to fix a day. Today is Friday, and the morrow Saturday, days which were inconvenient on account of fasting, so the feast was postponed until Sunday.

May 10th. According to the instruction given him by Adm. Cecille, the commander of the "Sabine" was not to land M. Leturdu except on my request. Last Sunday, if I have remembered rightly, Capt. Cecille had informed me of this and asked me, when I had formed a decision about this matter to send him a written demand for Leturdu's disembarkment. I needed some time to look around, examine and consider things before attacking a matter of such importance; and then, the zeal of Leturdu had created work for himself on shipboard which scarcely allowed him to go ashore immediately, so for those reasons and still others, the matter had been put off. Today, having weighed everything carefully and finding many advantages without anything to prevent the landing of this dear brother, I decided to claim him from the commander of the corvette by the following letter:

Forcade's Formal Demand for Leturdu

"Captain:
"Although I may not yet consider M. Leturdu's residence in this

kingdom as assured, yet, full of confidence in the known ability of Adm. Cecille and in his devotion to the cause of our missions, and reassured beside by his recent success in China, I venture to take the responsibility of demanding today the landing of my colleague. He has told me of all the good will with which you have deigned, Captain, to honor him, as of the kindness of which he was always the object, and which was shown him by your officers during his stay on your ship. All the French warships, and those of the China station in particular, have made poor missionaries like ourselves accustomed to similar treatment, but today I understand the duty far better; and I feel even more strongly the need of expressing to you in the present circumstance, both in the name of my beloved fellow-worker and myself, the profound gratitude with which I have the honor to be, etc."

Mass on Ship-Board

Toward nine o'clock in the morning, I celebrated holy mass on the deck of the "Sabine," where the sailors had improvised a pretty little chapel with the aid of flags. The commander, all the officers and crew were present in full uniform, and twenty sailors, prepared by the care of the excellent Leturdu, approached the sacred table in meditation. A fair number of petty mandarins and people who happened to be on board were posted on the poop and were witnesses of the ceremony, which went off very well. After this action of grace, my confrere and I dined with the commander, and then I returned alone to my house, leaving M. Lerturdu to edify his dear sailors for a few moments longer.

About 2 o'clock in the afternoon, the commander of the "Sabine," surrounded by his staff in full dress and followed by a company of sailors came to meet me at Tumai, asking me to guide them to the governor-general's dinner and to serve as their interpreter. I wore a cassock, but Leturdu, who was also one of the party, was dressed as a layman. The grand mandarin received us at the school at Tumai, where I had already been twice received by him in 1844 a little while after the departure of the "Alcmene." The reception and dinner differed not at all from the one which I saw before, and of which I spoke, if I remember rightly, in my long letter of 1845. The officials insisted upon offering presents, but these were refused. The party lasted two or three hours.

The Captain Makes an Excursion and Explores an Anchorage

At the beginning of the dinner, the mandarin spoke of the alarm which the presence of the corvette caused in the country, etc. Capt. Guerin answered that the French were far from coming here with any hostile intent, but that, on the contrary, to gain with the settled purpose of enjoying the most friendly and peaceful relations and to establish warm and sincere friendship between France and Loo Choo. However reassuring this declaration might be, it appeared to fail to calm their terrors.

May 11th. The captain came to get me in the morning, asking me to serve as his guide on an excursion. We mounted horses and first went to an old wall in ruins, which separated formerly, it seems, the Northern from the Central Kingdom. From the top of this wall, which rises over a mountain in a spot where the island is very narrow, the view was magnificent. To the north and south one could look off in the distance over the far fields and charming villages of Loo Choo. To the east you may see the great Pacific Ocean, and the blue sea on the west. From this same place, in the August of last year, the English captain, Sir Edward Belcher, had noted an anchorage on the Pacific which appeared excellent, and which he regretted to be unable to explore more closely. I pointed out this spot to the commander, and as it did not appear far, we resolved to go there at once. However, the height from which we measured the road deceived our eyes, and the way was very long. To cap our misfortunes, this port, which seemed so beautiful seen from a distance, proved, when nearby, to be very poor. It was quite shallow and surrounded by dangerous reefs which blocked the entrance. On returning to Tumai, we passed exactly through the middle of the capital. Our horses trotted past the walls, even past the gates of the palace of the king, and no one said a word.

The Story of a Letter and how it was Delivered in Person

May 12th. In the morning, a cadet from the "Sabine," in full uniform and acting as an officer, arrived at my house the bearer of letters from Capt. Guerin to the governor-general of Choui. Up to the present, I had been unable to present any letter directly to the great person in question, and in order that a note might reach him, it had to pass through

I don't know how many channels, and generally I could never know what became of it. From this, as one may well imagine, many inconveniences were felt; and this day's opportunity seemed a good one by which to alter this method. The cadet, not knowing exactly how to discharge his duty, and questioning me on this subject, was told by me that he ought to deliver his letters himself into the hands of the person to whom they were addressed. I offered to guide him and act as his interpreter in visiting the high mandarin. My guard of honor, which has not abandoned its post, seeing the two of us in rather fine clothes walking off towards Choui, asked me more questions, but I never said a word about our business until we reached the gates of the city. Arriving there, I clearly declared how things stood, and I asked them to guide me directly to the palace of the governor-general.

Hereupon, they pretended not to understand and tried to make us enter successively into two or three temples which stood over the entrance to the city. But it was trouble wasted, for we always came back to our text, and as they seemed little disposed to guide us to the designated place, which I did not know, we went straight ahead as far as the gate of the palace, which I knew quite well. It was closed, and I reiterated to the petty mandarins, in the name of the bearer of the letters, and of whom I was simply the interpreter, the demand which I had already made, asking to be guided to the palace of the governor. I insisted on the rationality of this request.

I said to them: "When His Excellency sends any person in uniform to the commander of the corvette, were he a mandarin of even the lowest class, he is always taken into the commander's cabin, and he may speak to him directly. Why does not the great mandarin of Choui treat the envoys of the French mandarin in the same way? Is the Kingdom of Loo Choo greater and more powerful than the Kingdom of France? Moreover, in China and in all the kingdoms of the world, the mandarins deign to admit French messengers before them, and why cannot Loo Choo conform to this custom which is founded on reason? Loo Choo must be a very strong kingdom, indeed, to treat French mandarins with so little respect."

Demonstration Before the Palace Gate

Nothing was said in reply to this, as they did not know what to answer; they only did us the honor of inviting us to enter a building which stood just before us, outside of the palace enclosure, and which, as far as I could judge by discovering from without one of its four-footed inhabitants, was a stable for the noble steeds of His Majesty. We thanked them, and while waiting for these people to deliberate and decide on something, went to smoke a cigar, (a thing which it is considered very swell to do in this country), on a kind of stone bench near the gate. This innocent occupation alarming no one, they made no haste; they deliberated, or did not deliberate at all. All that I know is that they made no answer. As long as the cigar should last, things might go on thus, but when the cigar was finished, that was another question. The representative of France arose, tucked his cap close to his body, took three steps in advance, seized his long sabre and struck the astonished gate three or four times with the gilded hilt. From the time of the flood down to our times, no such an attack had been seen or heard of in these latitudes.

The Letter is Read

The gate did not open of itself, but a yellow-capped petty mandarin, followed by two smaller red-caps, issued immediately from some place or other, and gravely advanced toward us. He said that he was sent out by the governor-general, and that we could hand over to him our dispatch. We replied that it was not fitting to receive the messenger of a French mandarin in the street, but in an official building, and that these dispatches could not be delivered to a stranger, but only to the governor himself. So we were then guided into a large house, which was indeed not that of the governor, but which appeared, however, to be a place where official business was carried on, and after some time and some more talking, His Excellency at last appeared. The bearer of the letters then delivered them into his own hand with admirable dignity and self-possession.

"Your excellency," I then said, "the letters are in French, and if you wish to gain a knowledge of their contents, you can open them at once, and I will translate them to you out loud." The great mandarin hesitated.

The case is so new, so strange. Yet he made up his mind, fell on his knees, and with trembling hand opened the first letter. He passed it to me then with the air of a man who thought that his head, or something of equivalent value, was to be asked of him. Judge the surprise on his features and the expression of his countenance when he saw that it was only a matter of thanks for his dinner of last Sunday and an invitation to dinner on shipboard for next Thursday. The worthy fellow had tea and cakes brought for us at once, smoked a Manila cigar himself with us, and we parted good friends.

A Toast in "Japanese." Troubling Guests and Spoiling Dinner

May 14th. Capt. Guerin, supported by his staff, gave the dinner to the highest mandarin of the capital to which he was invited last Tuesday. Leturdu and I were present at the feast. At dessert, while the champagne was being poured, the Captain asked me to propose in Japanese the following toast:

"To the warm friendship, etc... of the Emperor of the French and the King of Loo Choo." I translated as best I could and in a loud voice. Until then, nothing serious having come up for discussion, they had understood perfectly whatever I had translated for them, but all at once, they could understand nothing further. I was asked to repeat myself, though their faces betrayed their emotion. I repeated my words, and I expressed the thing so clearly that it was impossible to be deaf a second time. The great mandarin was perplexed; he did not know what to say, nor what to do.

Only one follower had entered the dining salon with him. This was old Agina, an able man, always in the foreground in the relations with Europeans. He was behind his back, and His Excellency and he talked together in a voice so low that I could not hear anything. But they discussed, assuredly, what action they should take in this serious juncture. But already the foam of the champagne had, little by little, disappeared. It vanished; it existed no longer. Without movement of life, the electrifying liquid stagnates in the bottom of the glasses. "*Conticuere omnes, intentique ora tenebant.*"

At last old Agina came and spoke in my ear. This may appear strange, for all three of us spoke one and the same language; but His Excellency never addressed me directly, nor did he deign to answer, if I had the boldness to speak to him. It was the old refrain: "Our kingdom is small, our kingdom is poor *et religna,* ...how can we form a friendship with the great, the rich, the noble realm of France?" I repeated this communication to Capt. Guerin, who said, "This has nothing to do with the other matter. I do not talk politics at the table, nor elsewhere. It is the Admiral with whom such things will be discussed; and all I have done is to express a wish of my own heart, nothing more."

The Governor Leaves the Ship. A Visit to Bettelheim.

No matter how reassuring this declaration might seem, His Excellency could not decide to accept the toast. While he hesitated, looked at Agina and confided something to him, I know not what, each guest, one after the other, drank off his glass in silence. Farewell to the royal toast!

After dinner, we tried to amuse the noble guest a little, but a death's head had been present at the feast, and he thought only of how to escape as quickly as possible. On the point of leaving the ship, he began his complaints, but, very rightly, we only answered him as we had replied before. Hardly had he embarked for the shore when he was saluted by France with nine guns, and by the skies with a splendid and generous shower. Both of these salutes appeared to give him about equal pleasure.

May 16th. I have finally paid a visit to Dr. Bettelheim. He was no longer in the temple at the entrance of the harbour of Nafa, but in another temple of the same town which the high mandarin allowed him to exchange for the former. This house is much cleaner and finer than mine. The poor man has, at any rate, as many difficulties with the authorities as myself; they want neither himself nor his medicine. He made many advances toward me, and appeared to desire to become intimate with me, but this is impossible for more than one reason.

On a Japanese Junk. Conversation with the Sailors.

May 17th. Some of the officers having taken it into their heads to go and visit a Japanese junk in the port of Nafa, Leturdu and I accompanied them. At the moment when we came alongside, the ladder was drawn up to bar the passage, but upon a word from the officers, two bold sailors scrambled up and were on the deck of the junk in a twinkling. Thus taken by assault, the Japanese smilingly let down the ladder and reopened the gangway. All of us then went aboard in a very peaceful manner.

"Where is the captain; guide us to the captain," I said to a member of the crew. We were then brought into the largest room, which was not far from being very fine, and received very politely, tea and preserved turnips being served us.

Soon I opened a conversation with the Japanese, and although their language seems to me to be a little different from that of Loo Choo, I can understand them, and they understand me. Their appearance was not at all hostile. Indeed, it was on the contrary, friendly. They talked freely and answered my questions, provided always that I did not take the liberty of pushing them too far, for in this case they turned a deaf ear and answered that they did not understand. These people were simple merchants, who of their own accord would not perhaps have been so mysterious, but a whole flock of petty mandarins who came on board and entered after us, watched them and kept them in awe. However this may be, Leturdu and I drank a cup of tea to their happy conversion. Though they did not understand this toast, proposed in French, may God, who heard it surely, deign to grant it!

At the moment when we withdrew, after having thanked him, I asked the captain to make a visit to the French ship. He replied in the affirmative, but, although in his heart he might ask for nothing better, it is certain that he would not come, as this would be too compromising. In passing in our boat near another Japanese junk, we remarked a man who seemed to make us a signal with his hand to come to his ship, but the lieutenant with whom we were did not judge it wise to answer this call. As for me, I was not able to believe that this call was addressed to us, but probably to some other ship of Japan or Loo Choo. In any case, we can hardly suppose that it was a mere motive of curiosity or a mere desire to see us more closely which led this man to such a bold act. It was full noon. We were surrounded by all the junks at the anchorage, and every eye was fixed on us. No man would risk his head as lightly as that.

May 21st. On behalf of Capt. Guerin I made the following communication orally to three of the principal mandarins:
"Today the commander of the corvette went ashore, and this time, as at all other times, he was himself preceded and followed by a crowd of petty mandarins and attendants who drove away all the women and shut up all the houses before him. To act in this way is to declare that you consider the French captain either a man without any morals, capable of outraging your women, or else a robber, ready to enter your habitations and to take whatever he might lay hands on. This is a serious insult, and it might have annoying consequences for you. The flag which the captain raises everyday over his ship is that of France, whose representative he is. By insulting him you insult France, and he would not be faithful to his duty if he tolerated this. He therefore asks you to denounce this action to your government, and he hopes that a similar insult will not be repeated. Not only should the houses not be closed, but he wants no guards or followers. Their presence is approbrious."

Oral Communication. The Guard of Honor.

The unfortunates to whom this harangue was addressed "lost face" at once. They demanded permission to take some notes and took their time over it as well. As these notes were written in Chinese, I asked Augustin to give me a translation of them. Here it is: "His Excellency, the high military mandarin, having landed yesterday, saw men who drove away the inhabitants of the country as if they were thieves. This did not appear right to him, and he asks that it shall not be repeated."

Oh, ye deaf and hard of hearing! Oh, ye faithless ones! "But this is not what was said to you. What does it matter to the captain if you act as if your people were thieves? Is that any of his business? Would he have any right to complain of this? What he does and should complain of is that you treat him like a thief, shutting every door in his face! It is he whom you treat like one without any morality in making the women flee upon his approach!" I replied.

At last, finally, but not without difficulty, they were made to write approximately what I had said.

I then added: "And notice this also: whatever is said about the captain ought to be understood in the same way and for the same reasons about all the French who come ashore. None of them appear here without the captain's order or permission. If they act badly, let him know of it, and be sure that full justice will be meted to you; but if the French on shore are well-behaved, by treating them as you do you not only injure honorable men who merit your esteem in different ways, but you insult in their persons the one by whose order or permission they have landed, and by insulting the captain, you insult the French flag, and thus insult France!"

Face was lost more and more completely. They did not know what to do, did not dare to speak a word.

I ended, "What is asked of you now is not a favour; you will show us no especial courtesy if you grant it, for you will only do us justice, and if you do no attend to this, steps will be taken... In some way or other, the thing will come to pass."

It was 10 p.m., and the officials retired, honoring us with whatever was most profound in the way of salutation.

"Interpreters" are Suggested. The Captain's Opinion.

May 22nd. A little before noon, the three mandarins of yesterday returned. They had given an account to the governor-general of the complaints and the request of the commander of the corvette, and His Excellency confessed that it was indeed improper to drive away the women and close all the doors before the great French mandarin.

"But would it not be wise," they added, "that at least two or three interpreters should always follow the French on their excursions ashore?"

I replied that it was not my place to answer them about such a question, and that I could do no more than refer it to the captain and transmit his reply.

When I went on board, for several good reasons, I found that Capt. Guerin would have none of these pretended interpreters. When I was back on shore, I made the following answer on his behalf: "The captain thanks His Excellency for having agreed to his just request. About the proposed interpreters, he thanks you also for this proposition, but he has no need of these men, since they do not know any more French than he knows of the language of the country, and so there would be no way for either side to understand the other. Moreover, when the French go ashore, they do not ordinarily go on any business, but only to take walks and see the country. This occupation does not call for any interpreters. But if there were any need of them, Augustin and myself are here, and they would address themselves directly to us. To the knowledge of the captain, we alone are able to act as interpreters between the French and Loo Chooans, and we are always ready to do so."

As under this specious title of interpreters, they were seeking nothing but the maintenance for all of this insufferable guard, which under the same ridiculous name has wearied me for the last two years with its perpetual and disagreeable presence and vigilant inspection, the answer of the captain was far from satisfactory. So they insisted strongly on the adoption of these pseudo interpreters.

"Their purpose is to show you honor and to prevent the plebes from lacking in respect, etc., etc. What prevents you from accepting them is doubtless a feeling of delicacy, the fear of the trouble you would cause. But that is nothing to us, *et reliqua.*"

Advice and how it was Taken. Victory?

One does not need to be a sorcerer to answer arguments like these. As moreover, during twenty-four long months I have often had occasion to hear and refute them, I am quite up on the question, and in a few minutes I put the mandarins back where they belonged. They appeared to agree with my reasoning, and I thought the affair was over. Wishing then to apply some balm to their hearts, I assumed a rather benign expression (a thing which I do not allow myself to do often with this brood), and I attempted to give them some charitable advice as to how to act under such circumstances. I spoke amicably about the French embassy in China, of the successes which it had obtained and the good results which should ensue for both nations. I told them, "Today you often say that you are afraid. Well, if you continue to use lies, petty tricks and much cringing toward the French and do nothing else, perhaps you are right in feeling fear. But if you would act frankly and sincerely toward us, believe me, you would have no reason to be afraid. We only wish you well. We will do you no wrong or any injustice, and everything will come out for the best, etc., etc."

Can you imagine what was the answer to this fine speech? Here it is: "And so we will have you followed by two or three interpreters. The great mandarin said so himself."

I had to show my teeth again, and this was what I said: "What! After the affair is settled you come back to the same question again? No! Understand clearly that hereafter not a soul shall follow us under any title or by any pretext whatsoever. This at least is certain!"

The interview was closed.

This took place at dinner time, and after we had eaten our lunch, we went out for a walk, and at last, for the first time, we were not followed. Or if they still did so, it was done at such a distance that we could not notice it. This was a splendid success, it seems to me, and a great step in advance. Let us thank God for it. Yes, yes, when the admiral comes, if he desires it (and who can doubt that he would not wish to do so), everything can be arranged, and we will achieve our end without conflict. Let us trust in Our Lord and in the heart of the Good Mother who pleads our cause with Him.

May 26th. In the evening I declared to the mandarins on behalf of Capt. Guerin that on next Saturday, the 30th of May, the corvette was to set sail for Port Melville. (Unten Harbour).

We asked, since we were not to be allowed to make purchase from private individuals, that they would kindly send agents of the government for this purpose, charged with the duty of furnishing the necessary fresh provisions for the ship.

At Timi-Gousi-Kou. A Voyage to Port Melville Planned.

May 27th. I had a fine horseback ride with Capt. Guerin to the very strange ruins of *Timi Goushi Kou (Tamagusuku)* to the southeast of Naha. This is an admirably placed old castle, of which nothing remains except the great walls. It appeared to go back to distant antiquity and must have been formerly the palace, or one of the palaces, of the king of the south. Its triple enclosure, where nothing grows except bushes and shrubs in the midst of the debris, seemed to me to be a very fine vacant site for a building. H.M. the King of Loo Choo would give me distinct pleasure if he should cede this ruin to me in order to build a church and a seminary on the spot. But alas! We are far from reaching that point at present. The worthy captain, on the way back, shared the frugal meal at the mission house without any formalities, and he hardly had regained his vessel when the following letter came to him:

A Letter on the Poverty of the Realm and the Need for Interpreters

"I who have prepared this letter am of the kingdom of Loo Choo, governor of the city of Tchong-Cheou. My name is Kiang-Ying-Pao. I now ask a favour. In attentively considering this vile realm, though it is poor, and though its products are very few, yet there are still a few merchants in this port, as it is near to Choui and Nafa, and also because the products yielded by the neighboring fields are rather abundant, when compared with those of more distant places. This is why, since the time of His Excellency's arrival in this realm, we have been able to procure the things he has needed in some fashion, with all sorts of anguish and unceasing labor. In the future we did not know how we could succeed in this. Yet precisely while we were harrowed with this care, behold, we received the advices of His Excellency as follows: 'That on the 6th of this moon he must leave on his ship for the north, to remain there for 30 days or more. And so, if trade is not permitted, men should be sent to supply him with all necessaries, etc., etc.'

"Now what we beg him to consider, what we are thinking of with great fear, is, namely, that the northern part of the island has nothing but many forests! Fertile and fat land is lacking, and its products, compared with those of the neighboring lands, do not amount to more than 20% or 30%. The roads are mountainous, steep and uneven and difficult, both for walking and riding, and it would be impossible to transport merchandise of all kinds overland. The people, beside the diligent care of their crops, have also the truly arduous toil of cutting fire wood. On the other hand, there has been famine and destitution this year. Nothing to eat is to be had. Only *soutitsi (sotetsu)* is to be found (a kind of heather (sic), the root of which is eaten in time of famine. It is a detestable dish). Thus it is that in some way our existence is secured.

"Now, if the ship should go to the north, not only would it be deprived of the conveniences of life, but moreover, it is to be feared that because of the scantiness of the products of the soil and the poverty of the people, it might not be able to procure even the most important necessaries of life. Even if men were sent to procure them, they could do nothing to remedy this state of things. Oh! When the poor people may not give themselves to agriculture, and when they do not have enough time to cut firewood, poverty is piled upon poverty, misery added to misery! How extreme is the sadness in which we are plunged!

"This is why we beg with insistence that His Excellency should deign to examine the preceding reasons to display his mansuetude and to abandon his project of visiting the north. In this case we would offer up thanks for his virtue.

"Concerning the demand that interpreters should not be sent to follow him, etc., as soon as we received this expression of His Excellency's opinion, we have had to obey him with respect. But the populace in this vile realm is numerous compared with the nobility, and there are only a few who know the ceremonies. This is why I have ordered that interpreters should follow in their train every time that their excellencies (the French) should go walking, as much that they might be at hand to receive orders and easily prepare anything, as that at the same time they should impose a respect for ceremony on the part of the common vulgar. Now if interpreters should not be sent to do honor or service, to follow, guard and protect you, not only would we fail in our duty, but there would be reason to fear lest the stupid people, failing in politeness, should cause offence. Now, if the vulgar people should give offence, His Excellency would feel generosity and indulgence, but the heart of the humble governor would not be tranquil. We ask permission to send interpreters in your train, and we have great hope that this will be granted. We have spoken sincerely.

> The 26th Year of Tao Kwang
> The 3rd of the Fifth Moon
> Governor, City of Tchong-Cheou
> Kiang-iung-pao
> Offered with respect."

Forcade Sends Leturdu to Pt. Melville.

I will not amuse myself by criticising, sentence after sentence, article by article, this very long letter. My readers know enough already about this country to be able to estimate, at a glance, the value of most of the facts mentioned therein. All that I will say is that on my own account I have often seen still better productions; better, I say, in exaggeration, falsehood, hypocrisy and ridiculousness.

May 28th. When taking a translation of the preceding letter to Capt. Guerin, I handed to him at the same time, the following letter of my own:

"Captain: When on the 10th of this month I asked for the landing of M. Leturdu, I had the honor of advising you that I could not yet consider his definite residence in this kingdom as absolutely certain. I counted then, as I still count, upon the presence of Adm. Cecille for the arrangement of this matter. Yet when on the 28th the flagship has not yet arrived, and you, on the other hand, are on the point of leaving the roadstead, I confess that I find myself in a rather embarrassing position. You can understand that the keeping of M. Leturdu with me, without having him presented to the government, might be very inconvenient, and to ask you to introduce him, or to attempt myself to present him to the government, would not be in accord with the instructions which recommend me to do nothing before the arrival of the admiral. One resource remains in this difficulty. That is to ask you to take my colleague back on your ship and to carry him with you to Port Melville. I venture to expect this favor from your kindness, which I have learned to appreciate during a full month of the happiest experiences, and in this way to arrange things for the present. About the future, this matter might become embarrassing once more if Adm. Cecille should not come, but in this case, which I hope will fortunately never be realized, I will go overland to you, and we will consult about what is to be done then.

"You told me recently that you would be very glad to have an interpreter with you at Port Melville, in order to procure fresh provisions for your ship. I therefore hasten to put at your disposition, and even under your orders, Augustin Ko, my catechist. His goodwill is already known to you, and I hope you will continue to be satisfied with him. For myself, I consider myself happy in finding this opportunity to discharge in some measure my enormous debt of gratitude to you."

Leturdu's Character. His Success on Shipboard.

May 29th. Two cadets of the "Sabine" who were on the point of being made officers and were both very capable, well instructed, and of good reputation, but who were somewhat corrupt of heart and mind, like most of the men of the present day, came to take communion very piously at M. Leturdu's mass. This double conversion is beyond dispute the greatest conquest of my dear brother on board the corvette. For its moral effect on officers and men, this itself is worth more than the confirmation of twenty sailors. Leturdu seems to be blessed a thousand times for it! Such a man is truly needed here, it is easily seen. Truly my venerated colaborer and dear friend, Libois, has made me a splendid gift, and I am very grateful to him. And I can assure him that as long as he sends me assistants of such kind, were it only once in two years, we will never disagree.

During lunch, a messenger from the ship brought me Capt. Guerin's reply to the last letter of the Governor of Choui for me to translate and present. The captain was astonished at the great difficulty which they felt in procuring the provisions which he had requested. Nevertheless, he assumed that he believed them at their words and expressed his gratitude, only observing that he had paid for everything without bargaining, and that they had lost nothing. He could not give up his voyage to Port Melville, as he had an order from the admiral, and his first duty was to obey it and go there. He also insisted upon getting fresh provisions, saying that less would be asked if the supply was small, and that if it were necessary, he was ready to pay more, taking their difficulties into question.

Guerin's Answer. Forcade is Left to Mediate.

The captain was astonished that they returned to the subject of those ridiculous interpreters who could not understand a word of French. He reminded the governor of the reasons why he had asked to be rid of their pursuit and remarked that no one has had the least reason for complaint about the conduct of the French since they have not been followed. He did not say any more, for he could not decide the question. So let His Excellency do what he wished. On his part he would endure anything without more complaint. The admiral was the person who would treat this matter and several others. *Vale.*

In the afternoon I went to put Leturdu and Augustin on board their ship. They were both quartered in the officer's wardroom.

May 30. The corvette set sail early this morning for Port Melville, and I am now alone in my temple. I do not find myself troubled by this, as I have spent the whole month of May in the midst of so much hubbub that I feel the need of repose, physical and moral. It is also very agreeable to be able to meditate a little in preparation for Pentecost and the other great feasts which follow. Alas! It is often when we have the most need to inquire at every step what is God's will and to hear His voice at every moment, that just at that time the agitation of the world comes to trouble us, and the speech of men deafens our ears and does not allow us to lend them to celestial accents!

The need for meditation: this was the first reason which deterred me from now following M. Leturdu and the corvette. There are others beside: the admiral seems to desire greatly that I should see him as soon as he appears, that, if it can be done, I should meet him before he comes to anchor. I desire this no less than he does, and from Port Melville I could not observe his coming. In a word, it is necessary that someone should be here now to keep open eye upon everything that goes on.

Chapter V
The "Victorieuse" and "Cleopatra" Arrive

Forcade as Pilot

June 3rd. This afternoon I received a letter from M. Leturdu sent overland from Port Melville. The "Sabine", which amused itself in doing some hydrography, took two days to get there. After anchoring, a petty mandarin accompanied by two followers came out to offer Capt. Guerin four hens, fifty eggs and some sticks of firewood to cook the same. Of course, this was refused. My dear brother has obtained a house where he can say the holy mass. I answered him at once and sent on various things which he asked for.

June 4th. A European ship was announced about 9 a.m. By the aid of my telescope, I could clearly make out the ship and her flag. She was a French corvette, and therefore the "Victorieuse." I asked for a boat, and though I could not get it as soon as I wanted, I set out as soon as it was ready. Capt. Guerin had taught me how to act as a pilot for my harbour, and my plan was to let the ship, which was in sight, profit by this. I made my half-dozen bad rowers hasten as much as possible, because the corvette, favored by a fine breeze, was coming on quickly. Already the ship's head was pointed toward Nafa, and as the lower sails were being furled, she seemed to be preparing to anchor. But what a profound deception, when I was far from land and near the much-desired goal of my voyage, the unworthy "Victorieuse" suddenly loosened her sails and, changing her course, took flight toward the north. She must have seen neither myself nor the red handkerchief which I waved as a signal above my head. And not discovering her sister ship, the "Sabine," anywhere in harbour, she went off, without doubt, to Port Melville, in the hope of finding her there. I lost all hope of catching up with her and limped back to shore as I had come.

June 5. Providence itself managed my misadventure of yesterday. If I had caught the "Victoreuse," she would in all probability have carried me off to Port Melville, and to my great regret I should have missed the admiral, whose beautiful frigate, the "Cleopatre," my old acquaintance, appeared this morning. I set out like yesterday in a badly equipped boat, though the sea was bad, and it rained in torrents. As much soaked with salt water as with rain, I reached the ship, though not without trouble, and with still more difficulty, I came alongside. With the help of the boatswain, the carpenter, and any number of sailor experts, I finally came in through a port and stood on the deck. Admiral Cecille was waiting anxiously for me there.

"You are crazy," he said, "to come to meet me at sea in such a boat and in such weather!" Then he took me by the hand to his quarters, and falling on my neck, kissed me on both cheeks. I was greatly moved by these signs of affection. He who showered them on me is the friend and benefactor of all missionaries, the liberator of the Christians of China.

Osculation. The Voyage to Port Melville.

Adm. Cecille did not exactly know whether he should put into Nafa or not, but my presence and what I told him caused him to determine to go to join the corvette at Port Melville, and he at once set out on this course. After luncheon, the good admiral took me into his own cabin and told me this was to be mine while I was on board. He himself had the habit of sleeping in a cot hung from the ceiling of his gallery. He also deigned to invite me to share his table. So, behold me treated like a lord, and I am scarcely equal to it after my two years of privation and captivity in the dirty, filthy temple.

June 6th. The wind was strangely against us last night and yesterday, and now we are still quite far from Port Melville, although it is only some 15 leagues from Naha. This morning a corvette appeared, and to my astonishment, we discovered that her flag was French. It was the "Victorieuse" which I had seen passing me with a good wind the day before yesterday, and which I thought must have arrived long ago. We learned afterward that a squall of wind struck her on Thursday afternoon and drove her back to sea, and so she had not been able to reach harbour.

Toward 2 or 3 p.m., the commander of the "Sabine," after having guided the "Victorieuse" to the anchorage, came out to meet us at sea to guide us in our turn. Under the direction of his excellent pilot, the "Cleopatre" easily cleared the narrow and difficult channel that leads to the port. We had almost reached the spot chosen for dropping anchor when the fore-foot of the frigate touched a bank that was not indicated on the map and which the approach of night rendered invisible. We were aground. It was no small matter to get off, but thanks to the clever means employed by the admiral, the efforts of our large crew and the help given by the two corvettes, we were again afloat at ll p.m. We had just struck when two petty mandarins with yellow caps came on board to honor the admiral with their salaams. The poor fellows had chosen a bad time, and they were informally sent off, if I should not rather say they were told to go to the devil.

The Admiral's First Callers, the Governor of *Fou-Kou-San*. (*Hokusan*, or Northern Mountain)

June 7th. Early in the morning I went ashore to go and celebrate holy mass in the house obtained by Leturdu. This was larger and better arranged in every way than my temple at Tumai, and a little chapel, which was not at all bad, had been already built there.

The rest of the day on shipboard was spent in putting things in order, for last night's adventure had turned everything topsy-turvy. Poor Adm. Cecille, who spent the whole night on his feet, was terribly weary. He felt severe pain in the legs and went to bed without being able to dine.

June 8th. The admiral had had a good rest, and he felt fairly well this morning. At noon, a purple cap followed by a somewhat numerous suite of red and yellow ones, came out to the ship. The admiral received this dignitary, who declared himself the governor of the city of *Fou-Kou-San* (the Northern Mountain, *Hokusan*). We are now in his province. After the regular compliments, Adm. Cecille asked that a mandarin of a rank equal to his own should be sent from the capital to treat with him. They replied that it took three days to go to Choui, and as long to return. And that this request could not be gratified for six days. To this the admiral replied that he would wait as long as it was necessary. He also insisted that in return for money his ships should be supplied with the necessary provisions. He warned them, also, that his sailors would not go on shore under any conditions for fear of disturbances, but that he and his officers would use the right of walking about on shore. These two points, which were long ago carried by assault, can now pass without any opposition.

"When will you leave?" the mandarins asked.

"When my business is over," was the answer. "If you transact your part quickly, I will go soon. If not, I will not go away for some time."

It is not necessary to say that the inevitable subjects of presents was broached, and that the greatest insistence was used to have them accepted. But the admiral, who knew the cards, would not accept anything and persisted in his refusal in spite of all that was said or done. This is the list of the gifts intended for him: One ox, two goats, fifteen hens, 150 eggs, fifty pounds of vegetables and fifty bundles of firewood. The mandarin bethought himself of going from the frigate to the two corvettes and repeating this politeness for the commander of these ships. Warned of this by me, the admiral then declared that his presence annulled the authority of these captains, his inferiors, that he was the only person in command, and that he alone should be addressed in all cases.

Port Melville and the Island *Koui* (Kouri), or Herbert's Island

Before letting the governor go, the admiral ordered Baron Reille, his aide-de-camp, to take him over the ship. She was the largest and finest vessel ever seen in these islands, her dimensions were astonishing, and her armament caused fear.

"Is this the very largest thing in the way of ships?" our astounded islanders asked me.

"No," I replied, "this is manned by five hundred men. There are other ships with a crew of a thousand or twelve hundred."

The governor did not deign to impart to me his impressions about the matter, but his face told them clearly.

When the visitors left, the admiral, accompanied by the captains of the three ships and your humble servant, made an inspection of the bay in his barge. It is composed of a long series of sufficiently deep basins perfectly protected by the surrounding mountains. In a word, a splendid anchorage. Unfortunately, of the two entrances supplied by nature, one is not navigable, and the other, narrow and fringed with reefs, is difficult of access. It appeared, however, that if this port were in the hands of Europeans, this state of things could be easily remedied by dredging and other harbour works.

June 10th. In the afternoon I accompanied the admiral on a walk ashore. The country near this port is not as rich as that around the capital, but it is fertile, nevertheless, and very well cultivated. Nothing could be more pleasing or picturesque than the scenes which met our eyes.

June 11th. With the admiral, I went for a trip to Herbert's Island, or *Koui*, as the natives call it. This was a very small island, as may be seen from a map, and it only has one village of the same name. There was some land under cultivation, but the larger part of the island was covered with rocks and such thick woods that one would take them for virgin forests. A landscape artist could make his fortune here, where each step would allow him to exercise his talent. A good guard was kept even at this isolated spot. I noticed a young boy occupied in reaping millet, and as he was alone, I came near and asked him several little questions, which he promptly answered with the best of grace. But our conversation was short, for four fellows, with faces like gallows-birds springing out of the earth, dashed down upon us, and the frightened child took to his heels and fled.

A Sailor Buried. First Trip to Yagadji Island.

June 12th. Assisted by Leturdu, I officiated at the interment of a sailor from the "Victorieuse" who died yesterday with the consolations of religion and in the best frame of mind. This melancholy ceremony was accomplished according to all the formalities. A very picturesque spot was chosen for the place of burial at the extremity of a point extending into the bay, and a cross was planted over the tomb. The respect which the people feel for graves and for European cannon will doubtless preserve this sacred sign from all insult, though their chiefs are far from regarding it as that of their redemption.

In the afternoon the admiral communicated to me the notes which he had prepared for the high mandarin who was coming from Shuri and allowed me to express my views to him in the manner of acting in the present circumstances. I was already prepared on this head, for since the arrival of the "Sabine" I have often had time to think of this and talk about it with Leturdu. Without delay, frankly and simply, I expressed my way of thinking, and my observations were well received.

June 15th. A visit with the admiral to the island named Lyra, called *Yagadji* by the natives. It had only four villages, and all its surface must be cultivated or capable of cultivation. We noticed a pretty little river here of considerable size for an island of such small area.

June 16th. The arrival of the king's minister, *Couja* in the language of the country, and *Chang-ting-chou* in Chinese, was announced to me after breakfast. The high dignitary, summoned eight days ago, has made us wait for him a little, but here he is at last. The admiral will receive him tomorrow.

Negotiations Opened with Couja. The Letter to China Discussed.

June 17th. Between 12 and 1 p.m. the aide-de-camp and myself went ashore to fetch the expected minister in the admiral's barge. Two other boats were destined to receive the members of His Excellency's staff. After a few minutes wait on the beach, the great man arrived in fine clothes. He was a fat old fellow of 60 years with an excellent face, much more amiable and talkative than the governor of Choui, with whom we had been in relations before. The admiral, the commander of the three ships, the staff and all the crew of the frigate were on deck in full uniform and the best of order when the high functionary came on board. After the usual bows, he was led to the admiral's quarters, and there after some common-places, which it is useless to mention, diplomacy began thus:

The admiral: "When I was at Canton and treating of affairs with Kung, the Imperial Commissioner, His Excellency told me that the King of Loo Choo had written to the Emperor of China on the subject of the two men which the corvette "Alcmene" had left in the kingdom. Is it true that such a letter was written and sent to China?"

The reply: "Yes, we did write about this matter, but not to the Emperor, only to *Fou-king-tay-fou* of *Foutcheou* (Fuchow). This was our duty."

The admiral: "In this letter, a copy of which I have before my eyes, it is said, among other things, that Fournier-Duplan, captain of the

"Alcmene," landed these two men by force on your territory. Now, is it true that violence was employed on that occasion?"

The reply: "No, there was no violence, and we never wrote such a thing to China. We only said that two men were casually landed on our territory by a French ship."

The admiral: "Since these two men have been in your country, have they violated the laws of your country in any way?"

The reply: "Never. We have had no complaint to make of them."

The admiral: "Although Kung told me the opposite, I am happy to learn that this was the case. I am also especially glad that Fornier-Duplan used no violence, for in this case he would have acted directly against my orders.

"Among the complaints which you sent to China, the following appeared, namely, that one of the two men left with you was a Chinese criminal, a man who had escaped from the rigors of Chinese law. It is true that he was once arrested and even condemned to perpetual exile, because he belonged to the religion of the Lord of Heaven, and because he refused to renounce it. But this was the religion of his father and mother, and it is in no sense a crime to be attached to a good religion transmitted to us by our parents. I had hardly arrived in China upon learning of his misfortune, and I hastened to intervene in his behalf with the viceroy of Canton and the Imperial Commissioner. Letters were written to Peking; his case was retried, his innocence was recognized and, returned to liberty, he was brought to me at Macao. Be assured that Augustin is a worthy man. He enjoys my affection and my esteem, and he is worthy of the respect and love of all good men."*

The Interpreter and Augustin's Case. A Diplomatic Note

There was trouble painted on every face. In three or four words the interpreter repeated this statement, but omitting more than half of it. I warned the admiral of this.

The admiral: "You should not act in such a way. You ought to repeat everything I said without omitting a word."

---

* Author's note: There are certainly verbal differences in this conversation, for I do not have memory enough to recall everything word for word, but the substance is unchanged. This observation applies in all similar cases.

The interpreter: "When a speech is so long, I cannot remember everything."

The admiral: "We will henceforth say less at one time. You may take notes, if you wish. But be sure to retell all that I say."

Not without difficulty the panegyric of Augustin was written down, and the minister was made fully acquainted with it.

"Ah!" they exclaimed. "We never wrote anything like that!"

With an air of a person who was hardly convinced the admiral went on: "I am happy that your conduct was so wise, for if you had delivered up these two men to the Chinese, and I had not found them on coming here, you would have been in great trouble."

The admiral then read the following note, which he had prepared beforehand, and its interpretation was accomplished with difficulty because of the bad will of the minister's interpreters, who pretended not to understand and used a thousand other devices that from lack of patience matters might have been dropped.

"Excellency:

"As I have already let you know, France is a powerful nation, but like everyone who is strong, she is generous, because she has nothing to fear. Thus you have nothing to fear from France. I have come here seeking nothing but justice and possessing none but peaceful sentiments. My desire is to cause no trouble in your country, to respect your customs and laws, and, in a word, to do nothing which could sadden the king of this noble realm and its great mandarins. Up till now you have known us very slightly, since the intercourse you have had with Europeans has not been very frequent, and your suspicions have rendered even this difficult. I have come to scatter all these misunderstandings, to establish friendly relations, and this is why I will speak truthfully to you. I hope you will put faith in my words, for they come from a sincere and benevolent heart.

The Nations of Europe Which May Visit You.
(Note continues below)

"Until now you have only seen the English, and I do not think that you repent of the relations you have had with them. You have done them favours for which I know they are grateful, and you will have no more reason to repent of your relations with the French. It is probable that you will see the Americans, who carry on a large trade with China, and you also know the Russians, who have a legation at Peking, for some of your mandarins have visited their archimandrite when in China paying your tribute. France, England and Russia are the first three kingdoms of Europe. Their emperors command several millions of men. The seas are covered with their commerce, and their vessels travel to all parts of this world. These three great peoples are at peace, their emperors and subjects live in the most perfect harmony, and the Queen of England is even now in France with our great Emperor, to whom she has come to pay a visit as to her best friend.

"According to what I have said, you ought to understand that the Europeans do not form a single nation, as you might have imagined at the time when you only saw the English. Each nation is distinct, having an independent ruler, a peculiar language and a particular flag which serves to distinguish it from other nations. There are many other nations beside these in Europe, but it is probable that you will never know them, because they have few ships, with the exception of the Spanish, who once had a great fleet and who possess Luzon, a large island not far from this noble realm, as you probably know quite well. If I explain these things to you, it is in order that you may clearly understand the distinctions which exist among the nations, and so, if other men than the French should visit the noble realm and behave badly, you may not confuse them with us.

Power of the Europeans Shown in China. Louis-Philippe's Virtues.

"You have heard of the war which the English fought with China, and you have learned that the illustrious *Tao Kuang* was reduced to the necessity of buying peace at the price of twenty-one million Mexican dollars, having beside to cede the island of Hongkong to the conquerors. This example of the great Chinese Empire conquered by a European country may well cause anxiety to the kings of the neighboring lands. They may well fear that the victors may not stop here. For if the peoples of this part of the world continue as they have done up to the present, to act contemptuously and insolently toward Europeans, treating them like barbarians, and furnishing them by these rash insults with a ground for discontent, war will burst out afresh, and woe to those who have provoked it. For I tell you truthfully that they will be defeated and humiliated. The force of European weapons is far greater than you can imagine, and you will believe this when you know that the English only needed 12,000 men and some ships to defeat China.

"The French Emperor has too fine and beautiful an empire to desire to increase it by distant conquests. Moreover, the Emperor is a good man who desires only what is just. But he is quick to resent any insult, and if he does not love war, because it causes unhappiness, he does not dread it, because he has a large army and a great fleet which can easily assure him victory. But I repeat that Louis-Philippe is a sage, a friend of humanity and peace. What he desires is that his vessels may find in foreign ports, and especially in those of the kingdom of Loo Choo, a refuge from storms, and water and provisions as needed. What he desires is that his subjects shipwrecked on foreign shores may be taken in and treated with humanity until he can send his ships to fetch them, or until an opportunity presents itself of sending them back by the vessels of his allies. On these conditions, which are demanded by justice and humanity, you may be sure to have our emperor for your friend and to obtain from him the good offices which you may need in the difficult conditions in which you may perhaps soon find yourselves placed.

"No nation has ever repented of having France as its friend, and the Emperor has more than once acted as intermediary to protect the weak from the strong. By his genius and the respect which he inspires in other kings, he has been able to stop wars that were on the point of being fought.

The Results of Seclusion Compared with the Palmy Days of Loo Choo

"The system of isolation, in which you have lived like Japan and China up to the present, is bad. The example of China proves it openly, for when the war with the English befell her, she was seen to be like a person without a friend who in misfortune is reduced to his own resources, and who has neither help nor advice from anyone. Moreover, the Chinese Empire failed. But if the illustrious Tao Kuang had then had the French for friends, as he does now, it is probably that the war would never have broken forth, and that all the difficulties would have been solved by our great Emperor, who is, as I have already said, also bound with ties of friendship for the Queen of England.

"The Emperor of the French has recently made a treaty of friendship and commerce with the Emperor of China. It was not necessary to fight in order to obtain this, for on each side the treaty was made voluntarily. It has been for the mutual advantage of the two parties, and it was framed by the mutual desire of forming an eternal friendship. According to this treaty, the French merchant ships may traffic in five Chinese ports, to wit, Canton, Amoy, Foutchou, Ning-po and Chang-hai. In the care of warships, they may enter any port without exception in order to give rest to their crews, to make repair or to buy provisions or other necessary articles. What the great Emperor of China has granted to France, the King of Loo Choo, who is neither less enlightened or less wise, may well, so it seems to me, grant to us in case of the ports of his realm.

"The example which the great Emperor of China has given is a good one to follow. It is by commerce that kingdoms acquire influence, riches and force; it gives activity to the people and spreads prosperity over all classes of society. Remember the glorious times of King Chang-Pa-Tse under whose reign the kingdom of *Fou-kou-san (Hokusan)* and *Nou-san (Nanzan)* were joined to that of *Chou-san;* and the days of King *Chang-Chong (Sho Shin),* who did so much for the industries and commerce of these islands. Then this noble realm shone with great splendour and enjoyed unheard of prosperity. Then you had many relations with foreign countries. You then carried on much commerce with China, Formosa, and with Hinga, Satsuma, Arima, Amakousa and Hocata in Japan. It is even said that your junks were seen as far away as Corea, Cochin, China, and Malacca. This commerce procured such a large quantity of silver and copper coin to your noble realm that specie became scarce in Fukien and Chekiang provinces in China and complaints about this were made by the Chinese to their emperor.

Final Appeal for a Commercial Treaty. A Visit Arranged.

"What has become of these fine days of the noble realm? Where have the riches, of which your ancestors boasted, gone? Where today is the power and glory of the former kings of this noble realm? All has vanished. But this glory, these riches and the splendours of past ages may reappear, and it is by means of commerce that you will succeed in doing this. If you establish intimate relations with Europeans, your kingdom will become, as before, the center of commerce of China, Formosa, Japan and Corea. Your kings will reassume that elevated position and the great degree of power which they formerly enjoyed. This is why I propose that you should form a treaty with France, similar to that which we have just concluded with China."

At last, toward six in the evening, when the difficult reading of this note was finished, we promised, on the request of the minister, to translate it into Chinese and to give him a copy in order that without fear of error, he might refer the whole matter to the king. His Excellency could decide nothing by himself.

Then, "At what hour, and on what day, may I have the honour of returning Your Excellency's visit?" the admiral asked.

"I am in the country, lodged in a small and dirty house; so I beg the great mandarin to excuse himself from returning my visit as I cannot receive him properly," was the reply.

"I know quite well that His Excellency is not living here in his own palace. Yet whatever may be the house in which he is staying, I will go there very gladly, and I will know how to take circumstances into account," replied the admiral.

More than one means of making the admiral give up his idea of visiting were proposed, but as he remained firm, they at last told him that they would tell him later on what day he could be received, as it was necessary to make preparations, etc. Guided by the admiral, the minister visited the batteries of the "Cleopatre" before leaving, which were doubtless too fine to please him.

The Governor Leaves the Ship. Second Trip to Yagadji Island

Thence he returned to the shore as he had come, still accompanied by the aide-de-camp and myself. The salute of nine guns with which he was honoured at his departure, was magnificent, thanks to the echo from the mountains which surrounded the narrow basin in which the frigate was moored. He had never heard such a racket before, but far from being, or appearing to be, frightened like his honorable compatriots, he merely laughed and stopped his ears at every shot. I also noticed with pleasure that he listened without any formality to the remarks which I made to him now and then, and that he replied good humoredly to me. This is something truly fine and rare on the part of a great mandarin.

June 18th. 4 p.m. Just at the moment when the admiral, the captain and myself were on the point of pushing off from the ship in order to make a trip, a yellow bonnet sent by the minister came out in two wretched canoes joined together. He told me that he was charged by His Excellency to invite the admiral to kindly come, tomorrow at noon, to take some tea and cakes and thus return the call which he desired to make.

At the same time he asked that two tables and some chairs might be sent from the ship, as it would otherwise be impossible to procure them in this out of the way place. Of course, this was promised.

"Are the captains invited?" I asked.

"That," said the yellow bonnet, "depends upon the wishes of the great mandarin; let him bring whoever he wishes."

We went to make a second expedition on the island of Yagadji. We were not followed on this walk, and we met an old man of about 60 years with whom I began a conversation. After some words of no importance, he left us, but we soon met him again at the door of his hut with his old father of 80 and his two sons. While the admiral was lighting his cigar at the coals which they hastened to bring him, I again took up our talk without difficulty. These good people, who were delighted to hear me speak their language, talked with as much confidence as simplicity. We left them, saying to ourselves, "If we were free here, things would go very differently." This is my conviction.

The Governor At Ou-Ounting. Forcade's State Costume.

June 19th. At a quarter of twelve the Admiral, followed by the captains and a large part of the staff-officers of the three vessels, went in full uniform to the villages of *Chimo Ounting* (Lower Unten) near which the frigate was anchored. Two petty mandarins with yellow caps came to offer their services as guides to the admiral at the beach where a number of his sailors awaited him. We set out, fifes and bugle in advance, drums beating and our ensign displayed, and after 20 minutes of solemn march along a pretty little mountain road we arrived at the town of Oy Ounting (Upper Unten). There the house which served at present as the head-quarters of the minister was situated. The governor of *Foukousan* (Hokusan, or Nothern Castle) in a purple hat was at the door, and the great mandarin stood in the court to receive us.*

The impoverished palace, although covered with thatch, was all right within; at least the room in which we were received was fairly large, clean and well aired. A mahogany table brought from the ship was placed for the admiral alone in the most honorable spot, and much insistence had to be used to persuade the minister to share it with him. I placed myself at the end of this table to serve as interpreter to the admiral on his left, and his staff arranged themselves as they could around a long table of white wood. The purple governor had disappeared. Only five or six petty mandarins were present, among them the famous Aniah and Okouma, who leaned against the wall and stood upright. After the presentation of visiting cards, the exchange of compliments and all that followed this, the dinner was served. It was neither elaborate nor brilliant; some mouthfuls of pork and fish, and some bad cakes, the whole served up in rather ugly dishes made up the feast. But on the other hand the tea was good, and the *saki* (rice wine) not bad. People here always like to affect poverty, and, to be just, the place and the circumstances hardly allowed them to do better.

---

* Note by Marbot, resuming the author's note: "The missionary enjoyed the greatest success of all. His cassock had no decent color except when, at the hour of mass, it disappeared under his alb. So the officers did their best to equip him, but they could only do this by dressing him in "mufti." A long pair of trousers belonging to Capt. Rigault de Genouilly and a fine sky blue swallow tail coat with cut and gilded buttons which the admiral had made for going into society 20 years ago made up his equipment. As the captain and admiral were tall, the missionary had to turn up the legs of his trousers to the knees and his sleeves to the elbow. An opera hat was clapped on over all this. One of the officers who was not on duty and was returning from a hunt was convulsed, but not so the natives. The latter murmured discreetly after him, 'They were right to call him a dignitary. His clothes are not skimped like the others, and cloth was not economized for him in the least!'"

A Reference to Bettelheim. Edicts from China.

Soon the admiral began the conversation in this way: "Is it a long time since you have had any news from China?"

Reply: "Last year, in the 5th moon, our ships returned, but since then we have had no news."

Admiral: "Did your ships coming back last year tell you of the edicts which the Emperor of China had then just published in favor of the Christians?"

Reply: "We have heard nothing on this subject." (Now, Mr. Bettelheim had brought those decrees, and he has no doubt already presented them to the government).

Admiral: "I am surprised at this, for this was a much talked of event in China, which was a reason for great joy on the part of all the Christians there. But at least I can let you see these decrees. Here they are."

The three edicts were presented. Ania, Okouma and the other mandarins at once set about reading them. We offered to allow them to keep these awhile and make copies of them, and the offer was accepted.

A little later the admiral said, "we are now busy in translating yesterday's note into Chinese, and as soon as this work is done, it will be transmitted to His Excellency in order that he may carry it to the King."

Reply: "My intention is to return to *Choui* tomorrow in order to make my report to the king."

Admiral: "It would be better that His Excellency should only send the document, but remain here in person, for I will no doubt have other reasons to consult with him. I have other requests to make of him, and I must be able to communicate to him my opinions when the answer comes."

His Excellency then replied that this was an affair of such importance that no one but himself could refer it to the king.

Admiral: "But His Excellency cannot leave tomorrow surely. He must wait until my note can be translated, for how could he render an exact account to the king without that document?"

Reply: "At the time of my departure, the king was slightly indisposed; he may be sick today, and my prompt return becomes imperative."

Admiral: "But once more, what can be done without my note? This will be translated tomorrow evening, and His Excellency ought to wait until that time, and he ought at least promise to come back here with the answer."

After more trouble, these two points were finally carried.

What's in a Letter or in a Name?
Pleasures of Diplomacy.

The admiral now presented a letter of invitation to dinner on next Sunday to the great mandarin. This letter was written in French by his own hand, and he requested His Excellency to open it, promising him that it should be read to him without further delay. The poor inhabitants of this country are so suspicious in their intercourse with Europeans that this tiny matter completely upset them. No one knew what this letter was about. They feared to discover some horrid mystery therein, and even dreaded to break the envelope. The admiral undertook this and handed the paper to me, and I gave a Latin translation of it to Augustin in order that he could transmit the invitation in Chinese... But Augustin could not be understood, so great was the trouble of the interpreters. While he perorated endlessly with them, attempting to make himself understood, I lost patience, and addressing the great mandarin directly, I revealed to him the amazing secret in a few words of the native language. The old fellow understood me. His features expanded, and the invitation was joyously accepted.

Then came another grave affair. "Until now in China," said the admiral, "my name has been written in a very imperfect manner. It is written *Si-Sie,* and I am named Cecille. So these two words sound quite differently to the ear. Won't you write my name more exactly in the character of your country?"

Great embarrassment and profound uneasiness among my lords, the mandarin interpreters! They whispered into each other's ears and discussed how to act in such a dreadful juncture. The great mandarin, to whom nothing had yet been said, wished to be informed on the question, and Okouma flung himself down at his knees and explained matters to him in as low a voice as possible, but not so low that I could not hear him.

At last they seemed to resolve something. The council passed into the next room, and after a quarter of an hour brought back the desired information on a scrap of paper. I spoke: "But these are Chinese characters, and the admiral wishes it to be in the characters of this country."

"With the characters of this country," said a petty mandarin, "such a thing cannot be written."

"Why can it not be written?" it was asked.

There was no reply. A new deliberation took place, and more hesitations, until at last, as our urgings continued, they hastily decided to act, and in less than a twinkling the word "Cecille" was at last written in a different way. I examined the writing, and the characters were exactly those of the Japanese *kata kana*. The interview now closed, and we returned back on board in majesty by the same road as we had come.

June 20th. The surgeon-major sent a messenger to wake me in the middle of the night on account of the second master armourer, who had long been ill, and who had just sunk into a dangerous state. The poor man had full consciousness, but seemed far from considering himself so near his end. No matter what I said to him, he could not make up his mind to confess himself at once, and he insisted on putting the matter off until the morning of the next day. After I left, the 2nd and 3rd surgeons, who were watching the sick man, several times made the greatest effort to get him to call me back, but without success. The dying man did not say "no" to this plan, but he always put it off until later. As soon as I awoke, between five and six in the morning, I ran to the sick bay.

"How is our patient?" I inquired.

"He is not doing well. He is very low," was the reply. I approached his bed, but he had just passed into the other world without anyone noticing it. He could still speak a minute earlier, for someone had asked him if he wanted anything, and he had replied, "No, I need nothing." This was his last word. What a sad example of the abuse of grace! *Ne differas de die in diem.* None the less, such an event is fortunately rare. In general our sick sailors welcome a priest with eagerness and receive the last sacraments in the best disposition.

In the evening the admiral recommended that I send Leturdu back to *Tumai,* since his stay here was of no use. Though he has not been introduced to the government, he ought to first install himself without saying a word in the old temple where our belongings have been right along, and of which we will soon be the owners. Wise reasons led Adm. Cecille to propose this line of conduct to me. Augustin would have to accompany my dear brother, but he was to fetch his baggage and my own from the house and to return alone to the frigate as quickly as possible. This expedition would have to be made overland, for we are right at the season of the southwest monsoon, in typhoon time, and for this reason it would not be either easy or safe to send a ship to Nafa.

June 21st. Toward 3 p.m. I went ashore in the admiral's barge to fetch the minister who was to dine on board today. The governor of *Foukousan,* who was also invited, followed us in a second boat.

The Minister at the Admiral's Dinner. A Musical Surprise.

Everyone knows the ordinary magnificence of an admiral's life, and as Admiral Cecille wished to create a high idea of France, he attempted to surpass himself, and he fully succeeded. He had a table of twenty covers prepared and splendidly served, at which the major part of his staff seated themselves with the two mandarins. The poor excellencies, who had never left their native islands, showed themselves much astonished by the abundance of the dishes and wines, but they were especially dazzled by the splendid silverware. These simple folks, I am sure, imagined that all the plated platters and well-shaped covers which they saw were made of massy silver, and even the porcelain, which was very pretty, and still more the glass, which was considered to be made of crystal in these lands, was able to make them marvel. If they had ever heard of fairies, they might have imagined themselves transported to one of their palaces.

But that which produced the greatest impression of all was a nice hurdy-gurdy which a sailor caused to play in a small cabin in the poop. The sounds came directly to us by a winding stairway. The machine appeared to be present, yet nothing was to be seen. The minister, all ears, stretched out and drew in his head, looked to right and left, above and below, along the side of the saloon and in every corner, always hearing the admirable concert without being able to discover either the artist or his instrument. He seemed to ask himself whether he was awake or dreaming, in this world or the next. His puzzled expression gave us much to laugh at.

After the repast, he was led into the little room where the organ had been installed, and it was opened for him and the cylinders explained. Seeing nothing but bits of wood which turned, he was no doubt unable to understand how so simple a machine could produce such results. Indeed, he could not get over it. We now made one of his mandarins approach and caused him to willy-nilly take told of the handle. "Turn," he was told. He turned, and lo! he found himself a musician. His terror appeared to be great at the unexpected revelation of this unknown talent, and he fled at the third revolution as if he feared lest the devil would spring out in his face. The admiral, seeing the fascination which this marvelous object exercised over his guest, hastened to offer it to him, but he was unable to make him accept it. This was certainly not for lack of a desire for it, but His Excellency no doubt had his own reasons for not doing so.

Forcade a Children's Nurse. Leturdu Leaves. Politeness of the Mandarins.

Leturdu and I, it will be readily understood, were present at this dinner. The admiral had the kindness to place me on the right of the minister, and I had the opportunity of filling the glorious function of a baby's nurse for him. Although a novice at this trade, I attempted to acquit myself well, and I wearied my bones in order to choose the finest morsels for him. I chopped these up in mouthfuls perfectly proportioned to the size of his mouth. These grateful services had good effect. His Excellency and I soon became a couple of good friends, and I was the first to whom he deigned to offer the honor of his pipe after the feast. The petty mandarins of his escort also had their turn, for as soon as we left the saloon, they took our places, and Augustin, who was kept for them, did the honors of their feast. Before the minister retired, the admiral presented him with a Chinese version of his note of Wednesday the 17th.

About 9 p.m., I took Leturdu and Augustin ashore. They leave tomorrow morning for Tumai at 4 a.m. I had much regret at allowing my poor companion to go back there alone, for I knew by experience just how disagreeable such a situation could be. But there was nothing else to be done. Letdurdu was perfectly resigned to it, and I only hope that his solitude will not last long.

June 22nd. At nine in the morning the minister appeared in full dress on the beach, while a tom-tom was beaten. I was then on shore in the house put at our disposal in the village of *Ounting (Unten),* so I went to see what His Excellency desired. He told me that he had come to say farewell to the admiral before leaving for the capital, and he asked me to transmit his sentiments. He then departed. "A pleasant journey to him."

At the same time, the governor of the province went out to the ship without my knowledge to return the copy of the Franco-Chinese Treaty and the edicts in favor of Christianity which the admiral had left with him. The admiral, who was not expecting this visit and did not understand what was said to him, could not imagine what was wanted, and he sent a boat in great haste after me, requesting me to come out to him. I was able to explain everything on my arrival. The staff was quite astonished at such extraordinary and unexpected courtesies. But for my part, I was not much surprised, for I knew something of the manners and customs of these lands, and I entertained no illusions about the value of these demonstrations.

Graves for the Sailors. *Yagadji* and the *Foundjagawa.*

The governor, before taking leave of the admiral, offered him, on behalf of the minister, a jar of saki, some pounds of gingerbread, and quite a number of little cakes. In consideration of the circumstances, the admiral thought he should accept these presents for the first time. It would have been truly hard to know how to refuse them. After dinner we had a nice walk on the island, *Yagadji,* and I was again able to carry on a little conversation with a poor peasant, free from the presence of witnesses. This was a man of the same type as all the others, kindly and simple. A cigar and a pinch of tobacco was given to the old fellow, and he went off happy as a king.

June 23rd. Just when we were going to leave the table after dinner, a petty yellow-bonnet came out on behalf of the governor of *Foukousan*

(*Hokusan*), who asked if the admiral would agree that they should raise gravestones over the bodies of the sailors who were recently buried.

The admiral answered coldly, "Yes, I would like it very much!"

And I added that when Augustin came back, he would give them an inscription to be engraved on the tombstones. My intention is to give them in Chinese characters the epitaph which it is customary to place on the tombs of Christians in China. The wooden crosses already in position are to be retained, but on these the names of the deceased, their ages, the date of their deaths, etc., are to be written in French. Our mandarins are showing themselves more and more obliging.

After having gotten rid of this messenger in less than a minute, we went for a very agreeable walk as far as a very pretty water course, a veritable little river named *Foundjagawa*, which we discovered on the large island, about half a league from our anchorage. Splendid rice fields stretched themselves out here and there along its banks.

June 26th. In the morning I accompanied the admiral to *Foundjagawa* river, which we had already reconnoitered. We entered it from its mouth, and we went up it for quite a distance inland as far as the place where a dike used to carry a road across the stream. This barred our passage and forced us to stop. This stream is surrounded by wooded mountains of the most beautiful appearance, and the country which stretched from the foot of these hills to the river banks was covered with beautiful paddy fields. I cannot say how many delightful villas and castles in the air we built as we passed along.

Today the governor also began to build the tomb of our two sailors. We have to let him go ahead without seeming to pay the least attention to his actions in order to let it be understood that we are not deceived by the sycophancy shown toward us.

Leturdu's Account of his Journey. A Friendly Family.

This morning I received a letter from Leturdu, who had reached *Tumai*. Here follow some interesting passages from it:

"*Tumai*. Feast of St. John the Baptist, 1846."

"Here I am once more, back at *Tumai* after 30 hours spent on the way. We travelled night and day, at first on horseback and then in chairs. Poor Augustin is covered with sores and bruises which the horses and chairs, to which he was not accustomed, inflicted on him. What a road we have taken! We have followed the seashore all the distance from Pt. Melville to *Tumai*. At times it was necessary to go through water, at times to scramble over rocks, and sometimes to leave our horses and climb clear out of sight. At first I thought, with Augustin, that this was not the true road, and that we were taken on this way merely to weary us and prevent us from seeing the interior. Nevertheless, we saw many traces of travellers along the shore. We met many people carrying burdens who said they came from the capital, and we were completely persuaded when your belongings went off in the same direction. Several large and clean villages charmed our eyes from time to time, eyes wearied by the sand on the beach....

"At the village where we stopped for lunch I invited "Smiler" and "Skygazer"* and two other yellow-bonnets who travelled with us to share our bread and tea. I have only praise for them. In one village, the whole population gathered around us. I offered tea and wine to the headman and the man who appeared the oldest. They were both pleased. I asked them not to forget me, because I would not forget them, and that I would probably meet them again.

"We also made a short halt at the long bridge two leagues from Tumai in a house situated on the heights. There was there an old man and a great grandmother, a place which you have visited two or three times. The old man was not at home, but his large family came out to welcome us, all except the old lady, who did not appear. She was not forgotten, however, for I had bread and wine carried to her. I kept some for the old man, and all the children had their share, so I imagine that this good family will remember the fathers.

In Chairs From *Ouenna (Onna)* Village.
A Sailor's Pastoral Idyll.

"The chair coolies, baggage carriers and leaders of our horses had also a share in our largess. From time to time I served them with a glass of *saki* and a piece of bread, and at night they had rice and eggs for dinner. Their fatigue was not small.

---

* Author's note: "We gave nicknames of this sort to the petty mandarins with whom we had most to do that we might speak of them without arousing their suspicions."

"We reached the village of *Ouenna* at 6:30 p.m. and had something to eat. Here the horses were replaced by palanquins, and we set out with our caravan at 11 o'clock at night. There were more than twenty of us, six men for each chair, two who carried, two who had torches, and two who were resting. We travelled at a trot, and the poor fellows lost what little fat they had.

"At 2 a.m. we stopped on the shore, and we gave the men *saki*. So they went on better than ever.

"We reached *Tumai* at 9:30 a.m., having run abreast continuously for eleven hours.

"Before this we did nine hours on horseback, so you can judge of the distance. They told us it was 19 leagues. I think they could have added a zero to this!

"Five or six hours before arriving, the coast becoming lower, the road was rough. At every quarter of an hour we came to a brook, and I have never seen a country so well watered. Some of the rice we passed was admirable in height.... My solitude will please me. Already I feel my own master. None the less, may the good God preserve you and soon bring you back! I shall return Augustin when he has recovered from his weariness."

I immediately replied to this letter and sent off some things which were desired of me.*

June 27th. A little incident learned today will give an idea of how easily we could establish good relations with the common people were it not for the ever present eyes of our followers. A sailor has been landed daily in a little hole enclosed by the mountains and hidden by them near the anchorage of the "Sabine." He has been caring for two or three cows belonging to the ship. Here, far away from ordinary watchers, are four or five huts, also belonging to poor people. Well! This sailor has become the best friend in the world of the inhabitants of this spot. He is free to enter every door, and the ship's food and the yams of the cottage are habitually shared there in common. The women, far from fleeing from the western barbarian, come calmly to sit between him and their husbands.

---

* Author's note: The petty mandarins and their attendants, who daily travelled from the capital to Port Melville, and vice versa, supplied us in these days with a convenient post for messages.

Forcade and the Spies. Discomforture of the Headman of Yagadji

In my case, not only can I enter no cottage so freely, but it always is very difficult to get a moment of private conversation, even with the humblest peasant anywhere. Satellites no longer officially follow us on our walks since Capt. Guerin protested, but they have been replaced by a swarm of spies, who amount to the same thing. People are especially suspicious of me, considering that I can speak the language more or less, and that they know the reason why I have come here. Everything is in commotion as soon as I leave the ship, and eyes follow, observe and count my steps in whatever direction I may move, while indiscrete ears are on watch everywhere to hear me. They are found on every road or lie hidden behind the walls and bushes.

This evening I had gone for a walk with the admiral on Yagadji Island. We had been seated for some time near a village, and when some peasants came, I began a conversation. But the headman and some spies came up at once, and there was no chance to say any more. Nevertheless, we were polite to this magistrate. We offered him a cigar, and for want of anyone better, I began to talk with him. He did not wait to ask us agreeably when we were going away.

I replied, "I do not know; the time is not fixed."

He said, "The quicker the better, for the women here are all in terror. They are always scattering in flight."

I asked, "Why are they afraid? Has anyone done them the least injury?"

"Well," he said, "it is because they have never seen any men like you, and they are much afraid."

On this, the admiral, to whom I translated about all that I could understand in such cases, exclaimed, "Tell him now that they are not afraid of us, but that they are in terror of the attendants sent by the mandarins!"

I loudly translated the words of the admiral. There was an explosion of laughter in the audience, and everyone seemed to say by the expression of their faces, "How true that is!"

His honor, the mayor, completely put out of countenance, thought it was right to give up the game. He went away much less proudly than he had come.

Chapter VI
Letrudu Writes of the Mandarin's Council and Reasons With Aniah.

June 30th. I received a letter from Leturdu this morning dated the 27th. These are the principal passages:

"I was going to write to you when I received your letter. This morning Aniah came to ask some questions about the admiral's letter, and he told me that the council was quite undecided. Their great objection to the treaty is the fear that in consequence of it they could not carry on the necessary trade with the Japanese, for all their iron and copper comes from Japan. They fear lest the Japanese will be unwilling to visit a country open to Europeans.

"I tried to reassure him on this point, saying that the admiral would take the necessary steps so that they would suffer no loss, and that they would be supplied with iron just as before; that a treaty similar to that with China could not be hurtful to them in any way, but that it would procure them many advantages, as the admiral told them so clearly in his letter; that moreover, they could not remain long in their present condition; that sooner or later, they would have to fraternise with other nations, because all men are like brothers in the great family of mankind, with whom it was proper to live in friendship and good will; that they would be wiser if they accepted this fate freely instead of waiting to be forced to do so at the risk of seeing themselves spoiled of a portion of their country; that when the treaty was once made, they would have nothing to fear from other kingdoms, because these could not undo what France had done, and that besides, there would be no more reasons for war, etc.

"Then I gave him a lesson in history and geography, and I wound up as follows: 'You ought to accept the proposed treaty because you will not be long able to avoid it. Europe is absolutely intent upon opening up all these closed countries. You will please the Emperor of

China by following his example, while to act differently would seem to criticize and condemn his action. No harm will come to you from Japan, nor from anyone else. You will gain the great advantages enumerated in the admiral's letter. You will be safe from all trouble with the other powers. And finally, it is right that the children of a large family should not keep apart, but should associate and see each other often, and this is the will of the European powers,

"After this, he asked for more time, saying that eight days, including the journey in both directions, were not enough. I replied that I should not presume to postpone or hasten the arrival of the great mandarin, and that I could merely advise the admiral of his request. He is to come this evening to tell me the number of days they ask, and he will also fix the date of the mandarin's arrival at *Ounting.*"

A P.S. about Bettelheim. His Wine Cellar is Empty.

P.S. "Aniah has given me his answer. The admiral's letter must be communicated to all the orders of the state, and in order to do this, thousands of copies of it have to be made. The minister will be able to leave about the 10th of this moon, between the 8th and the 12th, and he cannot make the trip in less than three days. The 10th of this moon falls on Saturday, July 3rd, so with three days on the road, he will arrive on the 5th or 6th. Augustin will leave on Wednesday."

Another scrap: "I paid a visit Wednesday evening to the English doctor. He was well, but his wife and little girl were sick. Madame is unable to drink the water of the country without mixing it with wine, and this has materially diminished their supply. He begs you to see if he could not get some bottles of wine, and also some newspapers. He has just written me to warn me that if Augustin has not already gone on Monday, he would go with him to Port Melville to have the honor of saluting the admiral and to see the country. Setting aside the fact that he has not returned my call, he showed himself kind, even obliging, toward me. He twice invited me to dine with him every Sunday, and he invited Augustin for tomorrow. You will know that I accepted nothing, and if he invites me again, I will tell him plainly that my rule does not allow me to do so. I think this is the best way to escape from the situation. What do you think about it? He has displayed a signboard in

Chinese on the wall of his garden inviting the sick to have recourse to his art. He promises to give rice to those who have no means of getting it... He is contented with his guards and finds that they teach him the language very well."

Leturdu then told me that he was satisfied on this point, with those who were about him. These good people are happier than I was. They have arrived at a better time. This letter pleased the admiral. It gave him hope and suggested new ideas that would be very advantageous for us. He asked for a copy of the passage concerning his affairs. I answered Leturdu that the admiral, perfectly understanding the importance and the difficulties of the situation, gladly accorded as much time as the government would need to form a decision wisely. On my own account I urged my dear confrere to continue to give good advice to the mandarins who may apply to him. If this country should consent to a treaty with France, this would be a good piece of business for our mission (At least, I think so).

The Englishman's Wine. Augustin Returns by a New Road. A Grove.

About what concerned the Englishman, I answered that I could not undertake to get him any wine, and I praised my dear brother for not accepting any of his dinners. I advised him to always show himself polite and charitable, but quite reserved toward the doctor. While I was writing this reply, I received a new letter from Leturdu, dated the 28th, which announced the dispatch of my baggage by sea. They have just arrived in good condition by a native boat. Augustin was to leave *Tumai* tomorrow, and he will probably rejoin us Thursday night.

July 2nd. Augustin arrived from Tumai this evening. This time he made the whole journey by chair, and in two days, and he was not too tired. Leturdu has arranged matters fairly well, to judge from the letter I received from him, and he does not seem to fear his approaching solitude, but to be resigned to it.

One rather singular thing for this country! Leturdu and Augustin left here by the eastern road, and Augustin was brought back by the west in such a way that on this trip he has made the circuit of a large part of the island. He has seen charming spots and rich country on the eastern coast unknown to Europeans, and he thinks he has discovered some good anchorages. At four and a half leagues from Choui, he passed close to the ruins of an ancient city. But though he greatly wished to explore the place, the mandarins found means to make him keep away from it.

July 4th. After dinner, I went for a walk with the admiral on *Yagadji* Island. We halted near a clear spring in a grove of magnificent trees, which seemed as old as the world itself. This is a sacred wood, a holy spot where the poor people of this land come to worship their kami (the spirits). The mayor, the old fellow of whom I wrote on June 29th, joined us here with the purpose, no doubt, of merely honoring us with his presence. However, he showed himself decidedly amiable, talking with us, and even allowing some of his officers, who had not delayed joining us, to talk.

On arriving at the ship we found a yellow bonnet on the deck, who announced to us the arrival of the minister and asked for him at what hour tomorrow the captain could give him audience. His Excellency is to be received at 1 p.m. tomorrow, but according to what Leturdu had written us, we did not expect him so soon.

The Minister Salaams, Presents his Reply, and Embarasses Forcade.

July 5th. About one o'clock I went in the admiral's barges to meet the minister, and he was then received by the admiral, the three captains, and a part of the staff. After the usual compliments, His Excellency, with much ceremony, delivered the answer which he had brought, and then there followed, in a manner that was more comical than touching, three prostrations, his forehead against the earth, while the poor man demanded pardon and pity, as if we intended to shoot him.

The admiral replied that he would examine the contents of the letter with a clear brain when the translation had been made, and that then he would express his opinion about it. The pathetic salaaming was followed by the gift of presents. These were leaf tobacco and boxes of cake and vermicelli. There were gifts for the admiral, the three commanders and myself. These we judged it was proper to accept. In return for this politeness, the admiral asked the great mandarin to pass into the dining saloon, where a magnificent lunch was served. I was beside the minister, and this time he again showed me much friendship. During the feast he invited the admiral to dinner on next Tuesday.

After the collation was over nothing of importance took place. The admiral only asked for the Chinese and native names of all the islands of the kingdom in writing, and they promised to give him this information.

After the courteous exchange of a few words, the great mandarin withdrew. I accompanied him back to the shore, and in this short trip he showed me a courtesy truly extra-ordinary for a man of his rank and country. Suddenly, and without any preliminary remark, he took the lighted cigar which I had in my mouth and smoked it himself, saying that the tobacco was good. And he presented his pipe so that I could taste his tobacco, also. I accepted, as goes without saying, and after having tried two or three puffs, I assumed an air of great gratitude, while returning to His Excellency the honorable instrument he had deigned to lend me. The worthy man would not take it back. He told me graciously that it was mine, and adjusting for me his pretty silk tobacco pouch half full of tobacco, he contented himself with keeping my unhappy, half-smoked cigar in return for his double gift. I was quite troubled, as I had formed the resolution of neither receiving nor making any presents here. I felt, however, that the situation required that I should abandon my policy, and I accepted his gift, confused by so many honors!

The King Groans and States his Opinion to the Minister.

It was easy to see what was the cause of all these bursts of amiability. They were intended to ensure the acceptance of the following letter:

"Letter prepared to expose his feelings of friendship and to implore commiseration, prepared by Chang-ting-tcheou, Minister General of the city of *Tchong-Chow,* Loo Choo. The 28th day of the preceding moon, I accepted the kind invitation of His Excellency, who summoned me and directly gave a precious letter. After having taken this away, after having opened and read it, I left at once for *Choui,* and with respect

I laid the matter clearly before the King of this realm. The King said, groaning, 'This is a matter of very great importance; what can be done to act with safety? You should write the other mandarins, deliberate ripely with them and report it to me.'

"In conformity with this order, I immediately convoked all the mandarins, and after having deliberated about all things with the greatest attention, we referred them back to the king. We asked what was his will, and we received the following decision written in vermillion:

'His Excellency has come from afar with great difficulty in order to form friendship and carry on commerce with us. His purpose is good, and we owe him thanks without end for it.

'But the condition of a small kingdom is different indeed from that of great empires, and you must go yourself, as you have already declared, under the standard of His Excellency's authority, to make prostrations and implore his clemency.

'Now, respectfully and frankly explaining my true reasons, I fear to fail to please His Excellency, but in our deliberation, we have recognized that this kingdom is small as the bullet of a crossbow, and that the islands subject to it are also small. We lack silver and gold, copper and iron, silk thread and both fine and poor silk materials. Grains are not abundant. We have only a few products. Indeed, we cannot be called a kingdom. Since the last of the Ming dynasties to the present, our land has been graciously included among the countries upon which China has conferred the royal dignity.

The Tribute to China and Trade with *Foukiala (Satsuma)*

'From generation to generation our kings are invested with royal attributes by China, and we have discharged the duties of tributary nations. This is why, profiting by the occasion when the tribute is paid in Fukien Province of the Mings, we also buy silk, as much in order to make the royal robes as to make the hats and dresses of the mandarins, thus establishing distinctions according to the legal grades of rank. We also buy medicines to heal the sick, that men may not die at other times than Heaven may decree. As for the things which we pay as tribute, and concerning the various merchandise which is exported to China to be sold there, none of this is produced in this vile realm. We can only procure these by buying them from the island of *Fou-kia-la*. Moreover, rice, wood, iron kettles, cotton, tea, tobacco, mustard oil, yellow wax, and tools and instruments of all sorts are brought here by the merchants of this island, and it is thus that we are able to in someway satisfy our wants.

'They say also that there are severe laws in the kingdoms of Japan, and that they never have any communication with other realms, except at the Port of Nagasaki alone, where the servants of the mandarins are placed who watch the foreign merchants very strictly. The number of the ships and the quantity of merchandise having been fixed, the Dutch and the Chinese were at last allowed to come there each year to trade. But although the island of *Fou-kai-la* is subject to Japan, yet it is close to our kingdom. It is allowed to bring its products here to exchange them for *saki*, black sugar, the bananas of this vile realm, and the divers merchandise brought from the land of the Mings. When the merchants return from here to the island aforesaid, if they have any contraband among their other cargo, or if the merchandise exceeds the quantities stated in the list, or if any other offense is committed, as soon as the matter is discovered by the customs officials, all the merchandise is seized, and the offenders are very severely punished. This and other things have been told us.

'Now, if this vile realm should form a friendship with the noble empire for the sake of commerce, the merchants of the above-mentioned island would be surely prevented by the laws of Japan from coming hither. Then we would surely be obliged to be remiss in the duty of paying tribute to China, and we could not fulfill the obligations of subjects. We would be unable to procure anywhere the objects necessary for the mandarins and all the population of the realm, and should these objects be lacking, this kingdom would not exist on its own resources.

Laws Relating to Shipwrecked Sailors — An English Ship

'Now it is impossible for this kingdom to carry on commerce with other nations as His Excellency has urged. And when in ancient times the ships of this vile realm went to Corea, to Chochin-China and other places, it was not with the design of seeking the advantages of commerce, but it was in order to procure the necessary articles for paying the tribute down to the time of Kang-hi, who intentionally expressed his will concerning the articles to be paid as tribute, declaring that he did not value these strange objects. Since that time the custom of visiting other kingdoms ceased.

'Upon examination of the laws of the vile realm, we find:

'Whenever the ships of other nations have been cast ashore here by the wind, no matter to what nation the crew may belong, they shall be given water and provisions to satisfy their needs. Should there be danger from storms, or should the vessel or its rigging be injured, care must be taken of the men. Those whom we can send home shall be sent home, and to those to whom a ship must be given, a ship will be given them that they may escape from hardship to which they are not accustomed.

'Thus it is that when two English ships were driven on a subject island of this vile realm named Miyako *(Tai-pin-san)* and one of them striking a reef was broken up, we aided them at once, and giving them another ship, we sent them back home. These things are done not because of alliances and treaties, but because the rationality *(gi)* of succoring the unfortunate is coincident with the rationality *(gi)* of Heaven and man. This is the reason why, though mandarins are delegated for this matter, and though appeals must be made to the people for the necessary materials, when that from the public storehouses has been used, and the lower orders must give their toil, yet with great difficulty and by unrelaxing labor, we are able to achieve these results. Should any of the ships of the noble realm fall into these circumstances, according to our laws, it would be necessary to take care of them.

'We humbly reflect on the purpose by which His Excellency wishes to make a treaty of friendship with us like that which he has already made with China. In truth, this springs from the good-will of a great nation, and this is why we offer up thanks without end. But this vile realm is a land as small as the *Tamagondi* (etym: ordure of the beach) shell. It only has a very few products, and it is only by aid of *Fou-kai-la* Island that it is able to exist. Thus it cannot be regarded as on the same level as the great country (China). Now we ask to be released from ties of friendship and commerce. Although we are in great fear, yet as has been explained, there are truly great difficulties which prevent us (from acting as you would like us to).

'This is why we venture to expose this matter of His Excellency, begging His Excellency to clearly examine into the poverty and helplessness of the realm, and to extend even to us that clemency by which his great land is accustomed to show pity to the weak, and to distribute his favors and to grant which we request. We also pray that when he returns to his own country, His Excellency will expose the matter (to the King) in the best light that he can and will request that matters may be left as they are.

'Then the king on high, and the mandarins and people down below, will give thanks for the mercy of a new creation, and in all ages they will make this event the object of their religious commemoration, without ever forgetting it.

'The above is a detailed answer on every subject.

'26th Year of *Tao Kwang,* the 12th of the 5th moon, Chang-tung-tchou, Minister General of the city of *Tchong-chaou,* Kingdom of Loo Choo, deposes respectfully.'"

Leturdu Writes of Bettelheim's Desire to Visit the Admiral

July 6th. I transcribe some interesting passages from Leturdu, dated July 4th:

"Your letter reached me too late for the minister, but just in time for the Englishman, who without this was going to meet you the day after. On the eve of Augustin's departure, he wrote me that he would like to be one of his party and asked me if Augustin could not put off starting for one day, as he had still to watch his little daughter who had been sick. I answered that it was impossible for Augutin to postpone his journey, that he would lose nothing by not making the trip, that if he wished to know the country, I could give him a description of it, and that if he wished to see the admiral, I thought that the present circumstance was not favorable. This general officer was expecting the return of the minister from one day to another, and no doubt would not receive him. He replied that in spite of the details which I gave him about the country, he desired to see what I had seen with his own eyes. For his mind is such that in everything he wishes to say as he does in regard to religion: 'I believe not because I have heard, but because I have seen.' Upon receiving such a characteristically Protestant reply, I took my hat and sandals and went off to his house. I found him absolutely decided. He was going tomorrow evening. Fearing then lest more opposition on my part would appear inspired by jealousy, I gave him the necessary information about how to make a successful journey. But I was careful to give him nothing whatsoever for you. While I was here, a petty mandarin brought a reply to the request he had made for a female nurse for his child. He was told that the high mandarin was busy with the matter, and he could have one in a month. The interior of his house is open to all the petty mandarins, who come and go, prying into anything.

"At 9 p.m. your letter reached me in which you told me not to allow the Englishman to come and bore you at *Ounting,* and in which you gave me an answer about the wine. I wrote him again in the early morning that the admiral, being very busy just at this time, would rather see him later when the negotiations were finished. One reason which he gave me for visiting the admiral was that being the only Englishman in the country, he represented his nation, and that it was his duty to prove to the inhabitants of Loo Choo that France and England were friends.

The Gospel of John in Japanese (sic). Coudja Gives a Dinner.

"At 10 o'clock he came to my house quite satisfied with my letter and disposed to put off his trip. I gave him two bottles of wine to make up for it, and we parted good friends. He has begged me to ask you if you could not accept some copies of the Gospel according to St. John, translated into Japanese, to distribute them on your northern trip, or to place them in safe hands. He is commissioned by an English society to spread these as widely as he could. He has not been able to get any of them accepted here. I told him first that I would like a copy for myself in my capacity as an inhabitant of Loo

Choo, and also a Chinese translation, if he had one. He sent me these two works yesterday. As for you, I answered that if these translations were conformable to the Catholic Vulgate, I would gladly send them to you, but that we were not yet sufficiently convinced of this. He also asked you to make some researches, if you have any means of doing so, on the subject of the ten tribes of Israel, concerning which he is commissioned to collect data. Today his wife sent me a cake in return for the wine, and he sends 12 copies of St. John in Japanese, together with an English dissertation on the Ten Tribes and asks me to send on the bundle."

July 7th. Between noon and one o'clock the admiral set out for the minister's dinner in the same order and with about as much pomp as on the 14th of June. But this time it was not a mere collation, but an endless banquet. We ate what we could and said little, and nothing of what was said deserves to be repeated here. After the repast was over, gifts of very little value were brought in for the admiral, for all the other officers, and even for your servant. They offered us some paper, some rolls of poor cloth, some pipes, tobacco pouches, and fans, all of a very common kind. The admiral decided that these things should be accepted, but only on the express condition that His Excellency would no longer refuse the hand-organ which had been offered him. This condition was accepted, and we parted amicably.

July 8th. Toward noon the Minister came down with solemn march to repeat what he had done on June 22nd, and he posted himself majestically on the shore opposite the frigate. I left at once in the admiral's barge to find out what His Excellency desired. He only wished to salute Adm. Cecille from that distance and to thank him for the honor shown by accepting yesterday's feast. I urged the great mandarin to rather go on board the ship himself, as this would be more agreeable and more fitting, so he consented to do so.

There was nothing notable in this new interview. There were always many salaams on the part of the natives, but no one spoke about business on either side. The admiral merely said that he had written out his observations relative to the answer of His Excellency, and that he would communicate them to him as soon as they were rendered in Chinese, which would probably be on Friday. After returning from a walk about 6 o'clock in the evening, I found a letter from Leturdu, dated the 6th. Here is a little passage concerning our queer Englishman:

Bettelheim Advertises his Hospital Using Posters.

"Just a word about our friend, the Englishman. Day before yesterday he sent me advertisements of the hospital which he wishes to establish, asking me to put some up on the walls of my temple and to forward some to you for *Ounting*. As I do not know what these announcements contain, and as the hospital, moreover, is only a means of Protestant propaganda, I have not been willing to take them and thus render myself a tool of heresy. I returned them to him, advising him to do nothing before learning whether the high mandarin would not make some concessions to the admiral. I knew very well that this advice was a little tardy and that his posters were already displayed in several places, but this afforded a plausible excuse to escape from the difficulty. I will tell him the next time I have a chance that he must not speak to me concerning his religion, and that while we would live together as friends, we would draw a line at the altar.

"He replied that he was now unable to follow my advice for the reason I have given above. Furthermore, in such a country it was always best to act according to the light God has given us; that in present circumstances he ought to act as a representative of the English nation, independently of every other country, and a thousand other things more or less pertinent. But he did not send back the posters, and this is what I was wishing.

A Prayer for Bettelheim's Conversion.

"If the Blessed Virgin, of whom the church sings, *'Gaude, Virgo Maria, quae cunctas haecreses sola interemisti in universo mundo,* would only convert him! It is very difficult, even, humanly speaking, impossible. So many passions are opposed to it, selfish interests, and prejudices of sect and education. But what is impossible for God? Where is the rebellious heart which pitying Mary cannot enchain? Oh, what glory for her, and what happiness for this mission, if she should convert this agent of heresy, this enemy of her name, as well as that of her divine Son, since on the one hand he (Bettelheim) will have none of Mary, and on the other, he tries to lead into error those whom Jesus Christ came to redeem and to enlighten.

"But for such a task, how much am I lacking in prudence, in light and holiness! Mary would have to do everything here that her glory might be completely manifested. He is her special enemy, the enemy of her mission. Let us leave it to her to confound him, not in the abyss, but in the radiance of the truth. Consider where you judge it convenient for me to attempt this conversion, and think less of the difficulties, the obstacles, than of the mercy of Mary...

"If you judge that we ought to trust in Mary against all hope, then pray. For this will give me confidence, for there are many sins which make me timid, and with reason. On my side, I have not slighted prayer. I have forgotten to tell you of the desire which I have had to utilize these days when I have no teacher to make the retreat enjoined upon us by the book of instructions, when we first reach the field. I thought I ought to begin it last Sunday, and I warn you of this today. If you approve, I will continue; if not, I will break it off. This retreat has also as an object the conversion of the Englishman, in order, as we say, to kill two birds with one stone. And also to achieve my own conversion as well as his. Another reason has made me place the retreat at this time, and that is because, while you are treating affairs of the greatest importance, I thought that being far from the scene of action, I ought to have my hands and heart ceaselessly raised toward Heaven and Mary during this time...."

The First News of a Shipwreck.

July 9th. Between 8 and 9 in the morning, some petty mandarins came to tell me that during the evening of the 14th of the present moon (July 7th), a ship belonging to France was accidentally thrown by the wind upon their islands, that it struck upon a reef near Naha, that a boat being lowered to put cables in position, the boat was capsized and one man drowned. Also, that the fifteen other Frenchmen, aided by native boats, were rescued, and that the noble ship was now out of danger. It is probable, though not yet certain, that it has entered the harbour at Nafa.

But these shipwrecked men must have asked if there were any

French ships here, and they must have been told that there were three at *Ounting* Harbour. The admiral is unable to understand this tale, nor am I. We await fuller details with impatience, and it is not probable we will have long to wait before receiving them in a letter from Leturdu.

July 10th. Augustin came to wake me in the middle of the night to give me a letter from *Tumai*. It was dated the 8th, and consequently posterior to the wreck of the so-called French ship at Nafa. And yet he writes not a word on this subject. According to what I learned on shore this morning, it appears that the shipwreck was kept secret from my dear brother, and as the reef which caused it was not visible from the place of his abode, he was unable to discover it himself. I complained of such strange conduct to the officials and asked what was the reason for such secrecy in the case of a man who was called in his capacity of a fellow-citizen to give any useful service. I sent a letter off to *Tumai*.

The admiral, on his side, complained of having received no official notification either from the minister or the governor of the province, when the event was being told to anyone else who wanted to hear it. No response was made to these just complaints, and it was even impossible to obtain any new details. I wrote this a little after twelve, and then we knew no more. All is an enigma.

Leturdu Opens the Religious Controversy by a Letter.

Leturdu's letter contained the following news about his relations with the Rev. Bettelheim:

"The religious affair with the Englishman is getting on better than you would think, for he himself showed this to me in asking me several questions about Catholic principles. This is the answer I made him yesterday:

'Doctor: I bless the Divine Providence, which has taken us from our native lands and has brought us together in this island where our relations are necessarily frequent. What has been the purpose of Providence in acting thus, if not to achieve the conversion of one of us? If we had remained in Europe, calm in our faith, we perhaps would not have had the idea of examining before God our two beliefs in order to discern which one is true. For we cannot disguise the fact that they are opposed to each other in many ways: that what I believe, you do not believe, and that you have many dogmas which I reject. If then you are right, I am in error; and if it is I who possess the doctrines of the Divine Teacher, then you do not have the truth. Thus, if you are on the road which leads to salvation, I am in danger of perdition, for no one will be saved save those who follow the true religion. Or if they follow one that is false, they have not been able to learn the truth and are of necessity in error. But we are not in the condition of these last. Let us therefore silence, my dear sir, every human opinion, and let us seek for the truth, in all uprightness of heart, on one side and on the other. For myself, I assure you that if it is shown me that I am in error, and that you are in possession of the truth, on that instant I will become one of yours. For if I am Catholic, it is because I believe I am in the true religion. But in reality, what I am and what I wish to be is a partisan of the truth and a genuine disciple of Jesus Christ.

'I am sure, my dear doctor, that you are in the same frame of mind, that you love the truth no less than I do, and that you are no less disposed to sacrifice everything to this, certain beside that he who gives up all for the Kingdom of God and for the cause of justice, will have all things added to him. I send you *The Exposition of Catholic Doctrine,* by Bossuet, and you will find the answers to your questions therein. I should also be obliged if you could send me, also, an exposition of your faith and of your complaints against the Catholic Church. The first time that I shall have the honour of meeting you, we will discuss together that which we have read. Let us add prayer to reflection, in order that God may bless our studies, and I do not doubt that the truth, which is easily apparent to all, and even anticipates those who go in search of it, will also reveal itself to us. If it is I who am to be conquered, I will give a thousand thanks to God for enlightening me by your agency.

'You, my venerated fellow-worker, will perhaps consider that I have condescended too greatly. But I thought that I should act in this way to treat with deference the susceptibilities of a Protestant minister and the English self-conceit. Again, I am in need of your authorization. I ask an order from you, that the merit of obedience may be added to the virtues which I lack.'

Bettelheim takes up the Gauntlet.

"The Englishman replied the same evening that he saw this religious polemic opened with pleasure, and that he hoped that God would always preserve our friendship and let us live together in charity. But that he did not believe, as I did, that if one were on the path to Heaven, the other hastened to his damnation, because we could both have the doctrine of Christ. He speaks, no doubt, of fundamental points, which he will be much troubled to name to me and prove by the scriptures. All this is only the prelude. I wish first to finish my retreat.

"If you approve of my actions, indicate to me what road to take. Whether, for example, you judge it is expedient to go back to first principles, to examine what are the signs of the veritable Church of Jesus Christ...."

The Islands of the Realm. Of the Northern Islands.

In the evening the governor of the province came on board, and at last came to speak officially of the French ship stranded near Naha, but beside this he only repeated what had already been said.

The admiral asked the governor at what time tomorrow he could see *Coudja,* the minister, as his letter was ready, and he wished to hand it to him.

The governor replied that His Excellency would let him know the next morning. He then gave to the admiral the list of islands composing the kingdom of Loo Choo, but in the fear lest we should visit the northern islands, and that we should be badly received and some trouble might arise for his country, he also gave us the following note on that subject at the same time:

"These islands are lands originally subject to our country, but whose soil is rocky and where the crops fail. When the calamities of tempests or drought come upon us, there is nothing to eat, and it is only by the rice borrowed from *Foukaila* Island *(Kyushu)* that we maintain our lives. But the loan of this rice has risen to such a great quantity that we could not return it, and so it was agreed with this island that we should make restitution for the rice and give them satisfaction for our debts by the products of these islands. Now this island has sent mandarins thither who are charged with the execution of this agreement."

This is what was stated in writing, but they spoke orally of a complete cession made about two hundred years ago. It appears fairly clear, moreover, that this cession was not made for debts of the kind mentioned in this note, but as the ransom of a king of *Oukinia* who was made a prisoner of war about this time and carried off to Japan, where he was kept two years in detention.*

---

* Editor's note: An evident reference to the war with Satsuma of 1609, after which the King of Okinawa was taken to Satsuma and held for ransom.

Chapter VII
The Admiral Will Report to his Master the Loochooans' Refusal.

July 11th. At eleven this morning a yellow bonnet came to deliver to me the following note, which was to be sent to the admiral:

"At 10 a.m. on the 16th of the present moon (Thursday, July 9), a ship of the noble realm was brought to *Po-tsung (Tumai),* and she dropped anchor here. Then the captain and two of his men with him went ashore and saw Teacher Pierre (Leturdu) at the temple of *Amikou.* One mast of the ship was broken at sea, and this is why they have asked for a piece of pine wood six feet in circumference and five fathoms long."

This is, so they said, all the news that is to be known. The same yellow bonnet also asked, on behalf of the minister, that the admiral should not trouble himself to come ashore to meet him today, but that His Excellency would rather come out himself to receive the letter on board ship. This was granted without trouble. One p.m. was the hour fixed for the interview.

The minister, excusing himself on the ground that he had no watch and did not know the time, came out to us before noon. After the ordinary formalities, the admiral handed him his reply in an unsealed envelope and invited him to make himself acquainted with the contents at once.

"I would prefer to read it at home," he said.

But the admiral declared, "It will be better for you to read it now, for if there is anything which you do not understand, it can be explained to you; and you can, of course, reread it at leisure when you are alone and at home."

After some hesitation over this trifling subject, the minister summoned one of the yellow capped interpreters to his feet and had the document rendered into Japanese (sic.) by him, while he appeared to follow the Chinese characters with his eyes.

After having solidly refuted the bad reasoning put forward to justify the refusal of the proposed treaty, the admiral said that he could do nothing more except to refer the matter to his Imperial Master and to promise that within a year another ship would return to let them know His Majesty's decision. He closed his note as follows:

"In the meantime, Msgr. Forcade will remain in this country. It is necessary that he should learn your language perfectly, and consequently he must be furnished with an able teacher and the necessary books. When the emperor's reply comes, he alone will be able to act as an interpreter, for Augustin, of whom I have need elsewhere, will go away with me and not return. But Msgr. Forcade, who enjoys my esteem, and whom I place under Your Excellency's protection, must no longer be treated as he has been in the past. He must no longer be kept in surveillance or followed as if he were a criminal or an adventurer. He must be allowed to enjoy his liberty. He must be permitted to rent for money a house with a garden, for I do not want him to be a burden on this kingdom, which you say is so poor. His residence must be made inviolable, and no one can be allowed to disturb him there when he wishes to be alone. He must have servants of his own, whom he must be able to employ and discharge at will. Lastly, he must be able to send people directly to the market to buy whatever things he needs. Msgr. Forcade, moreover, is a man deserving of consideration, etc., etc..."

Provisions for Forcade's Further Residence. No Reply Made.

Nothing in this letter ought to have surprised the minister. He knew the whole of it from yesterday morning at least, since, with the admiral's consent, Augustin, quite tired out by his work, had used His Excellency's own scribes for copying the rough draft of this letter.

The minister, after reading the letter, replied: "This is a matter of great importance; I cannot answer at once."

The admiral: "But it seems to me that the matter has been decided, and that there is no answer now to be made. You have refused what I asked for; I have told you that I would refer the matter to the Emperor; and what more or less do you desire before the Emperor has spoken?"

The minister: "This is an affair of great importance. I need to reflect about it, and I will then make an answer."

The admiral: "Can Your Excellency make answer here, and upon your own authority, or is it again necessary to return to *Choui*?"

The minister: "This is not certain. I will see when I have reread the letter and reflected on it."

The admiral: "If Your Excellency can on your own authority promptly give me an answer, I will wait for it; but if it is again necessary to go back to the capital, your answer will have to be delivered to the commander of the "Sabine," which I will send back here in two months. I myself cannot wait here longer, for a serious affair summons me to *Corea*. We have learned that three Frenchmen have been put to death by the government of this country, and I have the Emperor's order to go thither to examine whether their execution was just or unjust. Now, if it was unjust, I must demand complete satisfaction for it. For, you must remember, the French people, in whatever country in the world they may be found, are still the subjects of the Emperor, and he always covers them with his high protection."

The minister (visibly moved): "When will you leave?"

Admiral: "As soon as possible."

Minister: "I see that I must act very quickly in this matter, and I will give you some sort of an answer tomorrow or the next day."

Admiral: "It is possible that in returning from the expedition to *Corea* I will myself come back by this way, and then I would go to *Choui* to obtain a definite answer from you."

The minister appeared little flattered by such great complacency, and he made no reply to this friendly proposal, so the admiral went on: "I am taking Msgr. Forcade and Augutin with me to act as interpreters in *Corea*. As I said before, Augustin will not come back again, but Msgr. Forcade will return by the "Sabine," and will then live under the conditions indicated by my letter. During his absence, Msgr. Leturdu will watch his property at *Tumai*. And then he will remain there to keep Forcade company."

The Minister Leaves the Ship in Haste.

I cannot remember if anything was said in answer to all this. Somewhat like a sheep in the presence of a lion, the poor minister ceaselessly kept looking toward the door, rising at every instant, beginning his farewell bows and seeming quite upset that he was always being asked to wait a little, as the business was not yet finished. Finally, seeing that we wished to attack the question of the wonderful island of *Fou-kai-la,* hearing us ask the name of its harbour, and no doubt foreseeing that much more besides was to be asked of him, he exclaimed in a broken voice, "We do not know! There is no one here who can tell you that!" On this, he turned definitely to the door and withdrew.

Details of the Wreck of the "Pacifique."

July 12th. At about 1 p.m. I finally received a letter from my friend, who had not written me earlier because the captain of the stranded ship appeared to be ready at any minute to go off overland to reach the admiral. According to the information furnished by Leturdu, the vessel in question is a merchant brig called the "Pacifique." Her captain is named de Servan. Leaving Bordeaux in September, 1845, he has visited several archipelagos in this ocean, such as the Marquesas, Tahiti, the Sandwich Islands, etc. He was sailing toward China when a typhoon broke his bowsprit, and as he was pretty close to Okinawa, he steered for Naha in order to make repairs. But because he had no charts, and the watch was not close enough, he was cast, in the evening of the 7th, on two banks of coral to the south of the point of land named *Saki Barou (Point Abbey),* and was stranded there, remaining on the rocks from 7 p.m. to 4 a.m. Fortunately, the wind went down, but the sea was rough, and the ship continuously was wracked by violent shocks during the whole time. However, as she was new and very strongly built, she does not appear to have suffered and does not make even an inch of water.

The captain praises the Okinawans greatly, who gathered in large numbers to help him, and they worked all night long with admirable intelligence and good will. It seems that all would have been lost without them. The captain, his associate, de Laurencel, and our Englishman ought to arrive here tomorrow.

Bettelheim Visits the Admiral.

July 13th. The three above-mentioned persons indeed came, as M. Leturdu had announced to us. The admiral extended a warm welcome to the two Frenchmen; he received the Englishman politely, but coldly. He invited the three of them to lunch and dinner. M. de Servan and M. de Lawrencel seemed fine men and quite distinguished persons. The first especially, some of whose relatives being priests, showed a great deal of interest in missions. He makes me hope that he will revisit us next year.

July 14th. The Englishman, who has not had the fortune to please the officers of the squadron, and who had been very coldly received everywhere, judged it wise to retrace his steps in a hurry. His palanquin is to be ready at 4 a.m., but his two travelling companions do not leave until tomorrow.

About 1 p.m. *Coudja,* the minister, who had announced his visit in the morning, came on board with his usual suite. The admiral thanked him, first of all, in the most suitable and gracious terms, for the help and assistance lavished on the stranded ship by the government and people of Okinawa. He offered him two large and handsome mirrors as a token of his gratitude for the salvaging of the ship, and as a souvenir of his personal relations with His Excellency.

The Minister of the King Presents a Reply

The great mandarin then replied several times that the country had only obeyed its own laws and done its mere duty in coming to the help of castaways. Consequently he refused the gift offered to him by the admiral. But as he was still pursued by the admiral's strong insistence, he ended by yielding. Following the custom of his fellow-countrymen, he refused out of politeness and in deference to politics also, but in the bottom of his heart he must have been enchanted, for the gift that he received was a magnificent one for this country, and quite priceless. I do not think I exaggerate when I say that the cheapest glass-wares are esteemed almost as highly as precious stones in this land, for the same name is given to them. I have more than once seen men who did not belong to the lowest class of society go into ecstasies in my house over a prism, a drinking glass, or shaving mirror of the slightest value.

Up until now, everything went easily and quickly, but what was to follow was more difficult, as will be seen. Soon the minister delivered his fresh reply to the admiral, and as before, we could judge from his embarrassed face that it would not be satisfactory. Hardly had the letter been handed over than the minister prepared to repeat his triple prostration, and it was with great difficulty that the admiral could stop him, declaring that such honor was given no man in France, not even the Emperor, but that it was reserved for God alone. Everyone having seated himself, the admiral opened the letter, and without further delay had it orally translated to him by Augustin. This was its tenor:

Request to be Released from Commerce and Friendship

"Letter prepared by *Chang-ting-tchou,* minister of the city of *Tchong-chou,* to again weary the ears of His Excellency, and to implore with tears his clemency. I have received with respect the opinions of His Excellency, and among others, this one: 'I will strive to inform the Emperor of the answer given me by the noble kingdom, according to your desires and to tell the reasons why you have refused our friendship and commerce; but as my duty is to report on the state of affairs truthfully and loyally, I would never dare deceive the Emperor with falsehoods, and so I could never tell him that the noble kingdom was as small, as poor as...'

"After having opened and read this letter, I was struck with such insurmountable terror that even when sleeping or eating my meals I have enjoyed no calmness of mind. Although I fear to weary the ears of His Excellency, what I nevertheless venture to again affirm is that upon examining this vile realm, as has been said before, one finds that it is as small as the bullet shot by the crossbow, and that the islands subject to it are also small. We possess neither gold nor silver, nor copper nor iron, and thread and silk cloth are also lacking. We have only black sugar, saki and banana cloth as products.

"This is why we visit China and why we keep up communication with *Fou-kai-la,* for thus exchanging our products, we procure in this fashion the things necessary for use in the kingdom. Now, if we should open up larger commerce and communicate with all nations, this would truly be beyond the resources of the realm. For if we should form friendship with the noble realm, that our land might become a centre of your commerce, then all the other countries might come down on us in swarms, and that would surely mean breaking off communication with *Fou-kai-la*. That which is still more to be feared is that we could not procure many things needed by our manner of life, and the kingdom would thus fall into a real state of ruin. These are true words which spring from a sincere heart, and they are in no wise vain or misleading. This is why in my preceding letter I asked a dispensation from commerce and friendship.

"Concerning the ships of the noble realm, many of which put in here in transit, if there are any which have need of provisions, we will furnish these. And if any may need water or firewood, we will also supply the ships with these things. We shall make it a duty to give them, with cheerful hearts, whatever we are able to procure in accordance with our means.

"It is our humble opinion that, although it is the Emperor of the noble land who is to make, by his wisdom and virtue, the final decision, still it depends on the favor of His Excellency, a favor which will be equivalent to a new creation, whether this decision is favorable to us or not. We therefore beg His Excellency that, letting his pity descend even on us, he will expose in the best way, as we have already asked, the state of affairs to the Emperor, whose bounty will grant that which we desire.

Request Leturdu's Removal. The Admiral's Answer.

"Behold, what we also have determined. When men from another country come here, we put guards about them on all sides, and they are to be followed on the roads. They are not to be permitted to rent houses nor to stay here for a long time. This is what is established by law. We therefore pray His Excellency to take Teacher Pierre (Leturdu) away with him. Then the King on high, and below him, the mandarins and the whole people from generation to generation, looking away toward the west, lighting incense sticks, and saluting with head and hands, will wish His Excellency great and eternal happiness. What I have explained is exact.

"The 26th year of Tao-kuang, the 21st day of the 5th intercalary moon. Deposed with respect,
 Chang-ting-chou."

It will be remembered, no doubt, that the admiral only spoke about me in his letter, and he did not say a word about Leturdu. And now notice, this is just why *Coudja* in his answer only spoke about Leturdu and did not breathe a word about me. It is in this fashion that questions are answered in this land. However, the real reason why he spoke of the one and was silent about the other was that they knew, no doubt, that I was going away, and that my companion was to remain.

After making himself acquainted with this letter, the admiral replied: "Since my arrival in this land, I have constantly admired the character of its inhabitants, the order and peace which reigns here, and I have conceived the highest opinion of its morality. It has always been far from my intention to do or to demand anything whatever which could be against the interests, or even against the will of the government. I am perfectly disposed to speak to the Emperor according to your desires, and I do not doubt that His Majesty, in his justice and great wisdom, will give as favorable a decision as you could hope for. Thus you have no reason to feel any sort of uneasiness on this head."

The Admiral Demands the Retention of Interpreters. He Asks for Teachers.

The minister and the mandarins had joy painted on their faces, and the warmest thanks expressed to the admiral.

He now continued: "But in order that the decision of the Emperor may be communicated to you when the ship bearing it arrives, it is necessary to have interpreters who know both our language and yours perfectly. And since, as I have said, Augustin is not to remain here, there is only Msgr. Forcade and Msgr. Leturdu who can act in this capacity. Therefore, it will be useful, and even necessary, for you to have these men live in your country. And as a language cannot be learned without books and teachers, you ought to find them teachers and books."

The minister, not without hesitation: "Yes, we understand that interpreters are necessary, and these men whom you propose may therefore remain, and we will take care to teach them, but they ought to go away on the ship which brings the Emperor's reply."

Admiral: "As I have said, as books are necessary for learning a language, will they be supplied with these?"

The minister: "In this vile realm there are no books in the native language. There are only a few in Chinese."

Admiral: "This seems inconceivable, for there are books in every civilized country. Tell me, then, how you teach your young people to learn their own language? Necessarily there must be at least some elementary books for this, and these are precisely what we ask for. Everyone here does not know Chinese. Even among the high mandarins themselves, I know positively that there are some who do not know that tongue, and how would they have obtained sufficient education for their posts without proper books for study?"

The minister: "There are no books in this vile realm."

The admiral: "Once again, this is unbelievable. Before me I have highly educated men in the person of His Excellency and his interpreters, and how have you gained so much knowledge without using books?"

The minister: "If you wish, we will write the characters used in this country for the interpreters, and teach them these without books."

The admiral: "That is not enough. One could never really learn these characters without books, and even if they could be learned, of what use would they be?"

The minister: "When I have returned, I will take counsel with the mandarins who I brought from Shuri, and then I will give you an answer."

Loo Chooan Books. "The Master of the Guests."

The admiral: "Indeed, I cannot understand why so much difficulty is made over such a simple and easy matter. This is not a subject for deliberation, as it is the necessary consequence of a principle which you yourself have admitted. You have recognized that interpreters are needed, and so you ought to recognize that they should be sufficiently instructed in your language and that books are necessary for this."

The minister: "After I have returned home, and after I have been able to discuss the matter with my council, I will give a reply."

The admiral: "But, once more, it is not necessary to debate over such a necessary matter or such a simple question. What danger do you see in the fact that foreigners should have a few elementary books between their hands? I have just given you a great proof of my good will in promising to speak to the Emperor in your favour, and I am astonished that you answer me thus."

The minister: "But at least I must confer about this with the mandarin named 'Master of the Guests,' who is especially charged with the care of foreigners."

The admiral: "What! Cannot His Excellency, who has been sent here to treat with us, decide anything by himself? And is it necessary in order to decide this tiny question for him to confer with one of his inferiors who has never been here, and with whom I have never been in touch and does not know me, and who might in a moment of ill-humour answer by a refusal at which I should be greatly offended?"

The minister: "If I have spoken of the Master of the Guests, it was because I feared that in granting this question without having consulted him, he might later feel unable to carry out your desire. But since you desire it, I will give him the order to teach the interpreters as well as possible."

The admiral: "And will they be given books? This is the question."

After fresh hesitations, the minister declared, with many little deliberations with his interpreters, without whose aid he never decided anything: "As you wish, they will be given to them."

The admiral: "It would be proper that some of your people learned French, in order that by and by, when there are no Frenchmen among you,* our ships can always have an interpreter among you. If you wish to choose an intelligent person, Msgrs. Forcade and Leturdu will make it their pleasure to teach him as well as they can, and he will be supplied with all the necessary books."

After having expressed his thanks for this difficult concession of the books, the admiral passed to another topic no less important.

Books are Conceded. The Question of Guards.

The admiral: "I have already said that Msgr. Forcade's position can no longer be what it has been. He must no longer be kept under surveillance, but he must be able to enjoy complete liberty."

---

* Forcade's note: "This speech hurt me, and I cannot yet guess why the admiral expressed himself thus when he had always previously been so well able to avoid this subject."

The minister: "According to the laws of our vile realm, if foreigners come here, they may not live here long, and they must be guarded wherever they are as long as they stay here."

The admiral: "These laws have been made no doubt for shipwrecked sailors or adventurers, and in such a case they are wise, for it is the part of prudence to closely watch men whom one does not know and who may be evil-doers. But the men whom I leave here do not belong to such a class. They have been brought here and introduced by warships, and they remain here in the service of the Emperor. His Excellency ought to understand that they must not be treated in the same fashion."

The minister: "Very well, then. We will only appoint a few guards, say four."

The admiral: "Even these are too many. There must be none at all. I beg His Excellency to consider that Msgr. Forcade has already been two years in this country, and that he must remain a year longer. It is a thing which is very hard in itself to remain so long separated from one's home, one's family, and from all that one holds dearest. But if the rigors of the captivity to which he has been subjected up to now should still continue, his situation which he has only accepted out of self-devotion would truly become intolerable. Moreover, His Excellency ought now to know that we French are good people, and that as we have done no wrong during these days spent in your country, you ought to have nothing to fear from us."

The minister: "If there were no guards, the people of this country might enter their house and do them some injury. And this would be a dreadfully entangling matter for us."

The admiral: "His Excellency has too unfavorable an opinion of the people of his country. For myself, after all that I have seen, I judge them much more highly. I can even say that I have nowhere met men so good and so peaceable. There is therefore no uneasiness to be felt on this point."

The minister: "The temple in which Msgr. Forcade has lived until now is very well situated. It is outside the town, and he has no reason to fear being disturbed by his neighbors, so I urge him to continue to live there."

Guards Abolished. The Temple to be Rented. Presents.

The admiral: "That is not the question. We do not raise any difficulties over this house, which we also think is suitable and good. Now we are discussing guards, and I demand that there shall be none of them."

After a little more hesitation, the minister finally yielded this point. The admiral thanked him and continued thus: "The house which Msgr. Forcade occupies is surrounded by a garden. Now, he must be granted the enjoyment of this, so that he can find some distraction here and be really at home."

The minister (without much difficulty): "This he shall have; I will give the bonze an order to yield this ground to him."

The admiral: "What is the indemnity to be paid to the bonze; or in other words, the amount of the rent?"

The minister: "I cannot determine this at once; it is a matter to be arranged with the bonze."

The admiral: "That is fine. Very well, then. You can answer this question on the return of Msgr. Forcade."

The minister agreed.

The admiral: "Now I desire that everything which has been agreed to may be at once put into execution for the benefit of Msgr. Leturdu. Especially I should like you not to delay in procuring him teachers and books, so that the coming two months may not be wasted."

The minister: "As soon as I return to the capital, I shall give orders to this effect."

The admiral thanked him for the third and last time. It was taken for granted that the question of servants, which was not mentioned by the minister in his reply, was granted like the rest.

Thus beaten at every point, the poor minister rose to take leave of the admiral, for he had already several times tried to do as much in vain. He was not stopped more than a minute this time, and frankly, he had no reason to object to it now. In order to thank him for the concessions he had just made, and, no doubt, in order also to pour a little balm of consolation on his sad spirit, the admiral presented him with two vases of Bohemian glass which His Excellency had previously admired, and he begged him to kindly offer these to his wife as a compensation for the grief and loneliness which the too long absence of her husband must have caused, though it is hardly probable, this worthy lady to feel. The minister accepted these after making a few objections out of pure politeness. The admiral finally announced to His Excellency, at the moment when he was leaving, that as everything was over, he would profit by the first fair wind and set sail. This last communication was manifestly that which caused the greatest pleasure.

Forcade's Opinion of the Negotiations.

Following my custom, I seated myself in the boat beside the minister and accompanied him back to the shore. The worthy fellow, although somewhat depressed by so many diplomatic failures, tried to put a good face on over his misfortunes. As for his three interpreters, they did not say a word. Their eyes were dull, and they seemed confounded. They, much rather than *Coudja,* the minister, had conducted all the negotiations, and never in their relations with foreigners had they been more soundly whipped than they had been by this clever Norman whom they had to deal with in today's interview.

The admiral has obtained everything for us that it was possible to obtain under the circumstances, and even more than we had dared to hope for. We owe him much gratitude for all of this. All has not been done, I know. Many obstacles have not been removed, and the success of our mission is at the present time still very doubtful, but let us learn to content ourselves with our new position, and profiting by it as much as is possible, let us leave the rest to time, and above all, to the Divine Providence.

Wednesday, July 15th. Captain de Servan of the "Pacifique" and de Laurencel, his mate, left *Ounting* this morning to return to Nafa.

During our lunch, the minister arrived opposite the frigate to say farewell to the admiral from that position. I went to salute His Excellency, who announced his immediate departure for *Choui,* and I brought back with me two petty mandarins charged by their superior with the duty of making some presents. The admiral accepted them, but in return for some bad pipes, paper fans, some rough cloth and some other objects of very little value, he immediately made gifts of mirrors and other European articles which were of great value in these parts.

After these envoys of the minister, other messengers came out from the governor of the province. These brought out an ox, three pigs, some hens, and some vegetables. The admiral was hardly disposed to accept these presents, but he resolved to do so in order not to displease or cross the mandarins in any way at his departure. He again gave much more away in European articles than he had received.

I wrote today to Leturdu to inform him of the happy results of yesterday's conference and to put him in a position to claim his rights, if necessary.

The wind did not allow us to set sail today.*

---

* Note from William Leonard Schwartz (translator): This is the end of verbatim translation from the book of Msgr. Forcade. The pages that follow summarize Forcade's voyage to Nagasaki. Here the French admiral treated the Japanese with much contempt. The following took place on board and shows how they had news of what took place in Loo Choo. The Japanese asked what was Forcade's name, because they were much astonished that he could speak in some sort of a fashion with them. They no sooner heard it than they had the air of saying, "This is the rogue!" They said to Augustin, "You two have come here, but there is still another at Nafa." Seeing them so well informed, Forcade asked, "Is Loo Choo a dependency of Japan?" Several voices at once replied, "Yes, yes!" (July 30, 1846). After a little, the admiral left for Corea, where he merely deposited a threatening letter. Forcade's further adventures will appear in the second narrative of the missionaries of Loo Choo.

Extracts from Chapter VIII
Departure

Bettelheim as French Poet. A Grotesque Ceremony.

July 17th. The "Cleopatra" left Port Melville at 8 a. m., but the "Victorieuse" could not clear the channel by 6 p.m., and the "Sabine" had to wait until the next day. Two letters arrived for Forcade. The first was delivered by a petty mandarin as we were setting sail. It was from the Protestant minister and written in the strangest sort of French verse. Here are the first two lines of this beautiful bit to allow one to judge of the whole: *'J'envoi des melons, A l'amiral si bon.'* ('I send some melons to the admiral so good'). All this was to ask me to present the admiral with four watermelons which our Englishman sent him. The second letter brought out by one of the boats which had remained behind was from dear Leturdu.

July 13, 1846. *Tumai.* A grotesque ceremony took place yesterday! I was returning from the "Pacifique" at about seven when I noticed an immense procession on the beach: torches, streamers, tom-toms and rattles. I could not imagine what it was all about. I came closer, and I saw children crowned with wreathes in front, ranged about a sort of banner, whose agreeable function was to scream and pound on kettles. After them came a long line of men who pulled on ropes under the direction of the governor of Nafa in uniform. At last I reached the object of veneration. It was a great tree which had been cut in the interior and which was thus being brought hither in order to make a bow-sprit for the ship. A bonze followed it together with an immense throng. Oh, what an excess of honor and adulation!

The Friday before, another tree was cut down on the beach. Before an axe was applied, a bonze, as the captain believes, came to make some libations at its foot, together with certain grimaces. Then he said to the captain, "Do not fear. Now it will never break." Unfortunately it was hollow and would not do.

July 18th. The "Victorieuse," "Cleopatra," and "Sabine" set sail in this order at 5 a.m. They passed *Jalo, Wakina* and the island of sulphur to the north of Okinawa.

Information from a Junk Captain. "Fou-Kai-La!"

July 19. The ships were in sight of unknown islands, one with a village on it. The weather did not allow of their exploration.

July 20. The ships returned to the same group of islands. On one of them, which had appeared uninhabited, a village and many cultivated fields were seen. It was larger than they thought and had two anchorages. This was thought to be *Ousima* (Oshima).

July 22. A new island was in sight. Forcade went off to explore it on the admiral's express desire. This is his story:

"On leaving the ship, our boat steered toward a little creek where a junk was at anchor.... Here we recognized subjects of the king of Okinawa. Far from appearing frightened, they made signs for us to approach, pointing to ropes which they had prepared to help us to come alongside. We went on board, and the captain, who belonged in Nafa, recognized me at once. After having quickly hastened to offer us tea, he told me that he had left port 27 days ago; that the island belonged to Japan (a thing which seemed hardly probable to me); that he had only put in here because of the bad weather. He asked me how long it had been since we left *Ounting*, whether Augustin was on our ship, and whether or not there was any other Frenchman in the temple at *Amikou*, whether or not the Englishman was still at the temple in Nafa, and whether or not the tribute ships had come back from China. I answered truthfully all his questions...

"I learned that this island was named *Akoucheki*, and that it was about three leagues in circumference, and that it was without a settled population.... In front of us to the southwest an island was in sight. This was the one we had seen closely the other day. I pointed to it with my hand, and I asked its name. Two or three voices immediately pronounced, to my great surprise, the name of *Fou-kai-la*. Turning to the Okinawa captain, I said, 'Is that, then, the island of *Fou-kai-la* which trades with you?' His answer was 'yes.' I remained astounded, for if we are to believe the people of Okinawa, everything comes to them from this island. It is the warehouse, the general storehouse for this country, and the island which I had under my eyes had very little area, and its arid soil appeared hardly cultivated at all. Thinking that they had misunderstood me or lied, I later addressed another person who had not been present, and he replied in the same manner. The fact hence appears indisputable, and I am forced to believe that we were shamelessly lied to on this point as well as many others in Okinawa...

"I tried to obtain some information about the islands we had met up till now on our voyage from Okinawa. Their names were given me in the following order, going from the south to the north: 1. *Yonno,* which is probably the island on the chart named *Julo.* 2. *Yrabon.* 3. *Toukonno-Sima.* 4. *Yourou.* 5. *Ousima.* 6. *Ki Kay.* 7. *Fou-kai-la.* Is this information exact? I do not know."

On July 25th, the coast of Kyushu was in sight, and Nagasaki was reached on the 29th.

Note by Schwartz: Chapter IX of this work describes Nagasaki and the insolence of the Japanese officers here. Also described is the voyage to Corea.

Chapter X tells of the voyage along the coast of Corea and of the admiral's dispatching a letter to the king, threatening him because of the murder of three French missionaries, Imbert, Chastan, and Maubant, on September 21, 1834. But lack of provisions prompted a return to China.

Chapter XI of this work describes experiences in China at *Ningpo* and *Chusan* Island, and explains how Forcade, wishing to be consecrated as a bishop, and meeting Adnet, who had come out for his mission, went to Manila, because the admiral positively refused to land more than one of them. Forcade, therefore, went to Manila by the "Cleopatre" in the hope of being ordained there, while Adnet went to Loo Choo by the "Victorieuse" expecting Forcade to return by the "Pacifique" or some other merchant vessel.

This marks the end of the record contained in *The First Catholic Missionary to Japan in the Nineteenth Century,* by Msgr. Forcade.

THE CATHOLIC MISSIONARIES IN LOO CHOO

Citations and summary of information from
La Religion de Jesus Christ Ressusitee au Japan (Yaso Jakyo)
Par Fr. Marnas, Missionaire Apostolique
Vicaire general honoraire du diocese d'Osaka
Delhomme et Briquet, Editeurs, Paris-Lyons, 1896.

I. From The Departure of Forcade (1846) to the First Abandonment (1848).

Forcade reached Manila, September 27th, 1846, but was disappointed to find that the Archbishop of Manila, like himself, had not been consecrated. He could not dream of regaining "his poor country," as he called Ryukyu, before spring. During his enforced stay in Manila, the Dominicans assured him that during the time of the missionaries in Japan, the faith had been preached by their fathers in this island, and that one of them had even suffered martyrdom there. Father Ferrando, rector of the College of St. Thomas, promised him notes on this subject, and even gave him a Japanese dictionary, a grammar, and an old prayer book formerly composed for the Christians.

The news brought him later by the "Victorieuse" was good. The promises made to Admiral Cecille had been fairly well kept. The missionaries were still watched, but from a distance and discreetly. Three language teachers had been given them. Their house, hardly habitable because of the winds in winter and the rains in summer, had been repaired, and the rent fixed at 5 dollars Mexican a month. They had the use of a fairly large garden. Fifteen days had been long enough for Captain Rigult de Genouilly to obtain everything from the authorities that the two missionaries wanted.

Forcade left for Hongkong by this ship and was consecrated at Hongkong, Feb. 21, 1847.

A letter from Adnet and Leturdu dated Nov. 8, 1846, reached him January 17th at Macao by the annual tribute ships going to Fou Chow. When the "Victorieuse" left, and the fear of the coming of another warship had been dissipated, Adnet and Leturdu had not failed to note a change in the disposition of the mandarins. "In spite of all his fine promises to the commander of the 'Victorieuse' the *Swi-Kwang* (minister) does nothing, and with the exception of language teachers, we are just as you were."

Forcade was not much disturbed by this, as the missionaries were at least able to study the language, and he thought that on his return by a warship, these conditions could be remedied more easily because of this breach of faith. A diplomatic affair troubled him most.

A Diplomatic Difficulty. Life of Adnet and Leturdu At Naha

Letter of March 12, 1847:

"The Government of Lieou Kieou which had dared to deny by the minister, *Coudja,* that any complaint had been made in China against me, has hastened to accuse Adnet and Leturdu to Kung, the Imperial Commissioner. The former at once addressed a letter full of bitter complaints to Admiral Cecille, and the admiral, with the best of intentions, has felt that his honor and even the interest of missions in China demanded that he should promise the Imperial Commissioner that Adnet and Leturdu should leave Loo Choo this very year."

Forcade formulated various plans to meet this contingency, but none were carried into effect, and this ultimately led to the withdrawal of Leturdu after Adnet's death. He himself now went to Cochiu, China, as interpreter for a French punitive expedition, and on his return carried the treaty which had been negotiated. The Congregation of the Propaganda sent him back to Hongkong (1848).

While Forcade was making this long and important journey, we learn from the "Memoir" of Leturdu on his stay in Ryukyu what he and Adnet were doing. This memoire is now in the archives of Summary of Foreign Missions at Paris and provides the substance of Chapt. V Pt. I of Marnas' book.

"Three professors had been given them: two ordinary and one extraordinary. This latter, who was habitually called 'the great teacher' was not so much charged with the duty of instruction, but acted as a spy on the two other instructors. He had to watch that the latter properly deceived their pupils, whether they became fond of the missionaries, and to keep himself informed of what the two noble guests in the temple at Amiko were thinking and saying. Every morning he spent a few minutes with the two missionaries, making the two professors talk, and when the latter taught the words of the written language in place of the colloquial, he did not fail to praise the happy choice and propriety of these expressions. However, the missionaries were not to be caught; they knew that these words were only praised because they were not in everyday use.

"Should they step out of their house, a throng of men at once followed them as if they were criminals. As they passed, all the houses were noisily closed and the markets were deserted. If they wished to buy anything, the translation had to take place through the *kikodun,* or public commissary, and the cheapest things were sold to them at an exorbitant price."

Leturdu Complains to the Prime Minister of the Crowds.

"Leturdu and Adnet decided to address a formal complaint to the prime minister of the realm. An interpreter took their demand to *Choui,* and an answer was promised in three days. When this time had expired, they made several consecutive trips to the capital, but they got no answer. The minister was always either sick or away in the country. Several times in these excursions they found themselves escorted by a few hundred people. One day, turning on this crowd, Leturdu read them in the language of the country the convention concluded between Adm. Cecille and the government of Ryukyu, according to which they were not to be followed in their walks. This act had no more effect than anything else they had done. He left then, resolved not to come back (home), refusing all the attentions of the mandarins until the prime minister had sent a reply. On the way as he was passing near Naha, the idea came to him of stopping at the governor's. He demanded to speak to him, but none of the servants deigned to say a word to him. Some pretended not to understand him. The others merely laughed at him.

"On the next day he addressed a letter to the governor of Naha to inform him of what had taken place the day before, adding, 'No doubt the inhabitants of Naha are ignorant of the agreement signed at Port Melville. Perhaps Your Excellency even does not know of it, and this is why I take the liberty of sending you a copy, asking you to publish it in the territory under your jurisdiction.' Then came the text of the convention. He concluded as follows: 'The Naha *Kwan* (governor) must understand the full importance of this act. Every treaty must be executed, and to refuse this is to insult the party with whom it was concluded and to expose oneself to his vengeance. Let the mandarins reflect on this and not risk the anger of the French commander who will come here next year.'

Admiral Cochran's Visit. The Minister's Masterpiece of Lies.

"In the meantime, two large English corvettes and a brig anchored at Nafa. They remained here three days. The English admiral did not show the missionaries the politeness of visiting them, but he required the kings' minister to come out to see him on his ship. The latter protested illness in vain. He had to come, and the admiral easily recognized that he had to do with a fat and healthy man. With the exception of this forced visit, he caused the government no trouble. He praised the civilization of Ryukyu and their form of government, and he adjured them to remain as they were and neither to accept European religion or customs. He refused any kind of provisions and tried so hard to please them that he preferred to cast into the sea the body of a dead sailor than to ask a piece of land in which to bury him. Thus the petty mandarins were unending in their praise of him. Admiral Cecille was kind, no doubt, but Admiral Cochrane — what an incomparable man!

"A short time after his departure, the Governor of Naha announced to the two missionaries, not that he was bringing a reply from the minister, but that guards were going to be placed over them to teach them to distinguish between private houses and public buildings. They answered that they knew perfectly well how to make this distinction, and if they had ever entered a private house, it was to escape from a crowd of five hundred people who followed them and gave them no repose. No matter what they said, they found on October 23rd, 1846, a cabin built near the entrance of their house, and four men were posted there ready to accompany them whenever they went out.

"The close of 1846 and the first months of 1847 were not marked by any important event. But on April 24th, they were not a little surprised to receive a visit from the Naha *Kwan.* After six months he suddenly brought the minister's reply, a little masterpiece in the art of falsehood. In answering everything, he had found the means of answering nothing. They soon had an explanation of this unexpected action, learning that several ships had been seen in the north. For a moment, the poor missionaries believed that their bishop was returning, but they received a letter from him a little later that told them of his trip to Chochin, China, and made the hope of seeing him vanish for a time.

"They continued their monotonous and sad life. What affected them most was that they were condemned to inaction and were unable to approach the Loochooans, who had been ordered to act as if they were lepers whose presence was to be fled. They also testified to all the good qualities of the people and deplored the servitude in which they were kept."

Leturdu's Estimate of the People.
Bettelheim's Congregations.

"Oh, what good people!" wrote Leturdu, November 27, 1848, from Hongkong. "They are poor, sober, docile, with an upright mind, laborious, having neither the love of luxury or the thirst for gold, nor a theatre by which to be corrupted!... But this people is enslaved and dares not resist its masters. They cannot do so without being exposed to the most terrible punishments. The least mark of esteem, whether it was shown toward us or our holy religion would be punished by the whip, prison and exile. And it is impossible to hide oneself because of the size of the country, the police, and that particular law which holds a father responsible for his family, one family responsible for its nine neighbors, and the headman responsible for a whole village.

"We have never preached in public, unlike the English Protestant minister, who perorated every Sunday in the streets. He has not been forbidden to do this, but the people have been forbidden to listen, and he has been made ridiculous. It has happened several times that when he was preaching to a circle of auditors and had reached the highest pitch in his harangue, a satellite blew his whistle, and instantly that half of the circle to whom he was addressing himself made a half-turn to the right and showed him their backs. On a second signal, the other half executed the same operation to the left, and the poor orator found himself surrounded by people whose backs and heads alone were to be seen. If he complained, he was answered without a smile that this was the greatest mark of politeness they could give him, as it was meant to show that they were unworthy to see his face. They have even gone so far as to place buckets of ordure at his feet while he was speaking...

"If we have never preached in public, we have done so pretty often in private whenever we found the opportunity. But when we spoke of God, these good people answered us: 'What you say is good, but we cannot listen to it. The government does not allow it, and we cannot disobey without danger.' Nothing could be more real than this danger for anyone who would try to listen to us. The prisons, the bamboo, death or exile would be his reward.

A Talk with an Old Man About Politics and Religion.

"This is what I have heard from an old man, who has been the governor of a small island. This kind fellow appears to feel real affection for us. One day he called to us as we passed his house, and after inviting us in, he offered us tea and tobacco in spite of the commands of some attendants who came up and reminded him of the government's orders. Thus began our acquaintance. Since then, whenever he meets us on the road, he begins by looking around him, and if he sees no suspicious person, he advances and enters into conversation with us. If, on the other hand, he does not feel safe, he stops on some pretext and merely says good morning.

"One morning, as I was walking along the seashore, he saw me, and making me a sign to follow him, he led me into a lonely hollow where there was a grave. There he said to me, 'Do you know that the *Yamatu* (Japanese) have forbidden anyone to speak face to face with you on penalty of death?'

'I know this,' I said, 'but this will stop soon, for a French mandarin will come in a little while who will speak to the king and demand that you may be allowed to communicate directly with us.'

'The king! Ah, he can do nothing; the Japanese mandarin is the person who governs!' he said.

'Where does this Japanese mandarin live?' I asked.

'At Naha, the principal port of the island,' was the reply.

'Well, we will speak to him!' I said.

'You will not be able to do so; he is invisible to foreigners,' he said. So speaking, he saw a man who was raking sand at some distance, and looking at me with alarm, he said in a low voice, 'Do you see that man? He is perhaps a spy; if he notices me, I am ruined.'

'You are mistaken,' I replied. 'He is not a spy, only an unhappy slave whom his master has sent to get some sand. Reassure yourself!'

'Ah!' replied he. 'It is because the spies are disguised in all sorts of costumes, some are well dressed, as there are also others in rags. They are in the town and the country, everywhere! But he is going off. Let us talk a little more. Explain to me a little about Jesus.'

'Jesus is a messenger from the Lord of Heaven, powerful in words and deeds. And the Lord of Heaven has created all that which exists, and He is One. For, tell me, can there be two suns in the same sky, or two kings in the same kingdom?' I asked.

'No, there must be only one,' he replied.

'In the same way there can only be one Lord of Heaven and earth,' I said.

'That is true,' he said.

'It is in order to tell you this that I have come here. Won't you listen to us?' I asked.

'Yes, yes. But it is dangerous. We cannot,' he replied.

'Very well! Promise me at least to offer Him this prayer every day: "Lord, let me learn of Thee!" And then come to hear us when you are permitted to do so.' Upon this, we parted...' (Close of the letter).

Another Strange Visit from an Old Man.
Leturdu Goes North.

Another time, an old man of seventy came from the north of the island, solely, as he said, in order to see the missionaries. In the afternoon, when Leturdu was out and Adnet alone was in the house, a venerable old man entered the temple, leading a fine child of ten by his hand.

"What do you want?" a servant, who was unluckily present, said to him.

"I desire to see the foreigners," he said.

"You cannot. It is forbidden by the mandarins," said the servant.

Upon this the visitor was going to withdraw, when Adnet happened to appear to inquire the reason of the noise. He at once had the old man enter the kitchen and offered tea to him. Later he regretted not having brought him into his own room, for the poor man was afraid in the presence of the servant and did not dare to talk. He only said that he had come expressly from the north in order to see the strangers, because he had heard them spoken of and wished to visit them once before his death. He did not say this immediately, but only as he was going away, and as if fearing the servant would hear.

He had hardly gone when, reflecting upon the strangeness of this visit, the missionary flew out of doors to try to find him again. But it was in vain that he and Leturdu hunted all over *Tumai* in every direction during the rest of the evening. Evidently he was not a mere sightseer! Perhaps he was descendant of some Christians, or an infidel whose heart God had touched.

Anxious to obtain the solution of this riddle, and hoping to meet the old man again, Leturdu resolved to visit the northern part of the island. The mandarins had no sooner learned of his plan than they made every effort to make him give up the trip. But seeing that all was in vain, they sent the order that he was not to be received, and that food was to be refused him in every town and hamlet through which he would have to pass.

People not Allowed to Speak. Note on Christianity in Loo Choo.

"They thought," Leturdu wrote in his memoir, "that, rebuffed on the very first day, I would retrace my steps, but they were mistaken, for one of our maxims was never to retreat. I therefore continued on my way, and when I became too hungry, I entered some hut and begged for potatoes. My journey lasted five days."

With the purpose of isolating him as much as possible, the mandarins went so far as even to impose silence on the inhabitants of the villages which he traversed. So that if he wished to speak with anyone, it was necessary for Leturdu to establish himself in people's homes and say that he would remain there until someone answered him. The people then confessed that they were silent by order of the mandarins. Nothing on this journey gave Leturdu any scent of the old man for whom he was hunting, but he retained the firm conviction that he must have been the descendent of a Christian.

The Death of the King. Adnet Seriously Ill.

The year 1847 closed without the appearance of any French ship on the horizon. Adnet and Leturdu, isolated from the rest of the world, did not know how to explain the delay. Adm. Cecille's expedition to Corea could not have lasted into the winter, for the winds would be dangerous at that season. No doubt some political event of considerable importance had taken place, perhaps the death of Louis Philippe. They lost themselves in conjectures over the matter. This last idea, that of the death of the French king, must have been suggested to them by the funeral of the King of Loo Choo, which marked the close of the month of October. This effigy of a monarch left a child of 8 or 9 yrs. Yet the kingdom was in no danger because of this, for the Japanese officers remained at Naha to ensure its safety.

The apotheosis of the deceased took place October 30, 1847. The mourning, which, according to the oriental custom, reached the whole people, was the same as that for a father or mother. It consisted of a fast of fifty days, during which the use of fish was prohibited. No doubt this abstinence was not very well observed, for the sea was covered with fishing boats as usual. Nevertheless, an attempt was made to impose these prescriptions on the missionaries, who refused to follow them. Adnet, whose health was already shaken, could not have stood it.

Already a sick man when he arrived at Loo Choo, September 15, 1846, he appeared at first to only suffer from an intermittent fever. Quinine was able to reduce the number of attacks, which instead of appearing every other day, finally only came on at intervals of two or three weeks. But now the sick man became completely prostrated. His companion soon recognized that the fever was not his only ill, but that he was attacked by tuberculosis. Thanks to his robust constitution, Adnet was able to struggle for twenty months against the devouring action of this disease. One can easily imagine what his existence in Okinawa was like. He languished and suffered there, offering his pains to God for the salvation of the souls he had come from so far to seek.

When the feast of Easter (April 23, 1848) came, the halleluias sung by the church above the empty grave of our Lord reminded the two exiles, soon to be separated by death, that the cross is the *via dolorosa* which leads the Christian, and above all, the priest, to the glories of the resurrection. They thought of their happy brethren who could offer Jesus Christ on this day some soul regenerated by baptism. "The other missionaries," wrote Leturdu then, "rejoice over having given new children to God, and new brothers to Jesus Christ, but this mission of ours is a barren bride who bears no offspring."

Last Words of Adnet. Grief of Leturdu.

Adnet dragged along as best he could until July 1st of the year 1848. He had lost his voice from January, and March had almost been fatal to him. Seeing him become weaker and weaker, Leturdu obliged him to stay in bed, at least until 6:30 a.m. But he could not prevent him from being present at the language lessons, which were, moreover, a distraction for the patient and a way of passing the time. The interpreters did not hide their fear of soon finding him alone from Leturdu. Alas! Of all the afflictions which could come to him, this was the greatest! The invalid, however, was resigned and even wished to die.

The month of April gave him more strength. He could take short walks and of course ascend to the altar every day. However, June 21st, on arising, he was utterly surprised to find himself short of breath. He was barely dressed before he had to lie down, and if he took a few steps, he was obliged to sit down and get his breath. He was no longer able to recite Holy Mass. As they were in the rainy season, the two friends attributed this oppression to the temperature and hoped that better weather would cause it to disappear. It is difficult to conceive what each of them felt, alone and as if abandoned in this land, deprived of all help on the eve of their last farewell.

"Fair weather came once more," wrote Leturdu, "but the trouble did not disappear. July 1st, the weakness of my co-laborer was much greater, and his breathing seemed more short. We were unable to disguise for ourselves the fact that danger was near, and he himself told me that he saw clearly he would not have long to suffer. In the evening

I noticed that he could only draw in his breath with effort, and that his eyes were dilated and glistening.

I said to him, "My dear friend, you are truly in a bad way. I don't know whether you will last long"...

"I don't think so," he replied.

"I believe that if you still have some last acts or wishes to make, it would be prudent to complete them at once. I will write to your dictation, and you can attach your signature," I said.

Then I added, "You recently spoke to me of making a general confession. I do not advise this. You are too weak, and you have done so often in the best frame of mind, because it was just after the close of a retreat."

"It is true," he replied, "that, thanks to God, my conscience reproaches me with nothing grave. However, before entering one's eternity, it is good to review one's past years in the bitterness of his heart. The sight of the bright day which approaches casts a light upon the soul which makes one better able to appreciate the greatness of his faults. This is why I will begin my confession tomorrow."

We rose together and went to sit down out of doors. I took his hand. It was wet with icy perspiration.

By Adnet's Death Bed. His Piety.

I turned my head to let a tear fall, and I begged him to go it. We recited the rosary and said the evening prayer just as usual, and then he went to bed. Then, as I was preparing to say a few words of edification, he said, "Wait a moment, until I breathe at ease." These were his last words. He had scarcely uttered them when two or three prolonged sighs escaped from his lips. I called him in an anxious voice; he did not answer. I opened his mosquito net, and his head was thrown back beyond his pillow. He was dying. I hastily gave him a last absolution. I applied in his case the indulgence for the death of a good man, and as I was finishing, he breathed his last, and his soul appeared before God to receive the reward promised to those who have left all to follow the Lord Jesus. Putting a check on my grief, I closed his eyes. I recited the vespers for the dead and the Way of the Cross as I had promised him to do a few days before. Then throwing myself on my knees before the lifeless body of my co-laborer and only friend, I offered up to God the death of this first missionary of the new Church of Japan. I adored His Divine Providence and adjured it to serve me more than ever as guide and friend. I continued to pray until, as midnight struck, the thought came that I would perhaps not have time to offer the Holy Sacrifice tomorrow, and I prepared to ascend the sacred altar in virtue of the privilege which we have of celebrating the mass one hour after midnight.

When mass was over, I felt somewhat strengthened. If I still remained in my affliction, I had the hope that my dear companion at least had entered into the joy of his Lord. With the exception of Extreme Unction, he had received all the comforts of the Church, and he had taken communion that very morning, as he had done ever since he himself could not say Holy Mass. I had asked him to notice the day before that few sick persons had the happiness of uniting themselves daily with the God of their eternity. He had recited his breviary right up to the end. For the last fortnight, in spite of his great difficulty in enunciating, he had wished to add the lesser office to the great. For a whole month he had only engaged in exercises of piety. His reading was in the "Lives of the Saints," in the New Testament, and in "The Imitation." He saw death approach with the resignation of a Christian, and at the end with the joy of a perfect missionary.

His Readiness for Death. His Patience.

At the beginning of his sickness, we made some novenae to obtain his cure from God, if that was His holy will, but since then, he desired to do so no more, except when he desired to obtain more patience. This patience was such that I have seen him almost always continuing his studies and persevering in tracing characters even under the attacks of the fever as long as his pen would write legibly.

He followed his rule with strict exactitude, and I had to make appeal to my authority to cause him to cease rising at five o'clock during the last six months. The thought that he died without having seen his bishop, and above all, without having baptised a single Japanese at first caused him trouble, but when he saw it was necessary to become resigned to this, he said that he consoled himself for it by the hope of praying in heaven. He has often repeated to me that if God gave him a choice between life and death, he would prefer the latter.

He has had the happiness of being among the first fruits of the new Christendom in Japan. Oh, how his fair soul must have been well received by those thousands of Japanese martyrs, St. Francis Xavier at their head, who have so long waited for the return of their land into the great family of the Heavenly Father. In Heaven, he adds his voice to theirs to draw the glances of divine pity upon this unhappy country.

For me, may the Lord recompense me for his death by giving me his virtues. While bowing humbly before adorable Providence, I cannot help from crying out: "Poor Japan, how art thou afflicted! For these two years thou hast been deprived of thy bishop; thou dost lose today an apostle who couldst so well contribute to thy salvation; thou hast now only a single man vowed to thy redemption, and who knoweth that even he may remain!....."

I then received some visits, among them those of three mandarins who came in the name of the prime minister, the governor of the capital, and the governor of Naha, to offer me letters of condolence. After this they asked to be allowed to attend the funeral, and this I granted. But one request of theirs which I could not grant at all was that of coming to make a sacrifice on some given day at the grave of the dear dead. I needed more than half an hour of explanations to make them understand that even in Loo Choo we could no more sacrifice to the dead than to the living. Even then they were only half convinced, until I told them that it was forbidden by law in my country, in order to finish the matter. On this word, "forbidden by my country," they were silent and had no more objections. I added that if the mandarins wished greatly to honor my friend, they could come to the temple, and that I would offer in their name a sacrifice to the Lord of Heaven for the repose of the one whose loss we mourned, but they did not reply to these advances.

The Mandarins. Three Letters of Condolence.

Letter of the Prime Minister:

"Kuja, Minister of the Kingdom of Loo Choo, transports himself in spirit to the house of mourning to worship there, and to salute the young afflicted Father. Master Adnet, having fallen sick on his arrival here, and having little by little become worse, has died on the first day of the 6th moon. He is the object of compassion of all. As for you, we beg you to moderate the grief which your affection for him causes you to feel. We salute you with respect."

Letter of the Governor of Shuri:
"Birth and death are like the spring which always follows autumn and like day which regularly gives place to the night. Master Adnet has long languished, couched on his mat. Finally, as the spirit of his sickness was unpitying, he has died. Creature of nothingness, at the announcement of his death, I have been seized with inexhaustible grief. But may you, reflecting that birth and death are the decrees of fate, condescend to temper your grief."

Letter of the Governor of Naha:
"Man upon this earth is like a leaf which the wind carries away. Master Adnet was in his third year of sickness: the remedies which he took were without effect. Now I suddenly hear that two baleful spirits, cutting the thread of his days, have dragged him into the subterranean prison. Life and death are coiled up by destiny. For this reason, moderate your grief and submit yourself to destiny. One should not regret a dead man excessively. I humbly urge this upon you."

Who would not say from this language that the mandarins were our best friends? This is because no one is stingy with politeness here which does not bind one to do anything. This is the politics of the country. When some bad tricks have been played on us, we are invited to dinner or presents are sent to us. The greatest pain which we were able to cause them was to refuse both the dinner and the hypocritical gifts. But this did not prevent them from troubling us at the first opportunity. I will say in their praise, however, that for fifteen days after the death of my companion, they caused me no annoyance whatever.

The Funeral and the Grave. The "Bayonnaise."

On the morning of the third, the three mandarins who had come before, presented themselves at the head of a numerous cortege in white clothes. I had draped the altar in black. After having recited Matins and Laudes before the coffin, I offered the Holy Sacrifice in the presence of the mandarins and their followers. We then directed our steps toward the trench, preceded by the cross. The place chosen for the entombment was a little wood by the side of the sea, a few steps from the temple. I had already buried a French doctor there two years ago. The attendants were struck by the burial ceremonies of the Church. They were considered very proper, and they have seen that if we do not worship the dead, we know how to honor them. I had a beautiful cross placed on the tomb.* In the center is a crown, half gilded, half plated silver, surmounted by a host surrounded by a halo, and on a large flat gravestone, this inscription has been cut:

"Ci-git le Corps du Reverend Matthieu Adnet
Pretre Francais,
Missionaire Apostolique du Japan
Decede Aux Riu-Kiu le 1er Juillet 1848."

Thanks to the cult of which this country professes for the dead, we can hope that this grave will be respected. It has been, indeed, until now.

A few days after the death of his companion, Leturdu received news from China by the annual ship. He learned that Forcade was just going to return to Hongkong as Pro-prefect Apostolic of that colony. The Holy See had assigned him this post as one most favorable for reaching Japan when the opportunity presented itself. He rejoiced over this, but as his mail did not bring him any orders from his bishop nor the announcement of a colleague, he thought of crossing to China in order to inform Forcade of the actual state of affairs and to plan with him how to reach their true goal. Such were his thoughts when the French corvette, "Bayonnaise," Capt. Jurien de la Graviere, arrived at Loo Choo, August 26th. "The Commander," he said, "told me that he came to fetch me. He read me the instructions according to which, if I did not wish to leave, he would have to declare to the mandarins that I remained on my

---

* Marnas' note: "The Cross, however, has been removed."

own responsibility. It was he who told me that the Port Melville convention, on which we had always depended, amounted to nothing definite.

Leturdu Leaves Loo Choo Forever.

Finding myself abandoned to my own resources, and not knowing when Monseigneur Forcade would send me a fresh companion, and certain, moreover, that nothing would ever be done in Loo Choo as long as the Japanese Government had domination here, I said that I would leave.

The next day, August 27, 1848, anchor was raised and the Loo Choos disappeared, for how long I do not know. (The above from Leturdu's diary, August 27, 1848).

The "Bayonnaise" transported him to Manila, from whence an English steamer carried him to Hongkong.

"Will we return to *Riukiu?*" he wrote on his arrival at Hongkong. "Shall we not rather turn toward some spot in Japan, in a wooded country, one that is mountainous and has few inhabitants, and is consequently better for us as we can more easily escape from the observation of the government? This last plan is more dangerous, but on the other hand, it offers greater chances of success, supposing that we are able to land, a matter which I do not consider impossible. But perhaps Providence itself will open the gate for us by means of the English or American cannon."

Verbatim translation. Chapter V, Book I, pp. 169-188.
Part I. Book I is entitled "L'Avant-Poste des Isles Riu-Kiu" (outpost)
Part I is entitled "Au Porte du Japan" (At the gates of Japan)

II. The Second Residence in Loo Choo
Hong Kong, 1848–Jan., 1855

The Missionaries at Hong Kong
Disadvantages of Having a Title.

At this time there were several besides Forcade at Hong Kong whose real goal was Japan. These had formed the plan of landing somewhere in Yezo or Saghalien in order to carry on a secret ministry among the Japanese. Mahon, one of the number, wrote as follows to the director of the Seminary at Paris, October 27, 1848:

"Astonishing, marvelous, providential, is the arrival here of good Father Leturdu, innocently bringing us from the distant Loo Choos the same project as we have already planned out!"

But the more Forcade reflected about this, the less inclined he was to approve the plan. He did not think that they could have any more success than in Loo Choo, and enlightened by his own experience and the accounts of Leturdu, he did not even dream of returning thither, but thought it was better to wait in Hongkong for the opening of Japan. The people in Loo Choo were helpless.

"The mandarins," wrote Leturdu to Paris, November 20, 1848, "do not expressly forbid us to preach. They do not have the courage to dare this, but what is worse, they forbid the people under the most severe penalties from listening, speaking or even paying the least attention to us... In fine, we had been taken to Loo Choo by warships, we had an official title there, that of Interpreters of the King of France, and everyone regarded us as French mandarins come to explore the country. Was this not of the nature to fortify the opinion which the Japanese have had since the former persecutions, that missionaries were nothing but the spies and envoys of their governments?... We vainly declared that we were not French officers, but priests coming with the intention of teaching the Way of Heaven. The people, the government, everyone, took us for mandarins, and not for *shen-fu* (Japanese: *shinpu*, priests). No doubt we were fortunate because Adm. Cecille carried us to the islands, for no one knew how to get there, and yet Rome urged us to send missionaries thither. Today, at least we have done our duty. We have gone there, we have lived there four years and a half, and we know the country. We know that we can return there whenever we wish, but humanly speaking, it is impossible to make a single proselyte there because the government is opposed to it, and even if the king of Loo Choo were in our favour, he could authorize nothing, for he does not govern, but the Emperor of Japan, acting through his envoys."

The "Beble." Forcade's Plans and Discovery of a Japanese Teacher.

The missionaries willingly made the sacrifice of their dearest ambition. Mahon wrote: "Oh Jesus! I have not been worthy of being broken on your cross!" Leturdu went to Canton, where he died. Only Monicoue and Girard were to see Japan. Forcade, from his post of observation, followed the expedition to Japan and Loo Choo, March to May, 1849, of the U.S. corvette, "Beble," which sailed to Japan for the purpose of rescuing some sailors, all of whom were obliged to trample on the cross, while those who made objections were caged up and only given salt fish and rice once a day.

Forcade was very uncomfortable at Hongkong, because his jurisdiction was so near Canton, and in 1849, he wrote to Paris asking to resign. Then he changed his mind and decided to take his missionaries back to Loo Choo to learn the language, and as he could not get a merchant ship, he wrote on September 18, 1848, "The missionaries will be transported to the island by some American warship which will be willing, as I have agreed with the commodore, to land them and withdraw without saying anything, in order not to make them appear to be sent by some government." But an unexpected incident reminded him that Japanese could be learned in Hongkong:

"As I was going from Macao to Hongkong on the 7th (September, 1849),... someone pointed me out a Japanese among the gentlemen surrounding me... He came from Shimabara and was a castaway. Alas, he had become a Protestant... You can judge of the conversation that soon took place between us. He spoke English as fluently as anyone in the world. I learned from him, among other things, that the language of Loo Choo over which I had taken so much trouble to learn without books or teachers during two years, was only a poor Japanese dialect, very difficult for the inhabitants of the large islands to understand, and as ridiculous to them as the vulgar patois of some of our provinces to the most scrupulous of the Forty (Academicians). Unpleasant discovery! Not only have I lost my time, but after this should we return to Loo Choo?... When I learned that this man was going to settle in Hongkong, I was not really able to thank God for this light cast upon my path... Evidently it is at Hongkong that Japanese should be learned with this Japanese who speaks well and is apparently well disposed, and not at all at Loo Choo with men who are opposed to us and who speak badly."

[On January 25th, 1851, on the Feast of the Conversion of St. Paul, this man was baptised into the Catholic faith by Forcade with the name Paul of the Holy Faith, the name of Anjiro].

Forcade Leaves China Forever. The Perry Expedtion.

Forcade's sister, Sister Alphonsine, who had been in charge of a foundling asylum in Hongkong from November 11, 1848, suddenly died of cerebral fever, October 13, 1850, at the age of 36. From 1849, Forcade had been suffering from dysentery, which had first attacked him in Loo Choo, and because of intermittent fever and other various reasons, partly ecclesiastical, he was glad to resign from the missionary society and to go home, carrying to Rome the acts of the synod of bishops in China which took place at Sicawei, near Shanghai, toward the close of 1851. He left Hongkong on January 27, 1852.

Mahon was left with the powers of Vican General (Deputy) of the Japan Mission. He watched the Perry expedition leave Hongkong to martial music, April 28, 1853, and even had an interview with Commodore Perry. Marnas gives this account of Perry in Loo Choo:

"May 26th, he anchored at Naha. It was only after long negotiations and much difficulty that he was able to get in touch with the regent. He did not see the king at all, a child of ll, whom he was told was sick. Although the native authorities refused to authorize his officers to live on shore, he had the principal island explored in order to find any deposits of coal. He sent two ships to the Bonins with the same purpose. On June 23rd the squadron was again united at Naha, but the negotiations attempted with the government ended in results of small importance. All the enterprising energy of the American was broken by the passive resistance of this supple and artful race. It is true that Commodore Perry, during his stay of several weeks at Ryukyu, collected interesting details about the inhabitants, and materials which were precious for geography and hydrography and other sciences, but that is about all he did.

"July 25th he was again at Naha. Knowing the people better, he threatened to land 200 soldiers to take possession of the palace at Shuri if he was not granted free trafficking in an open market, the permission to build a depot storehouse for coal, and the immediate abandonment of all espionage around his officers and men.

"It goes without saying that in spite of a thousand protests, the native authorities had to grant him all he asked. The 'Plymouth' stayed longer than the other ships."

Perry's Second Visit. Plans Made to Send Missionaries.

He returned to Hongkong, August 7, 1853, and set sail again January 4, 1854. He did not stop long at Naha, but received news here through the Governor General of the Dutch Indies of the death of the Dairi. He replied with condolences, but said that this should not delay negotiations and "that in case the Japanese government should refuse to treat and to assign a port of refuge for merchant ships or whalers, he was resolved to put the principal island of Ryukyu under an American protectorate."

The Council of the Propaganda had arranged a successor for Forcade. Colin, a member of the Foreign Missions and stationed in Manchuria, was named Apostolic Prefect of Japan. As soon as his nomination reached him (1853), he hastened to Hongkong, but death overtook him at Lientung (May 23, 1854). He had, at the same time, written Libois at Macao of his plans to send Girard and one or two others to Naha, where he expected to join them.

Mahon was now too much attached to the Asylum of the Holy Infancy, whose almoner he had been since October 27, 1848. Libois became temporarily charged with the mission to Japan.

A. At Naha, February 26, 1855 – The Landing.

Furet, Girard and Mermet Reach Naha by the Merchantman "Lion"

The death of Colin was not a hindrance to the accomplishment of his plans. Soon after the beginning of 1855, three missionaries, Girard, Furet and Mermet, were sent to the Loo Choo Islands. They had the prospect of soon being able to go from thence to Japan, for France occupied in fighting the Russians in the Crimea and sending for warships to attack them even in the estuary of the Amur River, could not fail to soon conclude her own treaty with the Japanese.

They set sail February 11, 1855, on a French merchantman, the "Lion," Captain Bonnet commanding. Three other missionaries belonging to the same society and on the way to Shanghai accompanied them. They also took three Chinese servants. In spite of head-winds and a very dangerous sea, their crossing from Hongkong to Naha was accomplished in fifteen days, and by the 26th, the "Lion" was in sight of Okinawa. Mermet recounts in these terms the difficulties attendant on their landing:

"Naha, February 26, 1855. Today to our great satisfaction, the anchor was dropped in sight of the harbour of Naha. The long-awaited pilots at least presented themselves on board. Our captain now made haste to send a box of presents to the governor, and this act of courtesy was soon followed by the arrival of three mandarins with a large following. They were charged with the duty of delivering a large roll of red paper to the captain. This was the modest visiting card of the governor. They had scarcely acquitted themselves of their message before they asked the following questions: 'From whence do you come?' 'Where are you going?' 'What do you want?'

"'We are going to Shanghai,' replied Captain Bonnet. 'Our ship leaks, and we want a few pieces of timber to repair her.'

"'You shall have them,' the chief mandarin gravely replied.

"But it was necessary to attack the burning question. The able captain attempted to prepare the way by inviting the three delegates to his dinner table. During the whole meal we were the special objects of their preoccupation. They could not look at us without allowing a significant uneasiness to appear on their faces. The interpreter finally became bold enough to ask me some questions. He asked for some details about the present state of affairs in China, and each of the visitors learned with evident pleasure that the French had beaten the rebels at Shanghai. The moment had come to risk a proposal: 'I have on my ship,' said the captain, 'some doctors (scholars), men of prayer, who desire to gain learning, and even to communicate their science to you while living on your island.'

"This opening was a terrible blow for them. It shook them to the bottom of their souls. The contraction of their features indicated this plainly enough.

Negotiations of Captain Bonnet at Naha.

"'It is difficult to visit our island,' replied the chief mandarin, 'but it is impossible to live here.'

"'Nevertheless,' Captain Bonnet went on, 'every people are opening their lands to strangers. When the Japanese come to France they would receive a friendly welcome... Why do you then refuse us the entrance to your land?'

"'Our laws are opposed to it; and then, such a thing is completely against our inclinations.' was the reply.

"'Maybe, but I am astonished that a civilized country has such laws.' ventured the captain.

"'But remember that our climate is very unhealthy,' said the mandarin.

"'That may be true, but fortunately you are all in splendid health,' said the captain.

"'And also,' I said, 'being doctors, we could take care of ourselves and easily cure you, as well.'

"'Our islands are too small; there is no room.' the abashed interpreter replied.

"This was their last word, and our visitors left on the pretext of a headache, and fearing to compromise themselves, they withdrew very quickly, making pompous demonstrations of politeness toward us. As it was too late now to achieve a landing, we have put this act off until tomorrow.

"February 27th. This morning at break of day, a new deputation, bearing the gifts which the governor sends to our captain, came on board. These presents consisted of pigs, fowls, eggs, turnips, sweet potatoes and a goat. The head of this embassy, after having acquitted himself of his mission, prayed us earnestly not to come ashore, offering to bring to the ship everything that was needed. These obstacles were not able to astonish us. We were prepared for anything... Girard, without taking into account the kind recommendations of the mandarin, went ashore with our captain, who had shown himself completely devoted to us. This is the result of their investigations. Everything has been refused us. There is no land and no food for us. Everything is needed, it appears, for the inhabitants of the country. We will therefore have to take ourselves what they refuse to give us, and we will land in spite of everything. At first we will occupy a hut open to all the winds and without any flooring. This prospect does not sadden us, but we grieved to see the natives flee or close their houses at our approach. Poor people! If they only knew the gift which we were bringing them! God alone knows all the annoyances which he has reserved for us. But we will love Him always, and we count ourselves happy to give Him, at the price of our own blood, the treasure of our faith."

The Story of a Peaceful Invasion by Doctors

March 1st. Girard and Captain Bonnet presented themselves before the Governor of Naha, but they only received absolute and formal refusals from him. The good captain was quite disconcerted at this, yet the missionaries, without allowing themselves to be depressed, fixed their landing for the next day, without waiting any longer. This is the story which M. Biet, one of the three missionaries going to Shanghai, has left us of this pacific invasion:

"Letter to the Director of the Seminary, dated March 4th, on board the 'Lion:'

"The weather was magnificent, the sea was calm and motionless as a lake. After having offered the Holy Sacrifice, M. Girard went ashore with the captain. While he was keeping the authorities busy, we went to join him by another route with the baggage and to meet in the house of the bonzes, occupied before by Messrs. Adnet and Leturdu. At the hour of noon, we were on the way, reciting the *Veni Creator* and the *Memorare*. Some magistrates of the island came toward us when we stepped ashore. We gave each of them a good handshake, and after polite salutations, we left these mandarins with our two confreres, Messrs. Mermet and Boyer and went off to find the temple.

"On seeing our boxes brought and put down here, the bonzes came out and their faces began to lengthen. One of the younger ones asked us in Chinese, 'Why have you come here?' We replied, 'To live here and learn the language.' The baggage continued to come. During this interval, there was a conference held among the bonzes. One of them, putting on a long black robe, came with a grave and severe air to express to us the order to carry away the trunks and to go. We answered by an affirmative sign, though we continued to receive and arrange our baggage, and soon we were joined by all our party, followed by a mandarin with two attendants and a large escort.

"This old functionary, a veritable patriarch with a long white beard, seated himself on a mat with his English interpreter, his assessors, the bonzes and young initiates of the temple, the servants and some inquisitive on-lookers. Tea was served and tobacco offered, and then a long conference began. Captain Bonnet played a generous part in order to plead our cause. M. Girard exhausted the wisdom of the old mandarin by the sagaciousness and aptness of his replies. This latter ended by telling them, 'I can decide nothing by myself. We must go to see the Regent at four o'clock.'

Audience with the Regent. Admitted on Certain Conditions.

"When this hour came, the audience was requested. But the old man told us now, 'You must wait until six o'clock, for the Regent is so greatly irritated to know that you are on these shores that he will not be able to talk for two hours.'

"We went in good order and very majestically to the abode of the Prince Regent who had come directly from Shuri. The governor of Naha, a grave and venerable person, received us solemnly at the entrance of a large hall filled with servants. There we were invited to take seats at a table loaded with dishes, and two old men, the governors and the Regent, placed themselves before us. There was a moment of profound silence, as if for the examination of our physiognomies. After the first course, a long letter from the Regent was handed to the captain. Our Chinese translated it.

"Our dear brothers had taken all sorts of precautions to be considered only as religiously minded men of science, but the letter of the Regent went to the bottom of the question at once. He said that the people of Loo Choo, having one religion, had no need for that of Jesus; that the foreigners who really come to plant their religion ought to go away, adding that they did not even allow the doctrine of Confucius to be preached here!*... He also said that other Europeans would not fail to come after us, and then the island would be invaded by them; that there was hardly enough room and food for the natives, so small and poor was the island, without other products than grass... The question was attacked boldly, the motive of all their refusals was disclosed, and the order for departure was categorical.

"At this, the Regent was going to leave, but we found means to continue the session. The Prince, very grave and sad, sat down once more. M. Girard eluded the letter by evasive replies and protests of sincere friendship, which the captain supported.

"'Well,' Girard said, 'we are here because it is our duty, and the captain cannot take us back on his ship. You are free to treat us with cruelty, but we cannot leave... You would better kill us rather.'

---

* Translator's note: This was either a lie or a misunderstanding

"These words produced a good effect... The Regent, seeing so much firmness and their unshakable resolution, and fearing also that the French admiral might refuse him his assistance against the pirates, permitted Msgrs. Furet, Girard and Mermet to occupy the bonzerie on the condition that someone should come to take them away in two or three months. In brief, we had gained the victory!"

The "Lion" Departs and the Missionaries Take Possession

"Politics was talked for a little while. The governor praised the noble and generous character of the French who were protecting the central authority in China against the attacks of the rebels. During all this long discussion, the Regent, the mandarin, the interpreter and the whole suite showed themselves admirable because of their gravity, politeness and calmness in this affair which was as painful to them in view of their fears and prejudices. During the whole time we did not perceive a single sign of anger or impatience, not one word was uttered crossly or with hardness, but all was grave, noble, and marked by moderation. The profoundest silence reigned in a room filled with people, and servants with red caps waited on us with perfect kindness and amiability. Captain Bonnet could not get over it; he often repeated in his admiration, 'I have seen many peoples, but I have never seen one like this!' What a misfortune it is that such good men should be pagans. May the light of the gospel soon shine upon them!

"Our adieus to the Princes of Loo Choo were solemn and polite.... Proud of our triumph, we brought our dear co-workers back to their abode to help them settle in it. It was half-past eight, and two men with torches preceded us. This act of taking possession was official, and the servants of the bonzes themselves came to help prepare our rooms for us. Before separating, we exchanged our last farewells, our hearts filled with joy at such a happy result. The next day, Captain Bonnet once more wished to assure himself that all was going well with the missionaries, and having done so, we saluted the Regent with 21 guns and set sail."

The reader who remembers what the missionaries had to suffer before in their first stay in Loo Choo, assuredly asks himself what happened to their successors after the departure of the "Lion." We will allow M. Mermet to recount their experiences.

The Conditions in 1855. Arrival of the "Sybille."

Letter of April 25, 1855:

"Our landing was so sudden, so unusual, and so uncanonical, that at first we only thought of how to maintain ourselves in the place we had taken by assault. And in fact, in spite of the fury of the greater and lesser mandarins, in spite of the exorcisms and maledictions of the bonzes whom we summoned to depart, here we are installed in the celebrated bonzery of *Amiko,* having as our guests several hundreds of gnawing rats who devour our books and go off in processions to eat the fat bellies of the gods in the neighboring *miya*. Our stubbornness has triumphed over the Regent. What could he do against three headstrong fellows determined in advance to match their wits against his and to laugh over all misadventures?... For two days our new compatriots refused us all sorts of provisions. All this had been foreseen, so we did not fast for a moment. Little by little faces ceased to frown, and they ended by agreeing that we were very polite scholars with good faces. Nevertheless, I feel assured that the policies of the government will be more harassing than to our predecessors. We have fifteen guardians lodged in real guardhouses. They are in order to protect us from thieves, it is said, but in reality they are placed here to watch us. When we go out, a large vanguard precedes us to announce the approach of the enemy to the women, children, and even to the men. So when we appear, everyone flees. We are followed by a rear guard no less numerous. One of the mandarins told me that the death penalty was fixed for any one who should ever venture to learn about our religion."

The missionaries had only been two months in the island of Okinawa when on Sunday, May 6th, about 4 p.m., someone came to tell them that a foreign ship was in sight. At this hour they were taking their frugal meal, but they at once rose and by the aid of a spy glass mounted on that corner of the enclosure wall which served as the observatory, they recognized the French flag with joy. At the same time, they distinguished a little boat which was making for the shore, and the large number of men in this gave them for an instant the sad idea of a shipwreck. Fortunately it was nothing of the kind. After a wait of about two hours, the missionaries were shaking the hands of Lieut. Sibour, a nephew of the archbishop of Paris, and of two other officers of the "Sybille." "Where is Father Furet?" said Lieut. Sibour with a kindly note of authority. "I have orders to take him away with me." At the same time he handed the surprised missionary a letter from M. Libois and another from the commander of the "Sybille," Capt. Simonet de Maisonneuve.

News. Conduct of Lt. Sibour at Naha.

Foreseeing that in a short time France would have to treat with Japan, and that our interpreter would be necessary for the negotiations which were then commencing, Admiral Laguerre had asked the authorization of M. Libois to take one of the missionaries to Loo Choo on board one of his ships which were going north to fight the Russians. M. Furet had been designated for that end. He was to embark on the "Sybille," which was going into Japanese waters. To speak truly, he did not know the language of this country, but as he had the prospect of remaining quite a while at Hakodate, where at least one of the ships would stay during the whole campaign, he could no doubt study it under favorable conditions, see Japan at short range, and if he did not succeed in settling there, he could return after the campaign to Loo Choo, supplied with useful information. He therefore made his preparations and got ready to leave on the next day.

Lt. Sibour, who was questioned by the mandarins immediately upon the goal of the "Sybille's" voyage, maintained the greatest reserve. In this he only conformed to the orders of his captain. "I have come," he said coolly, "to inform myself of the manner in which the three French scholars at the temple of *Amiko* have been treated." He demanded an audience with the Governor of Naha on the next day and went as far as to almost fix the hour himself.

May 6th. In the morning, while M. Furet finished packing, M. Mermet and M. Girard accompanied the officers to the governor's residence. Lt. Sibour soon put this personage at ease. He only complimented him on the kind way in which the missionaries had been treated, but his purpose in this was to obtain that they should be better treated in the future. Nevertheless, the governor's conscience was to give him a few twinges. Thus, when Lt. Sibour announced to him that he was going to take M. Furet away, and that the latter could bear the same favorable witness to the admiral, he was visibly disturbed. "Will M. Furet come back here?" he asked.

"Yes, in three or four months, I expect," was the reply. Lt. Sibour expressed the desire of going to Shuri, the capital, but he declared that he didn't intend to have any spies at his back, and that he only wished to be accompanied by two mandarins, who would do him honor and give him information which he might happen to require. Everything was granted. Finally, there was a unanimous shout of admiration from the authorities of Loo Choo when he told them that the Emperor of China had written with his own hand to Admiral Laguerre to thank him for having defended him against the rebels.

Furet Leaves for Nagasaki.

The moment of farewells had come. M. Furet quitted his co-workers, and after three or four hours in the boat, was alongside the frigate "Sybille," where Lt. Gibour introduced him to Captain de Maisonneuve, a man much devoted to the missionaries. He found a cordial welcome at his hands and those of the other officers. These brave sailors often said to him, "You missionaries are more courageous than we, for you come to these distant and often inhospitable lands to remain here until death."*

The "Sybille" was at Nagasaki for some time. Capt. de Maisonneuve had the happy idea of painting white crosses on both bows of the ship's boats in order to indicate to the Japanese that France was a Christian nation, but he could not allow Furet to go on up to Hakodate, as he was superceded in command here by an officer named de Montravel. Although English and American merchants had settled in the north, the officer felt that the presence of a French civilian might prejudice the Japanese. He was sent to Shanghai from Nagasaki by the

---

* Translator's note: Verbatim from "AT NAHA, FEBRUARY 26, 1855 – THE LANDING," Marnes, Pt. I, Bk. III, pp. 253 to 263.

"Syngappore," and thence to Hongkong. Here he found another missionary candidate, M. Monicou, who had begun the study of Japanese with a native of Nagasaki. Furet therefore put himself to work at the same difficult task, difficult because they had no books, and their teacher knew but little English. The two of them thus prepared to go to Naha to make a fresh journey to Japan.

B. Narrative from 1855-1857.

Rear Adm. Guerin at Naha. Furet and Monicou. 1856.

On the way back from Hakodate, the two French frigates "Virginie" and "Sybille" had stopped at Naha (approx. August, 1854). They had found M. Girard and M. Mermet wearing the cassock and still established in the monastery at *Amiko*. They had not yet made any proselyte, and they did not see how they could ever have one, for death threatened anyone who wished to become converted. The governor exercised rigorous and almost hopeless surveillance over them. None the less, the two missionaries were already well advanced in the knowledge of the language. Sometime afterward they were able to be useful to Rear Admiral Guerin, who, without being officially invested with diplomatic powers, concluded a treaty with the little kingdom of Loo Choo (1855).*

At the beginning of 1856, Messrs. Furet and Monicou were certain of going to Hakodate on Rear Admiral Guerin's next expedition. They were received as passengers and interpreters on board the "Sybille" and "Constantine" and sailed, April 6th.

Furet, after a stop at Nagasaki, and Monicou, who had visited Corea, met each other in Shanghai and exchanged their views on the situation. Japan needed six or seven missionaries, they felt, and Naha should have at least three.

---

* "This treaty, whose clauses were favorable to the Catholic missionaries, was ultimately not to be ratified by the French Government, whether because in fact it offered only advantages of small importance, or because it was neglected in view of the approaching opening of Japan, as is most probable." Marnas.

M. Libois decided that by way of making a beginning, M. Furet and M. Monicou should return to Hongkong. This missionary had made very rapid progress in the dialect of Loo Choo, as well as in the real language of Japan. It was as much for this reason as in order to allow him to strengthen his health that his superior wished to have him near. None was more capable of being then employed as an interpreter than M. Mermet, and M. Libois foresaw that he could render real services at the time when negotiations were opened between France and Japan.

The admiral, going in the month of October (1856) to Loo Choo, carried back M. Furet and M. Monicou and brought back M. Mermet. Being rather dangerously sick himself and in a hurry to get to Macao, Adm. Guerin only stopped for a short time at Naha. He wrote a severe letter, however, to the Regent from this place in which he complained of the infractions of the treaty he had made the year before.

Mermet Leaves for Good. Change of Abode.

Before leaving Loo Choo, M. Mermet gave the following details concerning his residence in Okinawa:

Letter of October 26, 1856, at Naha, to the Superior of the Seminary at Paris:
"The year 1855 was for my dear co-worker M. Girard and myself only a year of struggle against the climate, vexations of all sorts on the part of the Japanese authorities, and a real imprisonment for our bodies. 1856 seemed to open under more favorable auspices. The convention concluded with so much prudence and energy by Adm. Guerin; and our acquisition of a house in the center of a populous town made us hope for some changes in our position.

"But if Japan, like China, but even more so, thinks that it is not prudent to refuse a treaty which some European power demands with firmness, it is done with the thought of cleverly eluding all of its clauses, and it will not be carried out until all the resources of crafty politics have been exhausted.

"Last year, sentry-boxes surrounded our temple at Amiko, and whenever we left it, it was necessary to fight for each foot of the ground with the satellites, or at least to employ mild force to enlarge the circuit of our walks. The government has not dared, it is true, to surround our new abode with a ring of soldiers (sic.), but policemen, actively on duty day and night, roam around us, guard every avenue of approach, and punish severely any impudent person who does not keep at a respectful distance of our habitation. Thus, although our house is in the centre of Naha, on town land in the middle of a thinly planted grove and admirably suited to become at some opportunity the site of a church or college, we live here as if in a desert. Formerly this was a place much resorted to for promenades, but today grass and thorns obstruct the roads, and the houses which faced ours have turned their backs on us and look in the opposite direction. It is forbidden anyone to approach us under the severest penalties, and only every other day or so, two petty mandarins chosen from among the most crafty in the country come to translate after a fashion for us some Chinese or Japanese books. For a long time their mission was only to amuse us and deceive us, and in that way to make us renounce our studies. However, after having laid bare their rascality, we have succeeded in obtaining some Japanese books, and so, to their great regret, we wrench from them both the dialect of Loo Choo and the language, either spoken or written, of Japan.

Language Study and Missionary Work.

"It is not necessary to tell you that it is almost impossible to attack the subject of religion with them. They repulse with fanatic obstinacy everything which could, from far or near, bring the conversation upon that head. On reflecting over their trouble and anxiety whenever a reflection about doctrine or morality seems about to appear, we are tempted to believe that our teachers are bound by some vow and obliged by their conscience to avoid all (religious) controversy. Yet we may meet less hostile characters, but no matter how happy the opportunity, we would have been unable to profit by it, so much do these two officials exercise threatening vigilance and redoubtable control over each other. But by an innocent ruse, we have made the Japanese policy yield on this point, and our teachers now come alternately.

"Beside these two persons, we cannot have the least intercourse nor exchange a word of any kind with anybody whatever. It is impossible to secure a workman or a servant except by the agency of the mandarins who give him instructions before sending him to us. If it is a laborer, he is always accompanied by another charged with spying on his conduct and himself condemned to the part of a mute. Thus our attempts at proselyting among such folks have always been fruitless. As for our domestics, they are changed every month, and they may not speak to us except about their work. However, in spite of the supervision to which they are submitted, God has permitted that one of them, a young man of 22 years, should understand and like our doctrine so well that he asked at once for baptism. After having been taught and prepared under cover of darkness, and in the midst of great silence, after a month of multiplied tests, he was baptised on Christmas night and consecrated to the Infant Jesus, whom he adored with a purified heart for the first time. Although this young man belonged to the humblest class, he was yet gifted with a force of character and a power of penetration that was out of the ordinary. He could become our catechist. This was our hope. The first-born of our apostleship, he had all our esteem and affection. We strongly urged secrecy on him, and, moreover, no one was more interested in this than he. When the day for the worship of his ancestors came, young Francis Xavier, for this was his baptismal name, profited by a slight indisposition and excused himself from taking part in this ceremony insulting to the God whom he worshipped, and from whom he demanded with so much ardour the conversion of his parents.

Young Francis Xavier. Persecution.

"His zeal, in fact, was so impatient, and the change which grace had operated in him was so noticeable, that he could not escape the observant and suspicious eye of his father. Our neophyte also had too tender a conscience to dissemble his faith. Then the most barbarous persecution began, but Francis remained firm, contenting himself by answering the blows and rages of his father with this simple prayer: 'Allow me to remain a child of the true God, and you will have no better son than I.' Exasperated by the perseverance and angelic resignation of this Christian, the father swore that on the morrow he would surrender himself with all his family to the rigors of the law. Young Francis, frightened not for himself, but for his kin, came to seek our advice in the middle of the night. The torment of his family seemed so horrible to him that he still doubted whether God required such a sacrifice of him. 'If it was my life only, said he, 'it would soon be finished.' It was only then that he revealed to us the hideous secret of which he had until now only allowed us to get an inkling, that whosoever should profess Christianity must die with all his relations in the first degree.

"Our answer could not be doubtful. If blood was to flow, it would fall back on the barbarous fanaticism of his father, while the son, an innocent victim of a savage law, would die for his faith and his God. There was nothing left for us to do but to ask for the strength of the martyrs. We remained for a long time kneeling together, our common prayer mingled into a single sob. Francis arose with tears in his eyes, but calm and reassured. He left us with courage in his heart. Our grief and our anxiety was keen. The palm cut down by the steel of the headsman is fair, no doubt, but the anguish which we then felt can only be compared with that of a mother who sees her firstborn torn from her arms to be led to death.

A Martyr? Other Inquirers.

"What has been the lot of this family? What has become of our neophyte? Is he dead? There is no positive news, yet we believe that we possess a martyr. When we asked a mandarin for some news about Francis, he answered us with trouble and marked embarrassment that he was no longer at the capital. All those who come near us have orders to feign completest ignorance of him. This subject of conversation has been placed on the Index *(Expurgatorius)*. Now if our disciple had weakened, not only would they speak freely about him, but the government would publish his apostasy as a triumph.

"Another adolescent was already giving the finest promise of his conversion when his family intervened and maltreated him so rudely that it was impossible to continue our talks on religion. This poor young man had not been fortified like Francis by the grace of baptism. In Japan, fathers not only have by law absolute control over their children, but they exercise incredible ascendency over them. You know the filial piety of the Chinese, but it does not approach that of the Japanese. This amounts to blind idolatry...

"In spite of the double and triple cordon of attendants which surrounds us, we are in secret touch with the father of a family. If he persists in his willing disposition, his conversion will lead to that of all his house. But after baptism, it will be necessary to prepare them for martyrdom, for a Christian, unless he compromises with his conscience, cannot live here unnoticed. He must, like the faithful of the primitive Church, choose between apostasy and death.

"This is the condition of our sterile ministry... The attendants appointed as our keepers do not leave us for a moment... They disperse crowds, order the closing of houses as we pass, announce our coming from afar, and create such a void before us that in broad daylight we pass through the most populous towns in the midst of profound silence and without meeting a human being. Along our path, the women and children have been ordered to flee at our approach. So the unhappy women from as far away as they can see us throw their burdens down on the ground, at the risk of losing everything, and do not feel safe until they are separated from us by a distance of three or four hundred yards. In the country, the peasant may not look at us, nor answer any of our questions. The only authorized word which he may use to get rid of us is, 'I do not understand.' Yet if our guards are at a distance, he will kindly ask us to withdraw in order not to risk his head. A conversation with us entails capital punishment.

"Beside the hate and contempt which the Japanese profess for the foreigner, beside the inflexible policy of silence and of exclusion sanctioned by the most rigorous of laws, Loo Choo has another quite particular reason for hating us. This motive arises from the organization of society which is not the same as in Japan, though the administration is identical. In our island there are two absolutely distinct classes, separated by an immense abyss. The nobles and the cultivators... These last form 29/30ths of the population, according to some, or 19/20ths according to others. All instruction is forbidden them. In the name of the heaven which has born them to be what they are, they must know nothing except the name of their farm tools, and, above all, to bow their foreheads in the need to humiliate themselves before the faces of their superiors... Proud of their vain science and making common cause with the government, the dominant class is interested above all in maintaining the status quo unchanged. They know that our teachings in the name of charity repulse this ignorance and servitude... With some liberty, light would quickly reach many minds, but without liberty, they are almost unapproachable. Loo Choo is not only a country tributary to Japan, but a province of Japan governed by Japanese officials. To keep the thoughts of the Chinese, who have some pretensions to this country, occupied, a junk goes every year to carry presents to the Chinese Emperor. The magistrates of Loo Choo, decorated with the title of mandarins, are only the effigies of officials, destined to play their role before the envoys of China or the Europeans."

Qualifications of a Missionary. Official Courtesies.

M. Mermet closed their letter by the following observation:
"When you send us new workers, be well assured that we have no use for mediocrities here. The language of Japan is complex and difficult. The Japanese people are intelligent and subtle. Besides ability and a solid grounding of acquired knowledge, we need men of extremely firm character, but patient and persevering, also. They must be polite and affable, with pleasant, mild manners, capable of enduring insults with a smiling face and of carrying on the most arduous affairs with imperturbable coolness; and lastly, they must be extremely prudent in their words as well as in their actions."

Thanks to the strong letter of Admiral Guerin, a certain amelioration was felt at first in the treatment of the missionaries. About three weeks after the arrival of M. Furet and M. Monicou, the old governor of Naha himself came to pay them a visit. He offered them some small presents, asked if they were well, and finally asked them, as well as M. Girard, to come to dinner in order, he said, that he might be able to talk with them. On the appointed day, two petty mandarins came to fetch the missionaries and guided them to the *Honkwan*. (This was an official building, and not the residence of the governor, which was carefully concealed from them from the beginning). The dinner was agreeable and the governor very attentive. Every time he emptied his sake cup, as large as a walnut shell, he showed the bottom of it to his guests to encourage them to do likewise.

Some time afterward one of the three ministers sent them his card accompanied by some cakes via a yellow bonnet. This act was due to the cold weather. The minister had the missionaries informed that he hoped the cold would do them no harm. But in reality, these obliging attentions did not change the most exclusive and vigilant policy of these islanders. The missionaries soon had proof of this. When they wished to return politeness for politeness to the governor and the minister, they were met by the same actions on the part of the population as in the past. When they reached Shuri, in the neighborhood of the castle, they asked passersby, "Show us the *kokwan* (city hall)." The general answer was, "*Wakaranu*" (I don't know). Some of the people slunk away; the others, lowering their eyes very humbly, did not open their mouths.

Letter of Furet on the Behavior of the Populace.

Furet wrote to the Superior of the Seminary, August 15, 1857, from Naha:

"It must be confessed that many played their role very well. The attentive air with which they listened to the very polite words of M. Girard, one hand lifted and carried to the ear, all seemed to say, 'We would indeed like to do you some service, but, *wakaranu!*' We were quite ready to give up our visit, when we noticed a house that appeared to us to be that of an interpreter. We entered into the court. No one was to be seen; we only heard doors being shut inside. After a moment, however, several individuals presented themselves. One of the more impulsive seemed disposed to ask us to go away, but another, who knew the ceremonies better, invited us to enter, to take tea and smoke. We refused and asked to be guided to the *kokwan*. After having consulted among themselves, they gave us a guide, who led us to the first house which one finds on entering the city. It was uninhabited and very filthy. Arriving at the threshold, we said to our mentor, 'Are you making fun of us? Is this the proper place?' The poor youth, not daring to accompany us any longer, withdrew, and we returned into the city. On the way, our Chinese servant, having entered the court of a house of fairly good appearance, came to tell us that many people were gathered in the rear apartments there. A man came out and at once offered to send after an interpreter for us. On hearing our griefs, he attempted to excuse his compatriots. 'Everyone here knows propriety,' he said. 'The man whom you questioned must have been crazy.'

"'In that case,' we answered, 'there must be a great many lunatics in Shuri.'

"Meanwhile, the interpreter had arrived. We explained to him the purpose of our visit, and he then conducted us to a neighboring house and introduced us this time into a reception room really worthy of the Regent. While a messenger was sent off to the minister's house, we exchanged a few words.

"How many inhabitants are there in Shuri?' we asked.

"Oh, there are at least five hundred,' was the reply.

"As two thousand would not have been an exaggerated figure, a smile of incredulity greeted this reply, and the embarrassed interpreter hastened to say, 'Oh, truly I have made a mistake!'

A Visit to the Governor. Conditions Improved.

"But here was the minister at last. After some words of politeness and some questions about the health of the Regent, we told intentionally, but in a joking way, the difficulties we had in making this call which we regarded as a duty. His embarrassment and that of the interpreter was evident.

"'Oh, the mandarin you questioned must have been afraid. His heart must have failed him,' they said.

"'We have questioned many persons, and the hearts of all failed them. However, is the word *kokwan* which we employed the word that is generally used?' we asked.

"'Yes... But if you had entered a house, you would have gotten an answer,' they said.

"'That is just what we did, and out of more than fifty people, not one was willing to understand us!' we replied.

"'If you had gone into one of our schools, there would have been no difficulty,' they replied.

"'Well, but how could we find your schools? The same difficulty would have arisen. But may your Excellency reassure himself; his presence here makes us forget everything!'

"Having noticed that orders were given to prepare a collation, we shortened our call intentionally, not wishing to accept anything from such liars.

"A few days later, on pretext of accompanying a new teacher, the minister's interpreter came to see us. The failings of the hearts of the inhabitants of the capital had evidently seemed to the authorities in contradiction to the promise made to Adm. Guerin that we would be treated as friends and that everyone would be allowed to communicate with us. The interpreter told us that henceforward the inhabitants would answer our questions and that they had received the order to do so, but that in order to be better understood, we ought to employ certain words different from those which we had previously been told ought to be understood by everyone."

The missionaries, none the less, remained without producing any effect on the people of Loo Choo. They could not make a single neophyte. The only results which they obtained were those of being able to learn from the teachers who were given them the language of the country and Japanese.

M. Monicou, thanks to his knowledge of Chinese, made rather remarkable progress in this study.

Dutch Castways, November, 1857.

One event came to interrupt the ordinary monotony of their life. This was the shipwreck in the last months of the year 1857 of a Dutch merchantman on *Majikoshima* (Miyako). The captain, his wife, and all his crew were brought to Naha to be at the center of government. The castaways, to the number of twenty-seven received such generous hospitality from the hands of the authorities that they did not fail to be surprised. The missionaries, on their side, did all they could to sweeten their lot, and they had the pleasure of seeing them bear their misfortune with patience. Seven of these castaways, five Hollanders and two Italians of the crew, were Catholics. M. Girard gave them a lesson in the catechism every week. They consoled him by themselves asking to be confessed and to take the communion. Although they were Protestants, the captain and his young wife were present at mass and sermon every Sunday for more than two months, the time that they stayed at Naha.

In the early part of November, a Dutch ship came to seek these castaways in order to carry them to Putana. She brought news from Nagasaki that Japan was about to definitely open the country to foreigners.

(Marnas, Pt. I, Bk. III, chapt. 2, pp. 279-290 verbatim, in this manuscript, from "B. Narrative from 1855-1857" to "Dutch Castaways, November, 1857.")

C. Last Years, 1858-1862.

Girard Leaves Loo Choo. A False Prophecy.

On the day when the treaties of 1858 had opened several ports in Japan, the nomination of a new superior of the mission who could go thither was immediately necessary. M. Girard was chosen for this post to which recent events had added so much importance. "He was a pious, zealous, prudent, erudite man and an accomplished missionary. We have seen him, after his laborious ministry in Hongkong, go to fix himself courageously in Loo Choo in the month of February. He was still there, and he had not had a visit from any French ship, when suddenly, October 25, 1858, the dispatch boat "Regent," returning from Yedo, Shimoda and Nagasaki, brought him all at one time the news of the end of the war in China, that of the treaties made with Japan, and the announcement of his nomination as superior of the mission."

At the thought of such an unexpected and heavy responsibility, M. Girard was disturbed, yet he accepted the burden reluctantly and left Loo Choo. Separated as he had been from the rest of the world for almost three years, he felt the need of informing himself about the situation and consulting with M. Libois before deciding the fate of his two companions.

In Hongkong he took the step of attaching himself to M. Duchesne de Bellecourt, who was appointed Consul General of France at Yedo, allowing M. Mermet to choose between Nagasaki and Hakodate, and in case he had to wait too long for helpers, he was ready to recall the missionaries at Naha. But he received orders expressing the desire that the Loo Choos should not be abandoned after so many efforts, and that M. Monicou should remain there with M. Furet until a new worker should arrive. M. Girard obeyed this order, though he was personally inclined to abandon the Loo Choos. "The Protestant ministers," he often used to say, "are not going to Loo Choo, but they will soon be in Japan!"

After four years of arduous labor as interpreter, chaplain, chancellor of legation, and school teacher, Girard returned to Europe after deciding upon the abandonment of Okinawa.

Language Study. A Strange Book form Satsuma.

At the time when the Loo Choo Islands were abandoned by the missionaries, the reader will perhaps not without interest learn how the last years that they spent there passed for them. After M. Girard's departure, M. Monicou and M. Furet remained alone in Naha. As much in consequence of the convention concluded by Adm. Guerin as by news from China and Japan, the situation of the missionaries became a little easier. However, the police surveillance over them had been in no wise suppressed, and the preaching of the gospel encountered always the same obstacles.

M. Furet, whose beard and hair began to turn gray, for he had entered the seminary late in life, resigned himself with difficulty to the apparent uselessness of his life. He also experienced rather great difficulty in the study of the language and sadly used to say to his co-worker that "an old noodle was not able to learn!" On the contrary, M. Monicou, who had formerly studied Chinese at Hongkong when he was assistant of M. Libois, had made remarkable progress in Japanese, as well as in the different idiom of Loo Choo. He could explain his books easily, and sometimes astonished his teachers in discussing the real meaning of the characters. Besides, it was not necessary to employ so much diplomacy to get language teachers. The mandarins had become very obliging on this point, and the missionaries had only to complain of the incapacity or unwillingness of their professors to see them changed at the first word. They were even able to put themselves in touch with some Japanese in Satsuma without causing the authorities to take offence.

Furet as Mathematician, Doctor and Dentist.

It was through these men that a rather strange book fell into the missionaries' hands.* It discussed the Trinity, the creation of the first man and woman, and the teachings of the doctors of the occident, "teachings," so the book said, "hard to understand, but which must be believed, however." In it, it was declared that the religion of China was false and had been invented by men. One of these Japanese, still young, polite, intelligent and kindly, ended by becoming quite intimate with the missionaries. Inflamed by a fine zeal for European science, he received some lessons in mathematics from M. Furet, and he begged his teacher to order, at his expense, a graphomotor, some sextants, an electrical machine, and even a telegraph outfit from Paris. M. Furet was already counting upon his pupil, whose devotion appeared sincere, to help him to reach the province of Satsuma, when he learned one day that his young man had killed himself by falling from a horse. After that he was never able to see the junks leave for Satsuma without sadness.

M. Furet did not gain the renown of a scholar only by this knowledge of mathematics. From the time that by the aid of an ointment well-known to the missionaries, the ointment of Father Libois, he had cured in a few days the child of one of his teachers, who suffered for a long time from an ulcer on the cheek, he passed as a physician of the first water in a circle of ten leagues. This title was the less contested because medicine had made such small progress in Loo Choo. It appears, or at least Father Furet says so in one of his letters, that the Galens of this country treated even internal disorders by the aid of plasters. If they happened to discover, and the cases were not rare, that a patient suffered from some internal itch, they made up a plaster and

---

* Translator's note: Hakuseki's, *Seiyo Kibun*, or *Sairan Igen?* He also wrote *Nantoshi*, a geographical work on Loo Choo.

had him swallow it, telling him that it would apply itself directly to the seat of the evil.

M. Furet was also led to practice the profession of a dentist. "Do you know," he wrote, "how teeth are pulled here? The patient holds his head in his hands and braces it against a pillar or mat. The doctor then approaches, armed with a little iron punch and a hammer. He places the punch against the tooth and weakens it by blows from the hammer. And then he pulls it by aid of a thread."

Out of pity for these poor people, M. Furet ordered instruments and a good instruction book from Paris, in order to become a "tooth-puller."

These details show that the missionaries entered more easily in touch with the people, and that they enjoyed greater tranquility, in fine. "We are too much undisturbed," wrote Furet on June 30, 1859, to the Superior of the Seminary. "And we are even too much honored. Some blows from a rattan, accompanied by the possibility of announcing the Good Tidings would be much more to my liking."

An Apology for Christiantiy Prepared. The Dutch "Bali."

As the peace in which they were left continued, the missionaries believed that the time had come to make a fresh attempt to secure authorization to openly teach their religion. Their language teachers were asking them questions on this subject which seemed to indicate that they had more liberty. This is why M. Furet conceived the idea of writing a brief apology for their religion in which he would try to indicate what the missionaries were and what they desired, in particular that their purpose was not to upset the country in any way, nor to change its policies and usages. Once this apology had been translated into Chinese by M. Monicou, they were going to get together and present it to the governor of the Loo Choos together with a clock and some other objects which had come to them from Europe. Granted or not, this document would very probably pass to the province of Satsuma, and who knew if God would not make use of it to put some souls on the way to the truth. This was the only means which M. Furet could see for evangelizing the pagans who surrounded him.

The missionaries were occupied at this work when, on Ascension Day, 1859, the "Bali," a warship of the Netherlands arrived in Naha harbor. She brought presents to the King of Loo Choo to thank him for the hospitality with which the Dutch castaways of 1857 had been received. But the "Bali" had another mission, that of concluding a treaty with the little country. Captain J. Van Copellen, appointed for this purpose, lacking interpreters, had recourse to the missionaries. On this occasion, the missionaries could meet the authorities at close quarters and gain an idea of their disposition. Their opinions had hardly changed at all. The mandarins could not form the resolution of entering into commercial relations with foreigners. They again consented to promise their friendship, but it still appeared necessary to avoid, as most dangerous, the exchange of their products with Europeans, or the invitation of the ships of the barbarians, these formidable vessels which gave so much reason for reflection, to their ports. After this, how could one hope to obtain the liberty to preach the religion of the Europeans in Loo Choo?

Arrival of M. Petitjean. His Trip on the "Medina."

M. Furet did not give up his project, however. At the end of several months, M. Monicou's translation was ready, and they were only waiting for a favorable opportunity to present it to the authorities. M. Petitjean's arrival at Naha furnished them with this. After having remained for two years without receiving any letters from France, and without being visited by any French ship, M. Furet and M. Monicou were agreeably surprised by the arrival of this new missionary on October 26, 1860.* (Verbatim, pp. 416-420, from top 163).

The chances of getting a ship for Loo Choo, whither he had been sent, were few, and M. Petitjean was obliged to stop at Hongkong, and he only reached his post seven months after leaving France. The last part of his journey from Hongkong to Naha was particularly tiresome. "The northeast wind," he wrote to M. Libois, October 20, on board Dent and Co.'s ship, the "Medina," "has made us greet almost every cape in China, from Hongkong to Formosa, then in Formosa, and then

---

* Translator's note: From "Language Study. A Strange Book from Satsuma," to here, verbatim translation of text.

in a great many of the Philippine Islands on our way. At last, here we are at Loo Choo, the long-desired terminus of my journey." But it was only after having tacked for about a week longer around Naha that the "Medina" ended by entering the harbor. It was quite time, for on shipboard they were beginning to murmur against the passenger for Naha. "Without you," they told him, "we would have long passed Kanagawa Bay." Thus, M. Petitjean was truly happy when on October 26th he could at last step ashore. "I cannot express the contentment which I feel in finding myself on these dear islands which God has given me for a second home," he said as he greeted his co-workers.

Monicou Quits the Islands. A Welcome for Petitjean.

M. Monicou had only time to pack.* On the next day he sailed for Japan by the same ship.

The arrival of M. Petitjean made M. Furet ten years younger. In interminable chats the poor exile attempted to revive the memory of his country and of those whom he had known and loved there, while the new arrival sought to make himself acquainted with the men and conditions of this little corner of the Asiatic world in which he was going to be confined, perhaps for long years. The curate and the vicar, for that is the way they spoke of each other, though they had neither a parish nor parishioners, got on very well together. The curate only made one reproach to his vicar, that of being sensible to the cold. "Because of you," he said, "here I am, condemned to stay in the house in the evening when the air is so good out of doors! I would reproach you with it if we did not have so much else to say to each other!"

M. Furet profited by the arrival of this new worker to make visits of courtesy, accompanied by small presents to the authorities. They went to Shuri and left their cards on the Regent, the ministers, and the interpreters. All of these thanked them and sent presents. Two *taifu***

---

* Girard learned of the arrival of Petitjean in November, 1860. He wrote that it was like the first mouthful of bread to a starving man. He at once ordered Monicou to come to help him and to leave Naha for health reasons, also.

**Taifu, a title of quality; high officials were chosen from among those bearing this title.

accompanied by an interpreter representing the Regent and the minsters came to return the call. The old governor of Naha, aged 70, himself visited them and offered them a kind of straw shoe containing fifty eggs. Then it was the turn of the interpreters. Wearing their holiday clothes and wide belts, they begged the new arrival to kindly accept a basket of oranges. M. Pettitjean marvelled at so much kindliness, and he asked himself if he would have received such a welcome in a Christian land. "Our good friends, the representatives of authority in Loo Choo," he wrote, November 11, 1860, to the seminary, "have paid us several visits since my arrival, accompanied by cakes, eggs and oranges by the hundreds, and with loads of compliments."

"You are going to bore yourself in our midst, Petitjean *Shinshi* (teacher)," said one interpreter, who spoke half in Loo Chooan, half in English. "You have left France, a very beautiful country! But we have nothing to offer you but a very small land, but with a good heart!" May their good heart allow itself to be touched and become even better.

The Arrangements for Presenting the Apology to the King.

M. Furet could not find a more opportune moment for the step of which he had been thinking for such a long time. After having thought and prayed for a long time, he presented himself with M. Petitjean at the capital, armed with his letter for the King, and he requested an audience with the Regent.

"The Regent," an interpreter told him, "only occupies himself with important matters. Explain to me the object of your visit, and I will inform him of it."

"No," said M. Furet, "our business is so important that we desire to discuss it ourselves with the Regent, or at least with one of his ministers."

"If that is the case, I will speak to the Regent, and you will have his answer in a little while," was the reply.

This took place on Sunday. On the next Thursday, men came to announce to the missionaries that the Regent had a cold, but that one of his ministers would receive them in the *Kokwan* on the morrow.

This is how M. Furet reported the interview in a letter of Girard, dated September 14, 1861:

"Yesterday about 2 p.m., an interpreter with white socks and wearing yellow ceremonial headgear came to fetch us. Two *taifu* in full dress were waiting for us in the street, and they conducted us to the *Kokwan*. When we had reached the court, the minister left his seat, and advancing in our direction invited us to step up into the reception hall. He was surrounded by a large suite of yellow, red and green caps, who observed everything in the deadest silence. We were asked to seat ourselves on two chairs near a table loaded with cakes, eggs, shrimps, *castera* and *sake*. The minister was seated facing us at another table. He had the kindness at first to have an inquiry made (for the conversation was carried on in a low voice and through interpreters) whether we were not in need of money, no French ship having come, and since also the ships going to Foo Chow had not brought us anything for a long time. I thanked him, and then opened up our business at once."

The Letter Accepted. A Mandarin and his Procession.

"I begged him, therefore, to kindly present our letter to the King, asking him to notice that the letter was about the Religion of the Lord of Heaven and the welfare of the King and his people. The letter was accepted. But one of the interpreters having passed behind the sliding screen where some big dignitary must have been standing, the scene was changed. The minister, after questioning the interpreter, changed his mind and wished to get me to take back my letter on the pretext that he could not present it without previously knowing what it contained. He added also that for centuries the people of Loo Choo had followed the teachings of Confucius and Mencius and had no need of the Lord of Heaven. Further, that they had made the same reply to our predecessors, namely, that the doctrine of Confucius was very good.

"Without allowing myself to be disconcerted, I had some presents offered which I owed to the generosity of my friends in France. There were some for the King, the Regent, and the three ministers. After some difficulties, the gifts, and also my letter to the King, were accepted. We then ate a few mouthfuls to give pleasure to the minister, emptied three walnut-shells of sugary wine, and retired promptly to eat our meagre fast-day lunch, for we fast on Friday in order to gain God's blessings on our beloved mission."

Some days after this interview, the minister himself came to our house. He arrived, preceded by a flag covered with large Chinese characters and a double file of individuals with yellow and red caps. He was borne in a brilliant chair, within which he was seated on his heels, after the custom of the country. Behind the chair were some samurai in ordinary costume wearing silver pins in their hair, while those of the minister were of gold, and the bearers' were of copper. On each side of the chair was an interpreter in full dress. On reaching the door of our house, the minister got down from his chair and withdrew his shoes from his feet before entering. He came to bring us the reply for which we were waiting. This answer was the same as that which came from behind the screen: "The *Komon** doctrine of Confucius has been followed for long centuries in our country, and this has sufficed us in governing the people. This is why we have no need of the teachings of the Lord of Heaven, which the people do not want. I beg you to take back your letter."

Lese-Majeste. Quotations of Furet's Second Letter. Attitude of Missionaries to Officials.

As the samurai were present, I profited by the chance to say some words to them. I said, among other things, "You have souls, you have declared! What becomes of these at death? The *Komon** tells you nothing about it, since Confucius himself declared that he knew nothing about things after death... We, however, do know about them, and one day the King, the Regent, and the ministers who refuse to hear us will see, in the presence of the Lord of Heaven, which of us was right."

The minister was embarrassed and said not a word. I was obliged to offer him a cake in order to restore him the power to speak. He retired almost at once with his numerous and brilliant escort in the same order as he had come. Two days later, I had a letter taken to him, letting him know that I did not ask for an answer. He sent it back to me unsealed, asking me to insist no more. "They could not," so they said, "accept our doctrine of the Lord of Heaven, but they thanked us, nonetheless,

---

* *Analects of Confucious.*

for our good intentions." If this was only a piece of human work, we would be completely discouraged...

We would reproach ourselves if we did not at least quote the letter addressed by M. Furet to the minister of the King of Loo Choo:

"Knowing your benevolence, I venture to ask you three questions: Mencius has said, 'The Way is one.' On the other hand, the great saint named Jesus has said, 'There is no other way than the Way of the Lord of Heaven. Whoso does not follow it will not have the joy of Heaven, but on the contrary, will have endless unhappiness.' Countless numbers of men, from emperors down to *hyakusho* (farmers), in the universe and even also in China, follow the same way. Yet the way of God and the *Komon* cannot both be true.

"It is said also in the *Chuyo*,* 'One must study widely, inquire carefully, think diligently, distinguish clearly and act with zeal.' After this, may not the partisans of the *Komon* study the way of the Lord of Heaven?

"Confucius says: 'Wait for the great saint who will practice the way perfectly,' and elsewhere, 'I do not understand life; how then should I know death?'

"On the other hand, we learn in the Way of the Lord of Heaven that the Perfect Saint has appeared in the world. This way teaches in detail the rules for human relations; and lastly, it clearly teaches the important matter of what comes after death. In order to obey reason and follow the method of Confucius himself, should not the partisans of the Kumo** study the way of the Lord of Heaven?

"Confucius says, 'If one is in error, assuredly one must not fear to correct himself.' It is not necessary to speak of anything concerning the teaching of superstition. In fact, Confucius says, 'If superstition is taught, the evil is very great. Moreover, can one not correct a way, no matter how ancient it may be, if it is bad or insufficient?'

"Having this great affair to confide to you, if I have laid aside all fear in addressing you these words, it is because in the situation that I find

---

* *The Way of the Mean* of Confucius.
**Author's note: Or "Kume," the Chinese community in Naha.

myself, I am the representative, though most unworthy, of the Lord of Heaven, and I must make known the merciful will of the Lord of Heaven toward the people of Loo Choo. This is why I believe that you will excuse my importunity. That which Mencius says, 'That there is nothing which does not come from Heaven, and that we must receive it thus, and conform ourselves to it,' applies perfectly here. The will of the Lord of Heaven is to be feared. One must not oppose it.

Signed: L. Furet"

Warnings and Prophecies from Furet. Dread Portents.

We have already said that this letter was sent back unsealed to the missionaries. A short time after, the ministers sent gifts to them, but they were refused. They did not accept the honor which was shown them of inviting them to the *kokwan* for a chat, either. They answered that they would not go there except to talk about the way of the Lord of Heaven. In spite of this refusal, the Regent sent to ask them if they did not feel well at the time of greatest heat.

They only replied by sending in their cards. To the *taifu* who had been sent to them with an interpreter, M. Furet said: "We are in no sense government officers. We are nothing but *shinpu* (priests). Consequently, there is nothing to be feared from us if presents are given and visits made, or not; nor from French ships, to which we will address no complaints. But tell your mandarins that we have two reasons for great grief. Every day some inhabitants of this island die without thinking of their souls or assuring themselves of their welfare in the other world. This is our first grief. Your King, though young, will soon die; soon also will the Regent and the ministers. After their death they will find themselves in the presence of the Lord of Heaven, who will judge them. And He will punish them rigorously for not having embraced His way and for having prevented it from being taught to the people. This is our second grief. Know that it is not in vain that the Lord of Heaven is to be mocked in refusing to admit His doctrine, which is the only true and reasonable one, into a country in which the doctrine of the bonzes, which is despised, is freely admitted!"

A solemn silence accompanied these words, and then the *taifu* and his interpreter had to go off with their eggs.

Another time, knowing that M. Girard was inclined to withdraw the missionaries from Loo Choo, M. Furet wished to give a last warning to this poor people, ready to see the light escape them without suspecting the fact. He summoned an interpreter and clearly told him: "Jesus, before leaving the earth to ascend into heaven, said to His disciples, 'Go out into the whole world and announce my law. If a kingdom, or a city, does not receive you, go carry the Good Tidings elsewhere. And woe to that realm, woe to that city which shall reject the truth!' Such were the words of Jesus to His disciples. And we, though weak men, have come as far as this to announce His way. If we withdraw from this kingdom, this will be the greatest misfortune which could happen to this land. If some chastisement should descend upon you, I would not be surprised at it. I do not ask for it, but I fear one!"

Now, after the missionaries had given these earnest warnings, several events took place worthy of being recorded here. A meteor, prodigious by the light that it shed and the noise it made in bursting, spread terror in Nafa and Shuri. "It was like," said M. Furet, "an eighty or one hundred twenty pounder had been fired off in the sky."

The ignorant and superstitious islanders asked themselves tremblingly what it portended.

Pestilence and Drought. Arrival of the "Dupliex."

A disease called *irigasu* or *fushika,* a kind of scarlet fever made horrible ravages at the same time, and for twenty-eight years this disease had not appeared in the island.

Finally, there was an extraordinary drought, such as the old men could not remember ever having seen. It brought a great famine.

Prayers were at first ordered. From their house the missionaries could see the banners and pennons floating about the bonzerie where prayers were taking place. Abstinences and fasts were then prescribed.

In these days it was forbidden to kill their hogs, or goats, or oxen, or fowls. Nothing was to be found in the market except fish and vegetables.

In spite of these supplications addressed to the *hotoke* to obtain a little rain, the rice fields remained dry and cracked in every direction. In their thirst, they seemed to open thousands of mouths. Yet finally, the rains brought by the storms allowed a few sweet potatoes to be planted.

Such were the last events in Loo Choo which marked their stay for the missionaries. Two years had already passed since the arrival of M. Petitjean. Though these islands were only two days from China, and though French vessels passed them at only a few dozen miles out to sea, the missionaries had not received one visit from them during two years. It was at the time when they were thinking least about such a thing that the "Dupleix" arrived to tear them from this soil where they had so long suffered to see that all efforts of their zeal remained fruitless.

Asked by the commander of the "Dupleix" whether they wished to complain of any infraction of the convention concluded by Adm. Guerin, a convention which had never received the approbation of the French government, they answered "no"!

Received on the second day which followed his arrival by the Regent and the Governor of Nafa, the captain was somewhat astounded to see these two old men prostrate themselves before him to thank him for the peaceful spirit in which he had come to Loo Choo. Father Furet then told them that his superior, M. Girard, having recognized that the residence of missionaries at Naha was useless, had decided to send them to some other spot, and that the captain had come to take them away!

"To take them away!" They could hardly believe their ears! The foreigners were going to leave! What unhoped for good fortune!

The Missionaries Withdraw after Full Reimbursement.

As the missionaries had made some expenditures at Loo Choo, an arrangement was necessary with the authorities. In particular, they had built a house on a hillock, and to protect it against the typhoons they had raised a wall on the north side. They could not think of renting this property. The government of Loo Choo, more polite and more generous than ever, wished them to be reimbursed for all their expenses.

"On the last day," M. Furet wrote to M. Libois, "they brought us the 900 dollars which had been spent for the house and in building the wall. We only wished to accept 600, saying that we had not come among them to live at their expense, but it was useless.

"When it was necessary to leave these good people of Loo Choo, it was a heart-break for me. May we at least do a little more in Japan!"

When the missionaries left the Loo Choo Islands, eighteen years had elapsed since Monseigneur Forcade had arranged to be landed there by Admiral Cecille.*

FINIS

---

* From "The Arrival of M. Petitjean: His Trip on the 'Medina,'" to here is to be found in Marnas, Pt. I, Bk. III, chapter IV, pp. 423-432. (Note by Schwartz).

THE PROTESTANT PIONEER:
DR. BERNARD J. BETTELHEIM

Introduction

There is probably no more controversial figure in the history of Protestant missions in Asia than Dr. Bernard Jean Bettelheim, a converted Hungarian Jewish physician. His most marked genius was in the field of language, though his work as a medical doctor benefited all classes of Okinawan society, and the message which he preached was more influential than some historians have imagined.

The judgment of Professor George Kerr is that it would have been difficult to find anyone less suited to the task of Christian mission work in the Ryukyus, and that Bettelheim was "more than a little mad."[1] He observes that this madness may have saved Bettelheim's life, since there were plenty of Christian martyrs in the history of Japan and records of mob violence in the history of China, whereas Bettelheim was only set upon with sticks and stones once in his eight-year residence in Ryukyu. The observation that Bettelheim avoided martyrdom because of his madness is not well taken, since official policy at the time dictated the treatment afforded him. And the record shows that Bettelheim was physically assaulted at least four times, not once, during his years on Okinawa. Persecution was allowed, but not martyrdom.

A Protestant missionary to Ryukyu of a later period made the mildly negative evaluation of Bettelheim that "from all accounts it does not appear that he was a man entirely fitted by disposition and temperament to make his effort successful."[2]

Others give him the credit of having been an important "trailblazer" and pioneer, calling him the first Protestant missionary to Japan fully thirteen years before the official histories recognized the presence of Protestants in the land. He is also credited with breaking open the seals of the closed land of Japan and thus directly influencing the forces leading to the Meiji Restoration of 1868.[3]

While there are widely varying appraisals of his influence and effectiveness as a Christian missionary, there is no question as to his unremitting zeal to present the gospel. There is great question about his wisdom, attitudes and methods. Perhaps the best defense of these is that he faced the constant opposition of Ryukyu officials determined to hinder his work. They were under orders from the Satsuma lords of southern Japan to carry out a dual policy of lenience and severity toward the missionaries. The Satsuma leaders from southern Japan then in control of Ryukyu had long since been confirmed in their opposition to Christianity by the official edicts of the central government of Japan, the Tokugawa Shogunate. In the face of such opposition, it might be expected that Bettelheim's activities would be a bit unusual.

Foreign Intrusions and the British Seaman's Mission

The background of the first Protestant missionary to Ryukyu is one of the most unusual in missionary annals. So also is the story behind the mission which sponsored him. The accounts of Captain Basil Hall, commanding officer of the British ship, "Lyra," and of John M'Leod, surgeon aboard the "Alceste," relating their visits to Okinawa in 1816 were published in beautifully illustrated editions and circulated widely in Europe and the United States.[4] The paradise-like descriptions of the Ryukyus and its peaceful and cultured people contained in these works greatly influenced the thinking of readers for three decades. Lt. Herbert J. Clifford, an officer with the "Alceste" on the occasion of the visit to Ryukyu, set forth an appeal for funds for a mission there under the title of, "Claims of Loo-Choo on British Liberality."[5] In the pamphlet he related an experience in Ryukyu which had a deep effect upon his thinking after his return to England. An official of the Ryukyu Government had asked why his party was dismissed from the "Alceste" on Sunday. Clifford replied that members of the crew were "chinchinning Joss (worshipping God)....just as you do." This remark gave him a bad conscience, but he says, "I knew not the Lord at this time and sinned ignorantly."[6] His subsequent conversion and deep sense of responsibility for sharing the message of Christ with the people of Ryukyu led Clifford, following his retirement, to call for the founding of the British Seaman's Mission.

A visit of the brig, "Brothers," to Naha in 1819 resulted in a friendly exchange between the British and the Okinawans during which a copy of the New Testament in Chinese was offered. William Eddis, one of the British party, reported that they could read the Testament fluently, but said that to accept the gift meant death.[7]

The later visit of the British ship, "Lord Amherst," in August, 1832, took place in the course of exploring commercial prospects in the China Sea and probing Japan's outer defenses. The ship carried an official of the East India Company, obviously alert to British business interests, a commander in the Royal Navy, and the well-known medical missionary, Dr. Friederich Augustus Gutzlaff. The alliance of military power and business interests was accompanied by a representative of Christian missionary thrust into new areas.[8] It is not difficult to surmise the immediate impression given to the people of Ryukyu, nor the alarm created among the officers of Satsuma, the Japanese clan which had conquered Okinawa in 1609 and from that time had exercised control over all economic and political matters in the islands. Satsuma controlled all contacts with the outside. The officers of Satsuma were without question fully aware that the great Western powers were looking for a gateway to the main islands of Japan for commercial purposes, and they also knew that Christian missionaries were intent upon entering the land. The identification of national interests of Western powers and the promotion of the Christian religion evidenced in the contacts of Japan with Spain and Portugal in the Sixteenth Century was symbolized again in their minds in the voyage of the "Lord Amherst."

A second visit of Gutzlaff to Okinawa took place in 1837 aboard the British ship, "Raleigh." In Naha he changed to the American ship, "Morrison," which was in the course of attempting the return of five Japanese castaways from Canton to the main islands of Japan. Aboard the "Morrison" were Dr. Peter Parker and the Rev. Samuel Wells Williams, veterans of missionary work in China. They made some exploration of Naha and the surrounding country. They attempted to demonstrate smallpox vaccination, albeit against the vigorous protests of many officials. It was during this visit that missionary strategy is said to have developed toward the Ryukyu Islands.[9] The area was considered an important one to which the Christian message must be taken, and it was also thought of as a stepping-stone to the closed land of Japan.

The first Anglo-Chinese War (1839-42) was occasioned by the Chinese government's forceful attempt to stop the illegal opium traffic being conducted by British interests. That such a war would eventually have been fought in spite of the problem of opium trade is beyond doubt in view of the relentless power of Western expansionism and the unwillingness or inability of Chinese institutions to change to meet the challenge. There is probably no more glaring example of Western aggression in the history of the Nineteenth Century in Asia than the onset and progress of this war. In the loss of the war, the Chinese Government failed to stem the opium traffic and also failed to maintain her traditional tribute system of foreign relations, with which Okinawa had been acquainted since 1374. The treaty of Nanking (August 29, 1842) opened five Chinese ports to foreign trade and residence, made Hong Kong a crown colony of the British, and granted Christian missionaries the permission to operate anywhere within a day's journey of one of the open ports. A subsequent treaty promised "most favored nation" status to Britain and led the way for other Western powers to attain privileges of trade in Chinese ports.

The provision of these treaties, soon known to both Japan and Okinawa, caused great alarm. Suppose the Chinese claimed the Ryukyus because of the centuries of tributary relationship? And suppose, further, that the terms of the treaties were applied to the port of Naha? The arrangement of dual fealty with both China and Japan which had obtained since the Satsuma conquest of Ryukyu in 1609 would be brought into question, and either China or Japan might have to give up claims of sovereignty in the Ryukyus.

The pressure of European power continued to be felt in Ryukyu as the French warship, "Alcemene," arrived in Naha in March, 1844, demanding trading privileges and offering to place Okinawa under French protection in order to avoid British seizure. Both the offer and the demand were refused, but it was at this point that Fr. Theodore A. Forcade and his Chinese assistant were put ashore. The reason given for this action was that they might study language in preparation for the conclusion of formal agreements between the Emperor of France and the Ryukyu Government. This show of military power combined with demands for trade privileges was again related to the presence of Christian missionaries, bringing to the fore once more the same type of threat posed by the Spanish and Portuguese in the Sixteenth and Seventeenth Centuries. But pressure from the Western nations was beginning to make impossible the enforcement of Japan's expulsion decrees.

Upon the arrival of the first French missionary, word was immediately forwarded to the Lord of Satsuma, Nariakira. He sought at once the direction of the Edo (Tokyo) Government concerning the course to take in relation of the presence of Christian missionaries on Okinawan soil. Senior Minister Abe Seiko followed the advice of Nariakira, deciding on a policy of combined leniency and severity, depending on the occasion and with a view to avoiding future difficulties.[10] It was decided, therefore, to permit communication and trade in the Ryukyus as being beneficial to Japan, but since the introduction of Christianity in the slightest degree would lead to trouble, it was decided to refuse all efforts at spreading that faith. For this reason, tacit permission was given to the missionary to remain in Ryukyu. Missionaries were not to be forcefully expelled; but at the same time their every effort at evangelism was to be resisted. In this way, the entering wedge for a Christian presence in Japan was allowed through Okinawa.

The confusion and consternation of the Okinawan officials was greatly increased when, in May of 1846, two other missionaries arrived, one a British Protestant aboard the British ship, "Starling," and the other a French Catholic aboard the French warship, "Sabine." Bettelheim arrived with his wife and two children on May 1, and the French priest, Fr. Leturdu, arrived on May 2. The latter stayed on Okinawa for a period of only two years, while Forcade left shortly after the arrival of Bettelheim in July, 1846. The residences in Ryukyu of other French priests is related above, including their first abandonment of the field in 1848 and their second attempt at establishing Catholic work between 1855 and 1862. Dr. Bettelheim remained in Ryukyu until 1854, his mission there spanning approximately eight years.[11]

Bettelheim's Early Life and Preparation

An account of Bettelheim's early life, Christian conversion and training for missionary service will help us to understand both his zealous perseverance in his chosen task and his impatient frustration at the many obstacles placed in his way. He had much to share as a Christian, as a scholar and as a medical doctor.

Bettelheim was born in Pressburg, Hungary, in June, 1811. When he was three months old, Pressburg was bombarded by Napoleon's soldiers, and Bettelheim's mother barely escaped being knocked down by a flying shell while carrying the baby in her arms. At a very young age, Bettelheim was placed in the rabbinical school of his uncle, Moses Saper, at Trebitsch. By the age of nine he is said to have been able to read Hebrew, German and French, a notable beginning in the process of becoming fluent in thirteen different languages. He left home before age thirteen and supported himself by teaching. He began the study of medicine as a young man, studying successively at Great Wardian, Drebretzin, Budapest, and then at Padua, Italy, where he finally took his degree in September, 1835.[12] He then journeyed to many places—Trieste, Unsine, Naples, Sicily, Malta and Greece—practicing medicine and giving special attention to the prevention of cholera. He is said to have followed the course of this disease about the Mediterranean area, this being one of his specialties. And while he engaged in practice, he found time to author some forty scholarly papers on scientific subjects.[13]

He subsequently served as head-surgeon of an Egyptian man-o'-war, and following that he moved to Constantinople, where he was appointed head physician of a Turkish regiment in the town of Magnesia, some forty miles from Smyrna. It was at this point that Bettelheim came into contact with two Church Missionary Society representatives, Fathers Jetter and Fjellstad, serving in Budjah and caring for the poor while a plague ravaged the area. From these new friends he received an Italian Bible, a French Roman Catholic Prayer Book, and a German Gospel. With these he began to read of the Christian faith, and after many sessions with his new friends, he was converted and baptized by the British chaplain of Smyrna, Rev. William Lewis.[14] In the same year, 1840, he entered into controversy with the local rabbi and published a controversial pamphlet against Jewish leaders entitled, "The Ruin of the Talmud."

His Church of England friends encouraged him to take up Christian work, and when they returned to England in July, 1840, Bettelheim resigned his position, spent five months studying the gospels while waiting to settle a salary dispute and finally proceeded to London. There he hoped to be recognized by the Church of England and duly authorized so that he could preach the gospel to the many Jews in the Mediterranean area.

He arrived in England in the fall of 1840 and sought out bishops, prominent missionary leaders and others preparing for missionary service. During this time both Bettelheim and David Livingston, pioneer to the heart of Africa, were at the office of the Church Missionary Society. They may well have been engaged in study together for their future careers as missionaries. The Opium War prevented Livingston from going to China, which was the land of his original interest, and other events kept Bettelheim from reaching Mediterranean lands to preach to the Jews.

There was considerable controversy between Bettelheim and the bishops of the Established Church. They wanted him to study for three years at Oxford and Cambridge before entering upon his ministry. It has been said that their refusal to recognize his continental degrees and their opposition to ordaining a Jew led Bettelheim to seek other outlets for his ministry, and he therefore became a minister of an independent church in London.[15] It is more likely that the refusal of the bishops was based upon the fact that Bettelheim was such a recent convert to the Christian faith and that they felt it unwise to ordain one to the ministry who had no specific training for that vocation.

Bettelheim was married on June 19, 1843, to Miss Elizabeth Mary Barwick, only daughter of a wealthy London thread manufacturer. Their first child was a daughter, Victoria Rose, born in April, 1844, and named for the Queen and Sir George Rose, President of the London Jews' Society.[16]

When the anti-state church movement began to show its strength, Bettelheim re-evaluated his position as an independent minister, and after prayer and study of the scriptures decided to re-affiliate with the Church of England.

The next stage in his career is somewhat vague. Bettelheim claimed that he accepted appointment from the London Jews' Society to go to Tiberias for evangelism among the Jews. The London Jews' Society claimed that two different applications by Dr. Bettelheim led to a probationary appointment, which after a short time was cancelled. In any case, he was prevented from sailing by a set of extraordinary providential accidents ("wind, water and fire"). The trip from Liverpool to Tiberias was cancelled.[17] He hoped for another appointment to Salonica, but his connection with the Society was severed, so he proceeded to pursue his medical practice in London for a period of time.

Lt. Herbert J. Clifford, founder of the British Seaman's Mission, had first tried to get various mission societies already established to take an interest in sending someone to the Loo Choo Islands as a missionary. He asked the Church Missionary Society, the London Missionary Society, and finally the Moravian Missionary Society, but failed to get a favorable response from any.[18] All were committed to the hilt in other areas and had no personnel or money for the small island chain. After fifteen years of trying to get other missions interested, Clifford organized the Loo Choo Naval Mission (or British Seaman's Mission) in February, 1843, for the purpose of sending missionaries to Ryukyu.

By the summer of 1845, Bettelheim had given up his comfortable medical practice in London, and on September 9, 1845, he sailed with his wife and daughter from Portsmouth on the "William Jardine" as the first missionary of the Loo Choo Naval Mission. There appears to have been an agreement with the Church Missionary Society that he was to be ordained after a year of service, but this was not carried out.[19]

On the voyage, about two hundred miles southwest of the Cape of Good Hope, a son was born to Bettelheim. He was named Bernard James Gutzlaff Bettelheim after the well-known China missionary, Gutzlaff, who had become secretary and interpreter for the British ambassador in China. The Gutzlaffs welcomed the ship when it arrived in Hong Kong after a voyage of four and one-half months. In Hong Kong the Bettelheims met the Colonial Chaplain Stanton, the Reverend George Smith (later appointed Bishop of China), Drs. Bridgman, Devan, Ball, Medhurst and others. These became later a corresponding committee in China for conducting the business of the Loo Choo Naval Mission.

With only a short period in China to study Chinese, January to April, 1844, the Bettelheim family embarked on the "Starling" with a Chinese interpreter and a child's nursemaid for the port of Naha, where their ship anchored on May 1, 1846.

The Landing in Okinawa

There was great expectation on the part of the sending agency as Dr. Bettelheim accepted the appointment of the British Seaman's Mission. Clifford wrote on October 20, 1845, "He has testimonials (testimonials perhaps unsurpassed by any missionary who has gone forth from this land to the heathen)."[20]

There was also great expectation on the part of the missionary and his wife. He wrote later in his diary: "One of the grounds which induced me to go to Loo Choo (rather than to a missionary post offered me in Ireland), was to delight my soul in the results of Protestantism on virgin soil."[21] It was indeed virgin soil, for at that time there was not a known Protestant convert in Formosa, Korea, Ryukyu or Japan.

The view of Okinawa from the ship pleased the missionary greatly, as his journal of April 30 indicates:

> The aspect of the Great Loo Choo is truly picturesque; hills crowned with trees, fine verdant slopes running down to the sea, and all on which the eye can rest, like the garden of the Lord. May soon the Rose of Sharon glow here in its original hue![22]

As soon as the ship was anchored, Father Forcade came aboard. Bettelheim was delighted to meet a European, and also to have visible proof that it was indeed possible for a foreigner to reside in Lew Chew. He also felt a deep zeal to have the British Union Jack accepted with at least the same privilege as had been accorded to the French tri-colored cockade, for the Union Jack was to him at that time "tantamount to the flag of Protestantism."[23] He established good relations with Forcade by making him a loan of money, since he had been without remuneration from Macao for a period of two years. He was glad he had done this, for the following day saw the arrival of the French ship "Sabine," and generous treatment was afforded the Englishman from captain and crew as a result of favorable comment by Father Forcade. The act also stood him in good stead with the entire French squadron which soon arrived under Admiral Cecille.

Unable to get the captain of the "Starling" to lower the ship's boats so that he could unload his personal cargo and household effects for a landing, Bettelheim prevailed upon the officer on guard to load as much as possible of his gear into two Okinawan boats alongside the ship.

Meanwhile, the missionary sought to keep the Okinawans happy with some liquor below decks. When the ruse was discovered, the Okinawans scurried to their boats and rowed away, unable to relieve themselves of the baggage, and also afraid to do it damage. Bettelheim was very pleased at this, for he felt that the natives were at least doing something to help their missionary, although under considerable protest.[24]

Getting permission from the captain to follow the native boats to see about his luggage, Bettelheim used one of the ship's boats and followed the Okinawans to Naha. Upon his trying to land his goods, some slight resistance was encountered, and some of his luggage got wet. But all the effects were safely landed with two more trips by the ship's boats, after which Bettelheim went to the Gokokuji Temple with his family. This was the place designated by the government for receiving all visitors.

There ensued at the temple a discussion between government officials and Bettelheim about his presence on the island, whereupon the chief official present performed the *kotau* before the missionary in an attempt to get him to return to the ship. The most repeated objection to his stay was that they could have no more *papatis* (probably meaning "papists") on the island. Bettelheim assured them that he and his family were not "papists," and produced a bottle of port to lessen the objections of his unwilling hosts. After getting them to drop the matter of immediate re-embarking, Bettelheim expressed surprise that the officials had not ordered his baggage brought from the beach, and at the same time he gave them to know that he would hold them responsible for any damage. A word from the officer, and all the goods were brought to the temple within fifteen minutes.[25]

Satsuma's resident minister reported that the Bettelheim family belongings were as follows: a mirror, a quilt (mattress), six chairs, a mosquito net, luggage for clothing, several leather boxes, an iron bathtub, two closets, two rattan-matting boxes, one umbrella and two dogs.[26] Because of the two dogs and his place of residence, he soon became known as *Nami no ue no gancho,* the "Spectacled man of Name no Ue," or *In gancho,* "Spectacled dog-man."

Bettelheim received an official request on the day following his arrival that he make plans to leave the island as soon as possible. It was dated May 2, 1846, and it begged him not to stop in the country for the sake of its tranquility. It gave as reasons the poverty of the country, a recent drought and the laws of the land which forbade foreigners to remain. The document noted that the French priests were refused permission to land, but were left by their ship in spite of the refusal. The purpose of the government to ask for the removal of the Frenchmen at the first opportunity was stated and compassion was asked for "this poor, worn-out country." The petition ended: "Give up the design of stopping in this land; wait until wind and weather be favorable, then embark in the same ship, and sail back to your country. This is what I anxiously hope and look for you to do."[27]

Bettelheim responded to the request with some gifts instead of an answer. He sent to the palace a showy American-made clock purchased in Hong Kong, some bottles of Price's aromatic spirits and oils, and a small silk purse with a collection of gold, silver and copper coins. Actually, the missionary tried first to deliver these in person to the king or his treasurer, but he was led on a circuitous route ending at the public hall in Tomari, far from Shuri Castle.

He and his family were soon settled in the Gokokuji Temple, which was to be his home for the period of his stay in Okinawa. He accepted the "interpreters" *(tsuji)* stationed at the temple as presenting an opportunity to learn the language, as well as to present the gospel to the country. Three groups of five each from the noble class were stationed in and around the temple on the pretext that they would serve as "guards" to protect the foreign family from the attacks of bad men, with whom they were told the country abounded.

Bettelheim was not so favorably disposed toward the Buddhist altar and images at the back of his bedroom. It was not only the rats which came to disturb the offerings of food, nor was it only that on a certain night something moved so fiercely up and down the paper partition that separated the gods from the rest of the bedroom near the head of the bed, leading all to conduct a snake-hunt the following morning, that bothered him. The continual Buddhist ceremonies vexed the soul of the missionary. He finally hinted that it was inconsistent for a Buddhist priest to come so often to view a foreign woman, while the wives of the nobility of the land were kept so out of sight of foreigners. This argument led to a suspension of rites in the temple, and finally to the shutting of all the idol cages by the missionary. He considered this cessation of idolatry in the "Country Protecting Temple" a great victory for Christianity.[28]

Beginning his Ministry

It is evident from the record that Bettelheim came to Okinawa with the purpose of being a physician to the people, a translator of scripture into their language, an evangelist communicating the Christian gospel, and an educator sponsoring a school to teach European arts and sciences.[28] It soon became clear that the organization of a school would not be possible, and the government put every barrier possible in the way of the accomplishment of his other objectives. There were some fluctuations in policy toward the missionary and his work, however, and these allowed him to make considerable progress at certain times during his residence in Okinawa.

Soon after his arrival, Bettelheim had sent to the authorities in Shuri a request for permission to practice medicine and to teach English and Western geography and astronomy. The answer to this request was some time in coming, but when it did arrive in early November of 1846, everything Bettelheim had requested was refused.

Undoubtedly the missionary designed to win his way into the community by providing for the Okinawans that which he thought they would surely want, namely, medical help and Western learning. From the very beginning he introduced himself as a doctor rather than as a Christian missionary. To Fr. Forcade he explained that he was a physician sent out by a philanthropic society in England to Ryukyu. Forcade, of course, recognized that he was undoubtedly a Protestant minister.[30] To the government he made request to serve as an educator and physician, but mentioned nothing of his desire to preach, though the government was aware of his intent.

The answer of the government at Shuri stated that Ryukyuan physicians had learned their arts from China, and there was no need for any further study of medicine or the introduction of new remedies. As for the study of English, the "interpreters" had already been ordered to study it, but the government stated that "our country is small and the people stupid, they cannot be aroused sufficiently to receive instruction, and become qualified to conduct important matters."[31] In the matter of studying geography and astronomy, skill in compass and rules for sailing had also been learned from China. The sea routes were well-known, and there was little danger of accidents, so there was obviously no need for further instruction along these lines, according to the reply.

This official reply destroyed hopes of establishing a hospital or school, so Bettelheim determined to enter upon the ministry of preaching to the people. He said, "The Lewchewans wanted neither physician or apothecary, charity doctor or master of language, neither would they know aught of geography or astronomy. What was I then to do? The answer was plain, *to be their missionary*." [32]

The missionary had begun some weeks before the exercise of his preaching ministry with memorized sermons, and in the preparation of these the "interpreters" were, in one way or another, a great help. Prayers from Robert Morrison's translation of the English liturgy in Chinese had been rendered into the dialect of Ryukyu and was read daily at Bettelheim's family worship. It was audibly followed by the servants and "interpreters."[33]

According to his diary, the missionary preached for the first time in public on November 10, 1846. It was evidently the same day he had been refused permission to teach Western subjects or to practice medicine.[34] The only occupation for which he had come which was not specifically denied him was that of preaching and conducting evangelistic work. Of course, he had not asked for such permission, probably realizing that it would have been denied before all the rest. But the fact that it had not been officially denied made it possible for him to proceed, and indeed for the first year of his effort he experienced what he referred to as the "golden age of the mission."[35] Though opposition did increase throughout the year, still the missionary had relative freedom to engage in his evangelistic ministry during this time. In his own words:

> ... crowds gathered, and were permitted to gather round me wherever I raised my humble pulpit upon a stone, in the corner of a street, in the market, in the roads or lanes, in Shui (Shuri) or in Napa (Naha), no matter where I halted, there all the passersby stopped, and inhabitants of the neighborhood opened their houses and slipped out, all of them, men, women, and children; the stalls were idle, sellers and buyers forgot their trade, while apparently

engaged in higher business. I have seen coolies lay down their burdens and quietly listen; laborers lean their heads on the handle of the rural tools and rest in pensive attention; thoroughfares were obstructed, and roads and open places rendered impassable from the masses of people crowded in the space around me; none forbidding, none driving them away, much less preventing their assembling as has long since been, and up to this time (late 1849) is, our sad case.[36]

At the same time, Bettelheim was continually offering gifts and medicines to the king and to various officials in the hope of winning favor and in the expectation of getting an audience with those in authority.

During this time Bettelheim realized that much of the liberty he was enjoying to preach the Christian faith was due to the regular arrival of French warships, which he said had a "deep, moral effect wrought on the whole nation, its rulers not excepted."[37] It is a question whether the effect should be called "moral," but it was unquestionably "deep." Neither the Okinawan authorities nor the Satsuma officers were willing to chance the wrath of a mighty Western power at that particular juncture by taking extreme measures against the missionaries residing in Ryukyu.

Bettelheim was not so grateful for the influence of a British admiral, Sir Thomas Cochrane, who visited Okinawa in October, 1846. It was after the departure of Sir Thomas that the official refusal came from the Shuri Government prohibiting Bettelheim from practicing medicine or opening a school. The admiral refused to intercede with the government on Bettelheim's behalf, even in the matter of being allowed to hire a female domestic. And he disappointed Bettelheim by taking a very mild and compliant stance toward Okinawan official requests to restrict shore leave of his officers to a small number at one time. But much more serious was the fact that the admiral accused Bettelheim of setting himself up as a British official and recommended that his naturalization papers as a British citizen be cancelled.[38] In response to the charge Bettelheim pointed to the fact that the Shuri Government was never led to regard him as a British official, a fact which was abundantly evident in their lack of response to his various requests. It was true that Bettelheim linked the honor of the British nation and the advance of the Protestant faith, and this could easily be misconstrued as an official claim to representing British interests. There were times when it seemed to British officials that it was Bettelheim's purpose to "engage Her Majesty's Government in a Missionary Crusade."[39] Admiral Cochrane made it plain in a reply to a Ryukyuan Government request to remove Bettelheim and his family from the island that the missionary was not an official of the government. In fact, the admiral went much further and stated that Bettelheim was not even a British subject. He gave his reasons for not removing the Bettelheims from Okinawa as follows: 1. Bettelheim came privately to the island and was engaged in a good work, namely, medical service for the people. 2. Bettelheim had the same right to reside in Okinawa as the French. 3. Bettelheim was not a British subject, anyway.[40] In Bettelheim's mind, the visit of Sir Thomas and the unfavorable response of the Shuri Government in early November were linked.

Growing Opposition

The opposition of the government to Bettelheim's preaching ministry began to appear in late November after he had conducted outdoor meetings several times. In early December, the people were forbidden to show any books to foreigners who were acquainted with the dialect of the islands, and one week later they were forbidden to reply to any inquiry made by foreigners in the native tongue or in the *kana* syllabary, the form of writing used to express the dialect.[41] Alarm had obviously risen in official circles over Bettelheim's ability in the Ryukyu dialect.

The first prohibition of preaching came on December 18, 1846, one month after the first public sermon, advising the missionary to desist lest he be injured. The same reasons were given for ceasing to preach as were given for refusing Western learning, that is, there was said to be no need for or time for learning a foreign religion. The religion Bettelheim preached was said to be only for the West. The way of Confucianism, on the other hand, was for the East.[42] The favorable response on the part of the crowds, and the official opposition of the government led Bettelheim to feel that the government was the great obstacle to successful evangelism and that the people must by all means continue to have the opportunity to hear the message. He began to suspect that either China or Japan was in control of the political situation, as is reflected in his diary entry of February 28, 1847. But it was another year before he understood the nature of the Satsuma overlordship in Ryukyu.[43]

Increased pressure was placed upon the servants of Bettelheim's house to stop attending family worship which was conducted there, and he began to lose the attention of the people as he preached in the marketplace during the first months of 1847. He continued, however, to go out each Sunday for street preaching until it became impossible to do so.

One of the events which seemed to increase opposition to the missionary was the theft of six hundred dollars in Mexican money from his house on July 5, 1847. The thieves were caught and exiled, one for life and one for fifteen years, but the event which really brought to a close the "golden age" of Bettelheim's preaching ministry was an altercation between a crowd of Okinawans and the three missionaries, Bettelheim, and Leturdu and Adnet of the Roman Catholic mission, as they were proceeding to Shuri to attend the funeral of King Sho Iku. The king passed away suddenly at the age of thirty-five years, leading Bettelheim to later reflect that there must have been some plot, and that his death was a contrived "theatrical exit" to make possible a change in policy with respect to the foreigners in Ryukyu.[44] The fact that a hundred Satsuma troops had been dispatched to reside in Ryukyu in the year 1847 signalled a strengthening of policy on the part of Satsuma toward the Ryukyu Government and toward foreign intrusions. One can well understand Bettelheim's suspicions.

Upon the king's death on October 27, 1847, Bettelheim presented a dirge for the king written in Chinese.[45] This should not have occasioned any adverse reaction toward the missionary, and it probably had no influence on what took place on October 31, the day of the funeral. The French priests urged Bettelheim to go with them to Shuri, and the three set out together. On the way they were set upon by a crowd of Okinawans using sticks and stones to drive them off the road. Bettelheim tried to go to the defense of Adnet, who was being beaten by the crowd, and was himself struck by their sticks. He protested to the crowd that they had only come to pay their respects to the king, whereupon the crowd calmed a bit and allowed them to return unmolested.[46] It was only later that Bettelheim learned that the French had been warned not to come to the capital. It was evidently because they defied the warning and got Bettelheim to accompany them that they were set upon. The Okinawans were also alarmed because the Frenchmen were carrying sticks and because Bettelheim had chosen to bring his dogs with him.[47]

It has been asserted that by contrast with the activities of Bettelheim, the French priests engaged in scholarly activities, "behaved themselves with patient restraint and made no overt attempts to win converts to Christianity."[48] But the record shows that they attempted to speak to their guards about Christianity, that they used various occasions to share their faith, that they actively sought opportunities for contact with villagers and that they entered homes to seek those who had expressed an interest in the Christian faith.[49] It was also their attempt to do evangelistic work in Shuri which led to their being asked not to come there. It is true that the French priests had been placed in Okinawa by the admiral to learn the language so that they might accompany the fleet as interpreters upon a later proposed entry into Japan.[50] Bettelheim, on the other hand, was sent out by a mission which bore the name, Loo Choo, and which was intent upon doing evangelistic work among the Okinawans. With this difference in purpose, there would naturally be some difference in the degree of evangelistic activity. But the attempts of the French to evangelize are well documented. When they attempted to speak to their guards, the reply was: "What you say is very good, but we cannot listen. The government does not wish us to do so, and we cannot disobey without incurring great danger." [51]

An old man who had been the chief officer of a small island attempted to talk with the missionaries on occasion. One day on the beach he signalled Leturdu to follow him to a secluded spot. There he asked, "Will you not explain to me who Jesus is?"

After replying, Leturdu said, "It is for the purpose of teaching these things that I have come hither. Do you not wish to hear what we have to say?"

The man replied, "Yes, but it is dangerous. We cannot do so."

The missionary said, "At least promise me that every day you will use this prayer: 'Lord, help me to know thee.' Then as soon as permission can be gained, come and listen to us."

The old man answered, "I will do so."⁵²

Others who came seeking could not later be found, though the missionaries searched for them diligently.

After Leturdu left Okinawa, he expressed the view that attempting to work there was hopeless under the conditions prevailing at the time. He wrote to Paris:

> We were carried thither by warships; we have there an official title — that of Interpreters of the King of France; and we are regarded as French officers sent to spy out the land. Is not all this fitted to increase the opinion which all Japanese have had since the former persecutions that missionaries are only spies of the countries from which they come?... Because of the opposition of the Government it is impossible, humanly speaking, to make a single convert. Even though the King of Loo Choo should come to favor us, he could authorize nothing, since it is not he that governs, but the Emperor of Japan through his envoys.⁵³

Bettelheim was not so easily deterred by this seemingly impossible situation, and as a result the change of policy toward his work on the part of the officials was quite noticeable.

The "interpreters" who were sent with Bettelheim everywhere he went, instead of standing by while he preached, scattered from the point of his intended street preaching to drive the people away from the site, sometimes dragging them away by force.⁵⁴ A period of real hardship for the work of Dr. Bettelheim was entered upon, and it lasted from October, 1847, until October, 1850.⁵⁵

Perseverence in Persecution

Undaunted by the attempts to stop his street preaching, Bettelheim continued to use methods which somewhat surprised Leturdu. He reported that when Bettelheim reached a point to stress, one of his guards would blow a whistle. At the sound of the whistle, half of the crowd would face right, turning their backs on the preacher. When the preacher complained of the tactic, the officials with great seriousness replied that they thought it was irreverent for the crowd to look upon his face and therefore desired in this way to show him the utmost courtesy. Occasionally, while he had been speaking, someone would leave a basket of excrement at his feet, and then would run away.[56]

Bettelheim himself described the situation a year after the king's death as follows:

> It took a year of persevering opposition, now hidden, now open, to enable even a despotic cabal like that we had fallen under since the king's death, to bring about a total desertion of the places where I halted, and of the streets and lanes I passed through. First, there was a bustle, a running here and there, a rattle and clapping of shutting doors and windows, as if a devil incarnate had come in their way; green grocers deserted their stalls, laborers ceased their work, and crews left their boats; women dragged their children indoors in such haste and fright, as to make them scream out when they saw me again afar off. Often the noise, confusion, and bewilderment rose to such a pitch that I was not always free from fear myself, and almost dreaded to walk about.[57]

Effectively stopped from his street preaching for a time, the missionary turned to the use of printed tracts and rolls of portions of scripture, mainly in Chinese, and addresses written in the Ryukyu dialect, which his wife had helped him copy off in the evening hours for use during the day.[58] The first notice of such distribution is in the journal of the missionary for January 23, 1848, at which time he attempted to preach and then proceeded to throw tracts into thirteen homes and the Confucian Temple. Although these materials were immediately confiscated by officials, this activity continued unabated for some seven months. All the tracts were returned to him on September 26, 1848, a total of five hundred seventy-six tracts.[59] There may have been some tracts which remained in the hands of those whom Bettelheim met on the streets, but it is rather doubtful.

As he colported his tracts through the streets, he offered at the same time cakes baked with his own hands. Some who refused the tracts took the cakes, but after a time the cakes, too, were refused, or the guards prevented the distribution.

Then he turned to attempting his work through the children who would throng around him in the darkening hours of the evening, attracted by the gifts of cakes and small coins. But this contact was also found out, and he was on occasion pelted with stones in the dark.[60]

When all hope of street work seemed gone, Bettelheim turned to house-to-house calls as a method of evangelism. He also worked more diligently with those close at hand, those to whom he had regular access, his guards. At the nearest guard hut to his house twenty men lived. Four of them served by turns each day, and the whole group changed about twice a year.[61] Presumably this was to assure that no group would be exposed to the missionary over too long a period of time. It was actually from this group that the greatest number of converts and "seekers" came. Bettelheim here had access to forty different men each year, and access to them could not be easily denied him. He insisted on placing Christian books from his own library in their hut to arouse their curiosity. He found them engaged on occasion in going through the books and maps which he left for their inspection, and this made him feel that his efforts were not entirely in vain. He also struck sheets containing the Decalogue on different walls in the house, as it was the custom in Okinawa to have scrolls or hangings on the wall with some classic word of wisdom. In addition, he pasted large oblong slips of red paper on his door posts inscribed with Christian thoughts. He copied large maps, lettering them with Chinese characters, and gave them to his guards, confident that through the guards they sometimes even reached the palace.[62]

As a result of this work with his guards, Bettelheim recorded on July 25, 1848:

> I heard today for the first time a plain satisfactory confession of faith in Jesus Christ from the mouths of two natives, one of the literati, and the other a peasant; and there is full indication of one more imbued with the faith.[63]

The chief guard, as a matter of fact, asked Bettelheim for some information concerning the Christian faith to be written on a sheet of European paper. He intended to hang it in his room. Such things were banned, but after the request was repeated, Bettelheim undertook the preparation of rather a detailed sheet, which he described as follows:

> In the central square, in prominent letters, is read, Father, Son and Holy Ghost. In a smaller square....of the Creed; further four largish ....squares contains (sic) the Lord's prayer, directions for spiritual worship, the doing away of all images, abstaining from sacrificing

to the *kamis* (the nature deities) or the dead, confession of sin, faith in the Lord Jesus Christ, the necessity of a total change of heart worked by the Holy Spirit, and the reading of God's Word.[64]

The guard taught the men under him some of the elements of Christianity, and Bettelheim discoursed regularly to a group of guards for about ten months.[65] The chief guard and his brother were removed from duty at the Bettelheim residence in April, 1849.

But being confined to trying to reach his guards alone was to Bettelheim a triumph of Satan, and to secure the small outreach which he had, he felt it necessary to strive for more. Although the situation might have dictated patience to a man of different character, the biblical commission to go to all nations plainly also said to Bettelheim that he was not to wait.[66] With this in mind, he started his house to house calls on June 4, 1848.

The record of his approach to the households of Naha are shocking to us today, but we must try to remember the interpretation Bettelheim gave to his own situation and to the situation of the people he was trying to reach. Passing through the streets of Naha, he saw doors closed against him as at previous times. He threw a stone at one such door, trying to get the shopkeeper to open to him. Similar attempts were made by him, according to his journal, on June 11 and June 18. They were largely futile attempts and only occasioned further opposition. He always sent payment for damages, or tried to do so, a few days after the events.[67]

When Shuri sent an official on June 24 to protest his action, Bettelheim replied, according to the Documents of the State Council, as follows:

> Though I am not a thief, every door has been closed while I was going along the street. Since I am a teacher (in Christianity) of this country, it is my duty to teach the doctrine of Christianity. To the intentionally closed doors, (I am) obliged to teach them, even though (I) forcibly intrude into the house.[68]

He undoubtedly made this reply in the full knowledge that it would be passed to Satsuma officials, and he probably saw it as a way of challenging their right to forbid him access to the people. From various statements he made, it is certain that he thought the people were on his side, and that they would gladly hear were it not for official hindrance. He said in this connection, "I only abominate the government, which brought about such a state of things all the while its officers made, and still make, professions of goodwill and friendly offices, whenever a ship calls in."[69]

Having been denied access to shops and homes while passing down the streets, the missionary eluded his guards, in so far as possible, and taking to the smaller streets and paths behind houses, he leaped over the gaps in dilapidated back walls to enter houses unannounced. Seating himself in the main room of the house, he would not leave until all had heard his message. The first time he tried this tactic, he created some pandemonium, but he himself was calm through it all. He reported of this occasion: "I was little moved with the cries of the women, or frightened at the screams of the children, but seated myself in the first room I could get access to."[70] He evidently started with the homes of the elite classes, remarking that this method of entering homes immediately occasioned considerable extra work for the stone masons, who were employed to fix the gaps in walls, so that the enclosures of those whom he visited and those in their vicinity were soon greatly improved.

On the first surprise visit to a home, some member of the family, if not the master of the house, would usually sit and listen to the missionary. On the second or third visit to the same house, the missionary's entrance was often blocked; sometimes the members of the house simply vacated the premises and left the missionary alone; sometimes the occupants of the house pled deafness and dumbness, motioning that such was their condition by movements of their hands; and sometimes the missionary narrowly escaped a beating. Such threats of overt opposition were attributed by him to the influence of official policy.[71]

As the opposition increased to his visits in the homes of the elite, he turned to the homes of the peasants. There were no walls to leap over. Accessible from all sides through the sparse bamboo planted around them, entry could be gained easily through wide open doors and through the simple bamboo door tied with straw.

At the same time, the public office in Naha, which was also used for a school, was visited regularly by Bettelheim over a period of eighteen months. At times from five to fifty people stayed to listen to him speak. At other times they all fled from the windows and over the walls to neighboring houses. He left books and maps at the school, but he was unable to recover them, and so discontinued the practice.[72] He also visited the Tomari public hall near the place where the French missionaries had resided, and in this place he continued a meeting mainly for children for a period of more than a year.

In January, 1849, Bettelheim received his second beating at the hands of the Okinawans. It had become difficult for him to get food. The people who had been supplying him and his family brought the worst possible produce, so payment was refused. Bettelheim took matters into his own hands and succeeded in getting a man with a horse-load of potatoes to come to his house. This took place in the early morning hours, so that the spies did not discover what was happening until the cart was in the lane leading to the house. A tremendous hooting by them drove the man away, but Bettelheim led the horse to the door himself. Then going out for other purchases, he was set upon in the following way:

> I had a servant with me at the time, and after selecting and laying down a good price for a piece of meat, ordered him to take it home. But on hearing the spies cry out and order the rabble to run after and tear it away from him, I took the meat into my own hand, and twice succeeded in dissuading them from attacking me, but they were repeatedly urged on, so I took to my heels. Through a whole long street they pursued and finally overtook, and tore away from me this purchase made in a way, for which we have established several precedents in the markets, where no opposition had been attempted, neither toward myself nor Mrs. Bettelheim, whenever we laid down silver coin for the articles we took from the stall. This public attack and disgraceful defeat frightened us greatly, and certainly there was much ground for it, considering the effect such scenes have on the mass of this populace.[73]

After this beating in March, 1849, the H.M.S. "Mariner" visited Okinawa on a mission to help a British ship which had been wrecked nearby, and Bettelheim used the occasion to appeal to the British Government for protection. He entrusted to Commander Matheson of the "Mariner" a petition to the Parliament asking that naval vessels might occasionally visit the island to give him protection.[74] The Ryukyu

Government, on the other hand, used the occasion to request again the removal of the missionary, pointing out that the French had cooperated by removing their missionaries in the previous year.[75] The British refused to remove Bettelheim, but the British envoy in Hong Kong, Bonham, did respond to Bettelheim's request to the extent of having British warships seeking trade relations with the Ryukyus show Bettelheim the kind attention that would "raise him in the estimation of the Loo Choo authorities." But they were not to give the doctor the impression that "he could use this naval support for his own ends."[76]

The visit of the "Mariner" itself did Bettelheim little good, for before the end of March he was refused passage on a public ferry-boat and was struck with a stone while addressing a group of people in the streets at their open shop doors. His complaint brought verbal reply that a boy trying to drive off some birds had missed and hit the missionary by mistake as the rock rebounded off a wall. The rock evidently caused a sizeable wound.[77]

Actually, that which was experienced by Bettelheim had been suffered by the French missionaries much earlier. Since they had introduced themselves as missionaries from the beginning of their residence, they were watched more closely at first than was Bettelheim. By the end of the year, 1846, the French were set upon by the Okinawans, whereas Bettelheim preached for another year before experiencing a great amount of opposition. Bettelheim's journal of December 26, 1846, recounts: "Heard this evening the French had been pelted with stones and threatened to be beaten with bamboos by some unmanageable natives."[78] They sought to publish tracts and started their house-to-house visits much earlier than did Bettelheim, concentrating on Shuri rather than Naha.[79] This was doubtless the reason for the warning to stay away from Shuri on the occasion of the funeral of King Sho Iku in October, 1947.[80]

It is well to remember that Forcade had left the island with the French warship "Sabine" in July, 1846, and was ordained bishop of Hong Kong on February 21, 1847. Adnet died in Ryukyu on July 1, 1848, having been in ill health since his arrival. Leturdu was removed by a French corvette whose captain had instructions to take him from the island in July, 1848.

But Bettelheim continued on, and he sought to increase his activities toward the end of 1849. In November of that year his journal indicates that he went out, jumped over low walls into several homes and six brothels. He called for the worship of God, distributed his cakes, religious tracts and some foreign coins. It was this increased activity on the part of the missionary that led to detailed instructions from the government to the four districts of Naha frequently visited by Bettelheim. The instructions ordered that when Bettelheim was roaming about every door and gate must be closed carefully. In the event the missionary forced his way into homes, it was ordered that:

1. Japanese books and important papers must be kept out of eyeshot in advance.
2. Women and children must run away from the house.
3. The samurai must stay at home. They must accuse Bettelheim of an unlawful act, saying, "You act like a burglar. Is this the morality of Jesus?" Then they must drive him out of the house.
4. If the missionary insists on staying, with the help of friends and relatives he must be forced out, and he must be declaimed as a rascal.
5. If he persists outrageously, "they are allowed even to twist his hand."[81]

Still further detailed instructions were issued on December 9, and the relations between the missionary and Shuri officials continued to worsen.

A fourth experience of physical violence came to the missionary on the first Sunday after the New Year in 1850. He had preached in the open air, and then entered a samurai's house to preach the gospel. He was thrown out into the street by six or eight policemen, and there was stoned. He lay there for some two hours, unable to rise. His wife was alerted by the household cook and rushed to his assistance. She found that he was unable to move hands or feet due to a bad blow in the back. For a time guards kept away all others from helping Mrs. Bettelheim with a mat upon which to carry the doctor home. She and the cook were left upon the largest thoroughfare of Naha with the immobilized doctor suffering the shivers and spasms of pain. Finally, after about an hour's entreaty, they were able to get a covering to put upon him and a mat to lay him upon; and then the guards sent two men with boards bound together to serve as an awkward palanquin to carry the missionary home.[82]

Improved Opportunites, Persistent Opposition

Relations were somewhat improved, however, with the visit of the H.M.S. "Reynard" to Okinawa in October, 1850. The Bishop of Victoria, the Rt. Rev. George Smith, was en route to conduct his first episcopal visit to the consular cities of North China. The ship's captain at this time presented to the Ryukyu Government a series of complaints which Bettelheim had sent to the colonial government of Hong Kong, and the government in reply sent the usual defense of its treatment of the missionary along with a renewed request for his removal from the island. Captain Craycroft replied to the Ryukyuan request:

> I am requested by the British Government to inform you that they regard Dr. Bettelheim with interest, and will view with great displeasure any attempt on the part of the Loo Choo authorities to compel Dr. Bettelheim, by any system of annoyance or persecution, to quit the island.[83]

News of this further request by the Okinawans to have Bettelheim removed resulted in an angry reply by Lord Palmerstone, British Foreign Secretary, to the effect that unless the missionary received better treatment, the visits of British warships might become less friendly.[84]

Bishop Smith saw Bettelheim cut off effectively from all contact with the people by the strict surveillance of the Okinawan officers, and he rendered the judgment that without improvement in the situation, the mission had better be abandoned.[85] After staying six nights with the Bettelheims at their temple residence, Smith wrote: "He sometimes uttered sentiments which savour more of a Joshua than a Paul...."[86]

The threats of the British Government had some effect on the situation, for Bettelheim could write two years after the visit of the Reynard: "The Reynard did us a world of good. We have since found door after door opening and the people now received us as friendly as at the beginning."[87] As officials neglected the work of suppression and gave up the attempts to expel the missionary, he had a great deal more freedom to engage in his work than previously. With the lifting of restraints there was an improvement of rapport with the officials and an increasing interest on the part of many people in the message which the missionary brought. The statement that after the first months of his stay on Okinawa the people became indifferent to him [83] does not accord with the record of his last years on the island.

After the visit of the "Reynard," Bettelheim sent presents worth $150 in Mexican money to government officials as a gesture of good will, and in return they held a party for the Bettelheims attended by many dignitaries. Bettelheim then arranged to welcome a number of officials to his house and wrote couplets for them expressing the new relationship:

> Like when the morning clouds disperse The world welcomes the sunny heaven, Now our griefs are vanished,
> The foreign family welcome
> The kind High Rulers.[89]

The improved relations with the officials was soon reflected in the response the missionary received in the marketplace. On February 6, 1851, he went to town and heard the people shouting a welcome to him in words he had often used in street preaching: "*Kamigwa Iesu, Shikin nu Matsiri*" (Jesus, Sor. of God, the sacrifice of the world).[90]

The record shows that Bettelheim saw more converts to the Christian faith in Ryukyu than have usually been recognized. Professor Kerr credits him with "one avowed convert in seven years."[91] But Dr. Teruya credits his ministry with five converts and about fifty inquirers reported during his eight years in Okinawa.[92] Gleaning the information from Bettelheim's diary, Dr. Teruya mentions those who entered the faith as including a carpenter, an interpreter, an old couple, and one of Bettelheim's servants.[93] Bettelheim also said in correspondence with Peter Parker in Hong Kong in 1851 that a harvest was ripening for the Christian church in Loo Choo, but he was concerned that Western governments, particularly British, ought to take a firmer stand to see that native Christians were not persecuted for their faith. Appealing in the main for the convert, Sachihama, who was evidently not helped by the visit of the "Reynard" or other British vessels, he said:

> The writer can point at several instances of persons secretly removed, and whole families ruined in consequence of their favoring the Christian religion. The sufferer now discovered justifies the suspicion that those persons have likewise undergone, or still undergo, ignominious severities because of their faith. Not to speak of the poor population, among whom I have found it possible to

maintain a good degree of intercourse, and among whom there is a considerable number of individuals, who, though well instructed, and confessing themselves believers before the missionary and his wife, yet cannot make open profession of their faith because of the terror of torture; there have been, during nearly five years, upward of two hundred of the class of literati, serving by rotation in the guard-huts already referred to, and also as *todzies* (interpreters); among this body likewise, there is a good number of well-informed men, who own that the fate of some of their companions is the sole obstacle to their assuming the name of Christian.[94]

The object of Bettelheim's immediate and great concern was the suffering which had been endured by Sachihama, about whom certain facts are well known. He had been one of Bettelheim's guards, and his uncle had also been a guard and a Christian believer. Sachihama had become a believer at about twenty-two years of age. He was confined by his own step-father on pretext of mental illness, probably under pressure from officials, since Shuri refrained from direct persecution at this point in time due to the recent visit of the "Reynard" and the threats of the British Government.[95]

The Bettelheims evidently discovered him being held in a cage quite by accident. He called out to them as they passed by where he was being held captive. His feet were in stocks bound to a heavy beam on the ground. He was being systematically starved, denied all comforts and beaten regularly with sticks, a practice which was supposed to help his demented condition. He begged for help of the Bettelheims, asked for their prayers and requested some books which he had studied in the guard hut.[96]

The missionaries discovered him on November 24, 1850. By December 29, when they found it possible to see him again, he was greatly weakened in body, and he told the missionaries that he had been declared mad and that regular beatings were administered to bring him to his senses. His Christian books had been taken from him, and he was compelled to read Confucian works. He begged to be sent to England, and Bettelheim promised to try to effect that as soon as a ship should come in.[97]

A third visit attempted by the missionaries on January 27, 1851, was in vain. Sachihama was gone. A request to officials to be informed of his location met with silence, and the father would reveal nothing. The father also shortly disappeared and no trace could be found of either father or son. Sachihama had told the Bettelheims that he knew he was to be killed. Yet they heard him shouting one day, "Jesus is true! Jesus is true! Why do you beat me? Jesus is true!" [98]

On March 13, 1851, the Bettelheims heard through their interpreters that Sachihama was dead. The shocking news reached them on Mrs. Bettelheim's birthday. The report was that he had been declared mad because he preferred Jesus to parents and Mandarins.[99]

There was some fluctuation in the treatment of the missionaries during the ensuing year, but the visit of the H.M.S. "Sphinx" in February of 1852 reinforced the requests made at the time of the visit of the "Reynard." The ship bore a letter from Palmerstone saying that a British ship would from time to time visit the island.[100] The captain of the "Sphinx" asked for kind treatment for Bettelheim, including access to the market. He also asked for toleration for natives interested in Christianity, but the request fell short of what was hoped for by Bettelheim, since it did not help solve the Sachihama tragedy.[101]

Palmerstone had been the only British Foreign Secretary who showed concern about the problem of Bettelheim's residence in Okinawa, and Bettelheim continued to write to him even after he was out of office, appealing for his support for religious toleration as the best way for breaking down the Japanese prohibition of trade. But Palmerstone was little interested in pressing the matter of trade or the connection with Japan. He was interested principally in supporting a British subject abroad and seeing that he got fair treatment.[102] After he was out of office, he forwarded Bettelheim's letters to Clarendon, but the new Foreign Secretary did nothing about the matter.

During the year 1852, Bettelheim made bold to try to open a work in Shuri, the Royal Capital. In October he acquired rooms for meetings in that city, but within a week he fell ill and had to return to Naha. His illness lasted for some days and became rather serious. Satsuma and Ryukyu officials, observing that he was ill, sought religious means to get rid of Bettelheim once and for all.

> Satsuma's representative, Nomoto, ordered a Ryukyuan State Councillor, Zakimi, to make Bettelheim die by exorcism. A portrait of Bettelheim was painted. In front of the portrait day and night the

Buddhist priests performed the secret prayer of exorcism to destroy the Christian priest in his sickbed.[103]

The prayer was not only offered to prevent healing, but to add a curse. The priest punctured the head of the picture in vital spots with needles and continued reading the sutras for cursing. Bettelheim, however, began to improve and was able to get out of bed to continue his work, leaving the officials who had ordered the curse completely frustrated.[104]

There was a subsequent attempt to preach in Shuri for a period of three months, but no results were achieved and the attempt was abandoned.

According to the missionary's journal of April 3, 1853, the number of inquirers gradually increased in the first months of 1853. The Nagamine brothers, one of whom was a spoon-maker, were baptised. An interpreter from Shuri took an interest in the faith and said he wanted to read the Bible. Bettelheim introduced him to Luke and Acts in the New Testament, laying stress on the Resurrection accounts.[105] There were hopeful signs of interest about, but Bettelheim's health began to fail. His eyes were affected with catarrh, and this disturbed his sleep at night. The concern over finances and the future of his mission work also caused him to lose rest. He had constantly appealed in his letters for the mission to send another missionary to help in the work, and the appeals appeared to have been in vain. There had been no contact with the outside world for fifteen months, and the missionary felt the isolation of his position. By the time Perry arrived with his "Black Ships," Bettelheim was exhausted both physically and mentally.[106]

Bettelheim's Medical Practice

One of the first approaches to his work attempted by Bettelheim when he reached Okinawa was to request permission to open medical service for the people. His plan was to open "The English Free Hospital" in another building on the grounds of the Gokoku Temple, but the government refused him permission. Nevertheless, he was able during the first year of his stay on Okinawa to treat more than fifty patients, most of whom were suffering from cutaneous diseases — leprosy, spora, lepra, elephantitis, tumors and so on.[103] The use of night soils for fertilizer, the prevalence of bare feet, and the almost exclusive use of pork for meat were given by the missionary as causes of these diseases. He noted that he and his family had also been subject to spora in many of its forms. They gave up the use of pork, and after the visit of the "Preble," from which they obtained shoes, they were able better to protect their feet from infection. The doctor noted that cataract, leucoma and staphyloma were not rare, but when he tried to treat a poor man whose eyes were both covered with leucoma, taking him to his own home for treatment, the guards removed the man on the second day of treatment. The missionary also noted that several nobles called from Shuri to receive itch ointment and eye-water, but from the time of the death of King Sho Iku in October, 1847, these visits were also stopped.[108]

Dr. and Mrs. Bettelheim both attempted to visit houses which were obviously much in need of medical aid. He stated:

> I took medicine to their houses, but on my next visit, bottle, medicine, all, had been taken by the emissaries, and the patients begged me not to expose them to danger and penalties, in addition to the pains they already suffered from illness.[109]

Bettelheim took note in particular of the number of deaths which seemed to occur about the time of the equinoxes. In 1849, he noted that many deaths took place in the neighborhood, deaths he attributed to bad water washed into the open wells by the long and heavy rains. He offered the magistrate of Naha twenty dollars to have curbs and covers made for the wells of their neighborhood, but the magistrate returned the money with a note explaining that no matter how long it rained, not a drop of run-off entered the wells. The official further refused advice about putting alum or coals into the water.[110]

During periods of persecution the medical treatment which Bettelheim was able to offer sharply declined. In March, 1851, in a letter to Peter Parker in Hong Kong, Bettelheim mentioned that he had had more than one hundred cases to date, but that fifty of the cases were during the first year of his residence.[111] This meant that the rate of the last three and one-half years was much less than for the first year. Often his medical services had to be offered over strong objections. A report of the Three-Member Regency of September 26, 1848, said that the doctor on a stroll near Naha observed the head of a certain household lying on a sick-bed. Although the man refused to receive medicines from him, the doctor promised them to him. The next day the doctor returned with the medicines, but found the man gone. He threw the medicines into the house and departed. On October 18 of the same year the doctor found a man in the east section of the city who had syphilis and gave him medicine. On the 20th he returned again to find the gate and doors closed against him. He forced his way into the house and found the man gone. On the 22nd he called again and was able to see the man, but the medicine was refused. He left some Chinese coins as alms and departed.[112]

Experiences of this kind apparently affected Bettelheim's approach to evangelism, also. He observed that people really wanted his medicines, but were afraid to receive them because of constant surveillance and the threat of punitive action by the officials. He inferred that the same was true of the Christian message. This, too, was something the common people would receive gladly were they free to do so, but they were being prevented from doing so, not only by their own government, but also by the orders of the Satsuma officials. He was therefore determined that they should have the medicines and the gospel, regardless of the methods employed to achieve this end.

Bovine vaccine for the treatment of smallpox was introduced into Okinawa by Dr. Bettelheim one year ahead of its introduction into Nagasaki, Japan, by the Dutch Army doctor, Otto J. Mohnike. In the introduction of this vaccine he had the cooperation of an Okinawa doctor, Nakachi Kijin. Nakachi had been trained in China, and also in the Satsuma domain of Japan. The two doctors met clandestinely at night on a nearby beach in order to avoid detection. Nakachi left a record of what he learned from Bettelheim in *Igaku Roku* ("Notes on Medicine"), a record which has become an heirloom of the Nakachi family.[113]

In the year 1848, after Bettelheim and Nakachi had examined many cows in the vicinity of Naha and Shuri to try to get more bovine vaccine to fight an epidemic of smallpox, but without success, Nakachi took a trip to the northern part of Okinawa. There he found a cow with pistules. Returning to Naha, he took a child of one of his servants to the place where the cow was and performed an inoculation of vaccine into the child's arm. The vaccination proved successful. [114]

Shortly after the departure of the American ship "Preble" in April, 1848, the government responded to Bettelheim's request that all children be sent to his house for vaccination by refusing all such treatment. They said they could get pox scabs from China, that it was too early in the year, and that the store of medicines was not ready. The officials returned a copy of the *New Vaccination Method* which had been sent them by the missionary, and they begged him not to vaccinate his own daughter lest the disease spread among the people.[115]

New vaccine was carried to the island by Bishop Smith from Hong Kong on the occasion of his visit in 1850. By this time the officials in Shuri were most anxious for their own doctors to learn the new methods and use the vaccine which had been brought. They sent word to Bettelheim asking for copies of the pamphlet on vaccination. With the new methods thus introduced, they were able to inoculate all recipients in a period of about three months, rather than in the year of work which had been planned.[116]

The treatment was so successful that Bettelheim had new opportunities to preach to the people. The missionary and his wife found new freedom in their medical practice, also. He wrote to the London Illustrated News as follows:

> Both myself and Mrs. Bettelheim have moved about like ambulatory dispensaries, carrying bags of medicine, cash and victuals with us for the poor suffering, and when healed, starving patients. We have introduced vaccination, have at the risk of our lives assisted the nation during the spread of small pox and subsequently during the epidemic of typhus.[117]

The inoculation program carried on by native physicians and by Bettelheim himself proved successful, so the missionary and his wife were able to spend six or seven hours per day visiting the sick in their home. They carried up to twenty pounds of medicines with them as they made their rounds. "Deeply impressed by his service, Shuri finally allowed him to use a palanquin with bearers for his medical care without further molestation, with their almost open encouragement." [118]

From this time forward various physicians sought the counsel and advice of the foreign doctor on many diseases up to the time he left the island. Unfortunately, the attitude of the government changed again as the epidemics subsided, and there was a renewed surveillance over the people seeking treatment. But it is important to note that the contribution which Bettelheim made to the health of the country was both immediately beneficial and lasting in nature.[119]

Translations and Linguistic Studies

The linguistic abilities of Dr. Bettelheim were early turned toward the translation of the scriptures in the dialect of Okinawa. It has been asserted that Bettelheim turned toward translation work when his evangelism failed, but it was clearly his intention from the time of his assignment to the Ryukyus to engage in the work of translation of the Bible. Notable work in the translation of the scriptures into Japanese had been done already by Gutzlaff and Morrison, and these portions were of help to Bettelheim in his production of the Gospel of John. But Bettelheim's work in the Ryukyu dialect was a pioneer work. The fact that he set out quite early in his translation efforts, completing the Gospel of Luke by July, 1847, shows that for him translation of the scriptures was not an alternative to evangelism, but rather an essential part of his basic plan from the beginning of his ministry. The Book of Acts in the dialect was then completed in August, 1848. These two books of the Bible seemed to be his favorites because they were written by a physician, because of their emphasis upon works of mercy, and because the authority of the Risen Christ is set forth with emphasis.

The translation of John was somewhat easier for him, since he had Gutzlaff's translation in hand to help him. He finished John's Gospel in December, 1850, and the Book of Romans was completed in March, 1851.

Later in the year 1851, Bettelheim found that his Ryukyu dialect translations were not suitable for use in Japan, and he applied to the government to provide him with a Japanese instructor.[120] Being denied his request, he determined to learn to use Japanese by reading the Chinese Classics with Okinawan scholars, noting how they used the *kunten* (marks for guidance in rendering Chinese into Japanese). His linguistic genius enabled him to learn rapidly, so that before the arrival of Commodore Perry in 1853, he had completed a Japanese version of the Book of Acts and had started on the Gospel of Luke.[121] With some revision, the gospel was later attempted in Japan. It was found, however, that there were too many Ryukyuan influences in the translation, and that it was not really comprehensible to the Japanese.

The efforts of Bettelheim in evangelism and Bible translation had a notable influence on a young sailor who came to Okinawa with Perry's squadron. He was Jonathan Goble, who was to become the first Baptist missionary to the land of Japan. Bettelheim had performed many services for the fleet, and in return he received various gifts and expressions of gratitude from the officers and men. At the time of Perry's visit, the living quarters of the Bettelheims in the Gokoku Temple were badly in need of repair. The first group sent from the American ships to perform the repairs became drunk and unruly, so Jonathan Goble was sent with a new group to direct the work. He was a man of deep Christian commitment, and he was impressed with the work of the missionary doctor, including his efforts to translate the scriptures.

Goble's faithfulness in this and other assignments given to him by the Commodore led to his being offered a promotion. Instead, he requested permission to go ashore when the ships reached Japan. This was granted, and he was allowed to visit the shore almost any time by simply giving notice to his superior officer.[122] His direct experience of being in Japan strengthened his resolve to become a missionary, and after studies in America he returned to Japan in 1860, just one year after the first Protestant missionary, the Rev. John Liggins of the Episcopal Church, had arrived there.

Goble was successful in getting the first portion of the Bible ever printed in Japan completed. It was the Gospel of Matthew printed from wooden blocks in 1871 in Tokyo by a man who evidently did not know the nature of the work. By the laws of Japan at that time, anyone who might be converted by reading the Bible could be put to death with all his family.[123]

A work of great historical importance was also done by Bettelheim in the production of the *Grammar and Dictionary in the Loochooan Langauge*. The main body of the work was completed by him in September, 1849. There were chapters on vocal sounds, syntax, exercises and vocabularies. His 1852 draft of the work included one thousand eight hundred compact quarto pages. But unfortunately, this monumental piece of work went unpublished and was finally sent to the British Museum. It was the first academic work on the Ryukyuan grammar.[124]

In the work of translation, also, Bettelheim often found his efforts blocked. Not only did the government refuse to allow him to study Japanese directly, there were many impediments placed in his way for the study of the dialect as well. His interpreters often refused to help, boycotted the study sessions or offered vague reasons for not being present. In spite of these hindrances, Bettelheim's accomplishments in the field of translation and linguistic studies were truly great.

Bettelheim and Commodore Perry

At the time of the first visit of Commodore Matthew Galbraith Perry to Ryukyu in May, 1853, Bettelheim had not seen any foreign vessels for fifteen months. He was overjoyed at the prospect of contact with the outside world once more. He ran up the British flag as a sign of welcome when the American ships hove into sight. He was early on board the flagship eagerly conferring with the Commodore and sharing his views in an interview which lasted two or three hours.

As a matter of fact, the views of Bettelheim conveyed through the reports of Commander Glynn of the U.S.S. "Preble," which had visited Naha in 1848, had helped to shape Commodore Perry's policy for his visit to Ryukyu.[125] Knowledge of Glynn's reports, which were formulated under Bettelheim's influence, led Perry to expect much duplicity and evasion on the part of Okinawan officials. With this and other voluminous information which he had gathered through extensive research into the situation in Japan, Perry determined on a policy of courtesy with firmness. He decided not to treat with lesser officials, but only with the highest authorities. He determined not to allow delays over minor matters, nor would he accept negative replies to the requests of his government. In this way the British missionary had influenced a policy which was destined to be successful in opening Japan to the West.[126]

Bettelheim's journal of August 5, 1850, shows that he had come to consider it a part of his mission to let the world know the true state of political affairs in Okinawa, where the facade of a kingdom existed with the real authority exercised by the Satsuma Clan of Kyushu and by the Edo Government.[127] Perry had evidently gleaned the nature of this relationship from Glynn's report. He therefore considered himself morally justified in a strong approach to the Government of Ryukyu, since in such an approach there was the possibility of actually ameliorating the condition of the Okinawans.[128]

Word had reached Naha about the movement of Perry's ships along the China coast, and the intelligence that they were on their way to Japan was conveyed to the authorities at Shuri. On April 9, Bettelheim noted that he had been asked to supply some information to Shuri about the application of steam power to ships, and he and his wife had prepared an illustrated text of the workings of a steam vessel and sent the text to Shuri on April 13.[129] So Bettelheim was in the position of supplying both parties some information about the other even before Perry's arrival in Ryukyu.

The missionary was overjoyed at the meeting with the Americans after his prolonged isolation, and he was very much impressed with the character of the Commodore. He recorded in his journal of May 26, 1853, "I offered to serve him as a son serves a father."[130]

He wanted very much to go to Japan with the squadron to serve as an interpreter for the Commodore, something suggested in a communication which Bettelheim had received from Bishop Smith. But there developed between S. Wells Williams, the interpreter accompanying the squadron, and Bettelheim a mutual suspicion and measure of distrust which probably influenced the Commodore in refusing Bettelheim's application to serve on the coming voyage.

Williams was a missionary serving with the American Board of Commissioners for Foreign Missions (Congregational) in China. He had been with the "Morrison" on its voyage to Japan and Ryukyu in 1837. He was a thorough scholar, publisher of the *Chinese Repository*, and an expert linguist. He had a good command of both Chinese and Japanese. Further, he had had extensive correspondence with Bettelheim about his work in Ryukyu and was deeply concerned about some of the reports which had been circulated concerning the missionary's methods and his claims to official sanction from the British Government. He was also disturbed by what he considered the erratic and annoying behavior which Bettelheim displayed at various functions arranged aboard ship and in meetings between Perry and Ryukyuan officials.

Bettelheim, on the other hand, very soon decided that Williams was not competent to act as interpreter-translator, since he used Cantonese dialect, and the Okinawa officials used the Peking dialect for official communication. In addition, Bettelheim was proficient in the dialect of Ryukyu, he had wanted for years to get to Japan, and he had long years of experience in Okinawa. It is not hard to see how the rivalry between the two missionary scholars arose.

In any case, both interpreters were included in the procession to the Royal Palace which took place on June 6. Every possible stratagem of the Okinawans had been used to try to dissuade the Commodore from undertaking this visit, but he was determined. It was said that the king was a mere boy who had not been confirmed by the Emperor of China, that the queen dowager was ill and could not receive visitors, and that such visits were not in accord with the customs and laws of the land. Nevertheless, Perry had decided on a display of pomp and power to achieve his objectives, and he would not be deterred.

"It was a matter of policy to make a show of it," according to the squadron *Narrative*.[131] The captain of the "Susquehanna" led the parade in full-dress uniform, flanked by Williams and Bettelheim. Two field pieces followed, displaying the American flag. Then came the band from the "Mississippi," followed by a company of marines in full dress. The Commodore was decked out in his finest, seated in a palanquin created by the ship's carpenter and hung with blue and red curtains. It was borne by four coolies and followed by a company of marines and a Chinese servant bearing gifts for the Royal House. Then came the band from the "Susquehanna" and another company of marines as a rear guard. Approximately two hundred men participated in the showy procession.[132]

Upon reaching one of the outer gates of the castle, the procession found it closed. The Regent Mabuni had sought to divert the company to his home to be received there, but this had been refused by the Commodore. Captain Bent of the "Susquehanna" requested through Bettelheim as interpreter that the gates be opened in accordance with the arrangements which had been previously made for their visit.

Regent Zakimi re-iterated that the queen dowager was ill and that preparation had been made in the home of the Chief Minister Mabuni to entertain the party. Perry is reported to have seen the discussion going on between the Regent and the Captain. He is said to have alighted from the palanquin and approached Regent Zakimi with a smile and hand extended, expressing himself through Bettelheim as follows: "Thank you all for your welcome. What great courtesy of you to close this important gate so that no one might enter ahead of us! Now that we have arrived, you may open the gate. Please proceed to open the gate." Such a bright and confident response to the closed gate on the part of the Commodore and his interpreter eased the tension and left Regent Zakimi with no reply. The Regent signalled with his eyes to the Chief Minister Mabuni, and at the order of Premier Ozato the gates were opened.[133]

There had been no preparation within the palace for the visit. Pleasantries were exchanged, and tea with very tough twists of gingerbread were served. The Regent was invited to take dinner aboard the flagship. After considerable embarrassed waiting, the invitation to go to the home of the Regent was renewed, and the Commodore accepted. There a multi-course meal was served, but the Americans withdrew after about two hours, having been served only twelve courses of a planned feast of twenty-four.

In this way an earnest wish of the missionary doctor was finally realized. He had gotten within the palace at Shuri, a feat he had repeatedly attempted without success during his years of residence on Okinawa. Further, he was in the process of playing a significant role in the opening of Japan to the West. The Commodore had refused the suggestion that the squadron should promote mission interests in Japan, a suggestion made by Bettelheim. But the presence of Bettelheim in the palace as interpreter for the Americans, decked out as he was in borrowed American finery, inevitably identified the interests of the Christian mission with those of the powerful American presence. It was somewhat ironic that the Commodore wanted to avoid such identification, while Bettelheim seemed to enjoy it. He preached aboard the "Plymouth" on June 26 on the text: "Thou has prepared a table before me in the presence of mine enemies." [134]

The squadron made its first visit to Japan in July, 1853, and

President Fillmore's letter to the Japanese Government was delivered at Uraga. It was some months before the full squadron again gathered at Naha in preparation for another visit to Edo Bay, and by this time the Bettelheims had decided to terminate their service on Okinawa. In fact, Mrs. Bettelheim and the children left Okinawa on the U.S.S. "Supply" for Shanghai on February 8, 1854. Bettelheim stayed on to put affairs in order and to welcome on the island a new appointee of the Loochoo Seaman's Mission, E. H. Moreton, who arrived with his family on the British ship "Robena."

From the time of Perry's first visit to Okinawa in May, 1853, Bettelheim found that the surveillance of his activities was lightened. He wrote on July 11 that he had baptized four natives, three in Naha and one in Shuri. Another convert came about a month later from a good family in Shuri, probably from the samurai class. Following that event, the number of inquirers increased, but there seem to have been no further conversions of record.[135]

After Perry's return to Okinawa following the conclusion of the Treaty of Kanagawa with Japan, March 31, 1854, work became easier for the missionaries. Moreton was learning very rapidly to converse in the dialect in preparation for taking over responsibility for all the work of the mission. Twelve Okinawa officials attended one of Bettelheim's Sunday sermons and listened respectfully for an hour. The missionary thought it was fear of the presence of the American squadron which led to their attendance,[136] and this may have been an accurate appraisal of the sudden interest.

In spite of the show of interest, however, Bettelheim was intent upon leaving Okinawa. It seems somewhat ironic that just as doors of opportunity seemed to be opening to him, and his requests for missionary reinforcements had been answered, he decided to depart. There were, however, other considerations. He had a desire to supervise the publication of his own Bible translations in Hong Kong. Both he and his wife had decided that the children should be educated in England. Further, the doctor's health was failing, and Mrs. Bettelheim had not been in good health since their arrival in Okinawa. Bettelheim thought he was going blind, and the strain of the years of frustration were evident in his attitudes. Also, the family had become alienated from the leadership of the Loochoo Naval Mission. They felt the Mission had not yielded enough discretionary power to the missionary, and there had been many delays of salary. Moreover, the stipend of three hundred pounds per year promised at the beginning of their service turned out to average only about two hundred pounds.[137] When the Bettelheims left the field without the specific permission of the Mission, the alienation became complete.

During the week before the doctor's departure a farewell banquet was held in his honor. All the money he had spent since 1846 was returned to him, as were his tracts. He was given various presents, including one from the Americans amounting to two hundred fifty dollars for his service to the fleet. His farewell address was given in Chinese, and it recounted his eight years of residence and service in Okinawa.[138]

He left the island in mid-July, 1854, on the "Powhattan" of Perry's squadron to meet his family in Hong Kong and work on the arrangements for the publication of his Bible translation.

It is worth noting that although Bettelheim was not allowed to accompany Perry's ships to Japan, his influence preceded the squadron in a way Perry could not have realized at the time, nor could the doctor himself have been aware of its extent. There had been a cultural and scientific awakening in certain fiefs of the "Outside Lords," those not related to the Tokugawa Shogunate which ruled Japan, and Bettelheim made an unconscious contribution to that awakening through the literature he introduced into Okinawa.

One *daimyo* (feudal lord) who was very eager to open Japan to Western learning and trade was Nariakira, Lord of Satsuma. He had come to power in 1851 in the powerful domain which had control of Okinawa. Not only was Okinawa the principal source of extra wealth which flowed into the Satsuma coffers, thus making Satsuma powerful enough to challenge the Tokugawa rulers, and in this way aiding in the restoration of Imperial authority. It was also a principal channel of information about the outside world.

This information in the form of reports, documents and publications came to Satsuma through Ryukyu and influenced greatly the Satsuma leaders in the formation of policy and in the exercise of power. Nariakira was almost unique among the *daimyo* of his time in recognizing the inevitability of opening Japan to the West. Under his capable leadership the profits from the Ryukyuan trade were invested in new industries which excelled those of other areas, and they were in some cases unique to Satsuma. Under the stimulus of a special institute called the *Shuseikan,* sugar, glass and porcelain were manufactured. Nariakira knew that in addition to wealth, modern science was basic to the power of the state. He planned the modernization of military forces, made gunpowder, built smelting works and constructed the first blast furnace in Japan for the production of cannon for coastal defense. He received permission from the Tokugawa Shogun to proceed with the building of steamships for trade and for war. And he also built up a large library of forbidden foreign books and sought to absorb as much foreign learning as possible.

It was at this point that Bettelheim appears to have made his unconscious contribution. Much of the literature which he had printed for distribution, as well as the publications which he forwarded to Shuri for information, was dutifully forwarded to Satsuma. Many of these items are to be found even today in the Nariakira Collection.[139] In addition to the religious tracts and publications, there were a number of periodicals published in Hong Kong in Chinese telling of events, arts and scientific studies in the West. There are thirteen copies of the Morrison Education Society magazine, *Kajikanchin,* which was published at the time in Hong Kong. These were given by Bettelheim to his interpreter, Itarazichi, and they were passed on to Nariakira. There are traces of his having had these copied for his officers to read.[140] Among the journals were also a number of scientific periodicals with a distinctly religious flavor. The influence of these on Nariakira and his policies probably awaits more comprehensive evaluation, but it has been said that one of the important sources of information about the Western world which Nariakira acquired was that which he received from the religious publications channeled to him by Bettelheim.[141] Thus the broad scientific interests of the missionary doctor probably made a larger impact upon Japan in the late Tokugawa Period than he himself realized.

Evaluation

The missionary work of Dr. Bettelheim was widely criticized by

S. Wells Williams and others of his missionary contemporaries. As has already been pointed out, Professor George Kerr spends a good deal of space in criticizing the doctor's personality and his methods.[142] But some of the criticism is rather prejudiced and lacks an appreciation of the situation in which the missionary was placed. Williams appears to have suspected Bettelheim of being mercenary, and Kerr refers to the "surplus cash" which he sent off to Shanghai as possibly derived from the sale of goods and services to the Americans.[143] But the record indicates that this money held by the missionary was his own, brought from England, and was being sent to the bank in Shanghai for safe-keeping.[143]

The personal differences which developed between Bettelheim and Williams could account for some of the adverse comments made by the latter. And accounts of the erratic behavior of the doctor toward the end of his stay in Okinawa fail to take into account the extreme hardship of the eight years of opposition he had suffered and his weakened condition.

The extreme methods which Bettelheim used on occasion to gain a hearing appear to have been based on the conviction that the common people were really ready to hear him, whereas the officials stood in the way. He was convinced that without importunity nothing could be accomplished. He was probably right, at least in part, about both the common people and the officials. Quite aside from the curiosity the foreign family stirred in the community, the genuine interest of the peasants was roused by the words: "All men, including the king and the noble, are equal before God."[145] This was revolutionary doctrine in Ryukyu and in Japan, and it could not be presented without great boldness.

The officials, on the other hand, could not be approached apart from the same kind of boldness, and the record of the number of converts and inquirers is quite remarkable in view of the situation in Ryukyu in the 1850's. In addition to the standard proscriptions against Christianity, the Japanese characters used in Satsuma documents for the word "Christian" conveyed clearly the prejudice of the times. They could be roughly translated in their literal significance, "Die, thou demon-possessed." Before anything at all was known of the Christian faith, Okinawans were taught to think of it as evil.[146] That Bettelheim was able to win a few of the nobility to the Christian faith was nothing short of miraculous.

The significance of Bettelheim's contribution to the treatment of smallpox and other diseases in Okinawa is widely recognized by Ryukyuan scholars, and it is regretted that his monumental *Grammar and Dictionary in the Loochooan Language* was never published. The Japan Bible Society has made available some of his Bible translations in limited editions, and these are very much in demand by scholars and students of Okinawan history.

Bettelheim's acts of philanthropy have not been widely mentioned, and the results are hard to assess. Most often his help for the poor was either refused initially or the gifts confiscated and later returned to the donor. But some items, such as medicines, were undoubtedly put to good use before they could be taken away.

The impression of the Rev. Francis Hawks, supervisor of Perry's *Narrative*, seems to hit the mark:

> He was a physician, a good linguist, with great energy of mind and activity of body, and most indefatigable perseverance. He possessed, also, a boldness of nature which caused him fearlessly to assert his rights as a British subject, and perhaps, not always with discretion.[147]

The mixture of zeal for the interests of the British Empire and commitment to the spread of the gospel was not unusual in mid-Nineteenth Century mission endeavors. It is hard to fault Bettelheim for manifesting this mixture to an excessive degree. One must remember that he was a British subject by choice, that his conversion was associated with British missionary effort, and that with the prevailing mood of the age it would be easy for him to carry to the extreme the tendency to identify the Union Jack with the advance of Protestant Christianity.

Bettelheim made many mistakes in approach and displayed many human errors, but his perseverance through eight years of extremely frustrating missionary work led to notable contributions to Okinawa and Japan in the fields of medicine, linguistics, Bible translation and Western learning. The fact that he was nicknamed "Bespectacled Dog Doctor," and not "Foreign Devil," tells a great deal about the way in which he was received by the ordinary people of Naha. There was a kind of intimacy and acceptance expressed toward the doctor, not the well-nigh complete rejection which has sometimes been portrayed.[148]

Postscript

The Bettelheim family left Hong Kong in August, 1854, and by February of the following year their ship, the "Sophia Burbage," had reached Bermuda, where she stopped for repairs. The Bettelheims decided to see the United States, so transferred to a ship bound for New York. They soon became very fond of America and decided to take up residence permanently.

Bettelheim's articles in the "Independent" newspaper of New York City, April 5 to 12, 1855, pleaded:

> "Dear Friends, let me tell you, what I ask of you, properly considered, is not that you should commence a new work in Japan, but that you may please to help me continue and extend my labors already carried on in a Japanese Principality for the last eight or nine years -labors, too, which under God, have been abundantly blessed."[149]

It was his idea to continue his efforts at translation of the scripture into Japanese, and he hoped eventually to return to Japan under another sponsorship. He presented his case to a group of New York clergymen, and Dr. Nathan Bangs of the Methodist Church investigated his request. Plans were started to raise five thousand dollars. Churches were asked to open their pulpits to the committee established for this purpose, its secretary being Dr. Bettelheim.

The plan was evidently not eminently successful, for Bettelheim moved to Illinois, and on December 18, 1860, he was ordained a minister by the Presbytery of Chicago (Old School).[150] He was appointed later on an evangelist to the destitute of Livingston County, Illinois. But for a time he worked in Chicago on a revision of his translations, assisted by a native Japanese (probably Niijima Jo, later the famous founder of Doshisha University in Kyoto, Japan) who was studying in that city,

Bettelheim served parishes in Pontiac, St. Anne and Cayuga, Illinois, and on August 16, 1862, he enlisted at Helena, Arkansas, in the 106th Regiment, Illinois Volunteer Infantry, as a surgeon with the rank of major. He participated in the siege of Vicksburg and was present at the capture of Little Rock.[151]

Following the Civil War, Bettelheim opened a drug store at Odell, Illinois, and devoted much time to lecturing on Japan and Ryukyu. In February, 1868, the family moved to Brookfield, Missouri, and on February 9, 1870, Bettelheim passed away, having been stricken with pneumonia.

A monument in memory of Dr. Bettelheim was erected in 1926 near the Gokoku Temple where the family had lived during their years in Ryukyu. The monument commemorated the eightieth anniversary of their landing. It had embedded in its base stones from each country where Bettelheim had lived. The monument was destroyed during the Battle for Okinawa in 1945, but it was restored in 1954, the hundredth anniversary of Bettelheim's departure from Okinawa. It is to be seen today just inside the entrance to the Gokoku Temple.

CONCLUSION

The Catholic Witness

The only Christian missionary effort of record in the Ryukyu Islands to precede that which is related in the foregoing pages of this volume was that of Fr. Juan de Los Angeles Rueda, a Spanish Dominican missionary. He was shipwrecked on the island of Ishigaki in the southern Ryukyus on the way to attempt a re-entry into the main islands of Japan from the Philippine Islands in about the year 1624. His story, the account of his activities and the results of his brief labors preceding his martyrdom I have related in a previous volume.[1]

The second such effort was that which is related above, including the pioneering work of Fr. Theodore Augustine Forcade of the Seminary of the Society of Foreign Missions, a society of French secular priests with their financial base of operations for Chinese missions in Macao.

The lack of fruit in the two phases of this second effort, one between 1844 and 1848, and one during the years 1855 and 1860 herein recounted, led to the abandonment of the Roman Catholic mission work in Ryukyu in 1862. Catholic mission activity was then not started again in Okinawa until 1931, at which time two priests of the Canadian Franciscan Province, Maxime Schiller and Peter Baptist Charbonneau, took up residence in Naha. The Catholics were forced out in 1938 by the increased anti-foreign sentiment of the 1930s prior to World War II. By 1938 the Catholic community numbered 128 persons, but being led entirely by foreign priests who were ordered out by the Papal Internuncio as the world situation deteriorated and local opposition to the foreign priests increased, the priests departed Okinawa.[2]

The extensive post-World War II work of Roman Catholics in the Ryukyu Islands began on September 5, 1947, just four days after the islands were officially opened to missionaries. There appears to have been no special historical connection between the entry of Frs. Felix Ley and Raymond Alban into Amami Oshima on that date and the pre-war ministry of the Canadian priests. In March of 1947, the Capucian Fathers of St. Joseph Parish in Detroit, Michigan, received a request from Rome to send missionaries to the Ryukyu Islands. At the same time Bishop Apolinaris Baumgartner of the Capucian order of Guam was made Supervisor of the Ryukyu District. Frs. Felix Ley and Raymond Bartoldus were sent by the Capucian Order to the Ryukyu Islands.

The work thus begun led to the greatly expanded ministry of Roman Catholics which is carried forward in the Ryukyus today.[3] During the first ten years of the labor of Frs. Ley and Bartoldus, twelve more missionary priests were added to the mission and thirteen churches and several institutions were completed.

The Protestant Witness

A Protestant work, which was somewhat inspired by the work of Bettelheim in the 1840s and 1850s, was begun in Naha in 1891. A wealthy Scottish lady, Mrs. Robert Allen of Glasgow, remembered on the occasion of a trip to Japan that she had, as a girl, contributed to the work of the British Seaman's Mission through her Sunday School offerings. Upon meeting Dr. Robert Thomson of the American Baptist Missionary Union in the Kobe Union Church, she inquired about the status of Christian activities in Okinawa. On being informed that there was no organized Christian activity there, she offered to support the beginning of a new work in the Ryukyus.

The agreement of Dr. Thomson to send a Japanese evangelist and pastor to Okinawa also led to the willingness of Mrs. Allen, wife of a wealthy shipbuilder of Glasgow, to finance a "Gospel Ship" for the Inland Sea of Japan. This was a project very much on the heart of Dr. Thomson. As Mrs. Allen expressed it, "If you will help me realize my desire for the Liu-Chiuans to hear the gospel, I will help bring about a ship for the Inland Sea."[4] It was thus that a plan began to be developed for a Christian witness to begin once more in Okinawa, and it was related closely with a plan to evangelize the islands of the Inland Sea of Japan.

The missionaries of the Baptist Missionary Union, meeting in Yokohama, unanimously approved the plan in the following words:

> Resolved: That this Conference approves most heartily the undertaking of work in the Liu-Chiu Islands to be supported by the money given by Mrs. Allan for this purpose.[5]

A young evangelist, Michinosuke Hara, moved to Okinawa, arriving with his family on December 20, 1891. He opened a mission in Naha which was soon well-attended. Meetings held by the mission were far more hopeful than the attempts made by Bettelheim many years before. Early in 1892 services conducted with the help of Thomson saw three to four hundred people in attendance. Though there were perhaps only a dozen people who during that first year confessed their faith in Christ and were baptised, yet it was a far more hopeful response than any which greeted the missionaries of mid-19th Century in Okinawa.

The subsequent work of Methodists, who sent pastors to Okinawa beginning in 1892, recognized the pioneering labors of Bettelheim. For some time in the early 20th Century their mission was called the "Bettelheim Memorial Mission" by the missionaries resident in Okinawa.

In this way, the approximately twenty Protestant churches which were established in the first four decades of the 20th Century remembered the importance of the ministry carried on by the first Protestant missionary sent to Okinawa.

The medical contributions which were made by Bettelheim to the practice of mid-19th Century physicians have been recognized in the 20th Century. A recent book by a descendent of Dr. Kijin Nakachi, an Okinawan physician who learned much from Bettelheim, pays tribute to these contributions. In particular, note is made of the introduction of cow-pox vaccines during a time of a severe small-pox epidemic. [6]

Bible translations of the gospels and portions of the epistles of the New Testament made by Bettelheim were reintroduced to Japan in 1977 by the Japan Bible Society. The first two weeks of June were promoted as "Weeks of Bible Reading," and special hand-made copies of Bettelheim's translations were available to scholars intent upon recovering some of the dialect of Okinawa of one hundred thirty years before. It must not be forgotten in this connection that one of the great values of Bible translation in many lands is the permanent record thus made of vocabulary and idioms of speech which might otherwise be totally lost to a given culture. Gospels of John with a special cover adorned with Bettelheim's translation of John, chapter one, were presented to all attending the Bible exhibitions and special Bible lectures were sponsored by the Japan Bible Society.

The labors of Bettelheim in the fields of Western medicine and Bible translation have borne fruit through the years since his departure and are alive today. His importunity in pursuing his evangelistic work does not today detract from his continuing significant and lasting contribution to the practice of medicine, to linguistic studies and to the continuing witness to the gospel of Christ throughout the Ryukyu Islands.

Notes
Author's Preface

[1] Edward E. Bollinger, (Pasadena: William Carey Library, 1983), 284 pp.

[2] *Bettelheim: A Study of the First Protestant Missionary to the Island Kingdom, 1846-1854,* (Unpublished Ph.D. Thesis, Univ. of Colorado, 1969), p. 1.

[3] Mgr. Theodore-Augustin Forcade, *Le Premiere Missionaire Catholique du Japon au XIX siecle* (The First Catholic Missionary to Japan of the 19th Century), (Lyon: Bureau of Catholic Missions, 1885), 201 pp.

[4] Apostolic Missionary F. Marnas, *La Religion de Jesus Christ Ressuscitee au Japan* (The Religion of Jesus Christ Revived in Japan), (Paris-Lyon: Delhomme et Briquet, ed., 1896), 432 pp.

Introduction

[1] George H. Kerr, *Okinawa: The History of an Island People* (Tokyo: Charles E. Tuttle Co, 1960) p.285.

[2] Edward E. Bollinger, *The Cross and the Floating Dragon,* (Pasadena: William Carey Press, 1983), p. 11.

[3] Edwin O. Reischauer and John K. Fairbank, *East Asia: The Great Tradition,* (Boston: Houghton Mifflin Co., 1960), pp. 596, 597.

[4] Yoshihiko Teruya, *Bettelheim: A Study of the First Protestant Missionary to the Island Kingdom, 1846-1854,* (Unpublished Ph.D. Thesis, University of Colorado, 1969), pp. 155, 156.

[5] *Ibid.,* p. 389.

[6] Otis Carey, *History of Christianity in Japan (Two Volumes in One),* (Tokyo: Charles E. Tuttle Co., 1976). Vol. I, pp. 272, 278.

[7] *Ibid.,* p. 279.

[8] *Ibid.,* p. 278.

[9] *Ibid.,* p. 282.

The Protestant Pioneer

[1] George H. Kerr, *Okinawa: The History of an Island People,* (Tokyo: Charles E. Tuttle Co., 1960), p. 287.

[2] Robert A. Thomson, "Glimpses of the Liu-Chiu Islands," *Gleanings,* Vol. 5, No. 4, March, 1899, p.3.

[3] Hattori Danjiro, *Okinawa Kiristokyoo Shiwa* (Talks on Okinawa Christian History), (Tokyo: Mishusha Printing, 1968), p. 20.

[4] *Account of a Voyage of Discovery to the West Coast of Corea and the Great Loo-Choo Island, and Voyage of His Majesty's Ship Alceste to China, Corea, and the Island of Lewchew with an Account of Her Shipwreck.*

[5] Kerr, note 10, p. 481.

[6] Quoted in Kerr, p. 257.

[7] Kerr, p. 261.

[8] *Ibid.,* p. 265.

[9] *Ibid.,* p. 270.

[10] Hattori, p. 47.

[11] Also called the "The Loo Choo Naval Mission"

[12] Earl R. Bull, "Trials of the Trail Blazer, Bettelheim," *The Japan Evangelist,* Vol. 32 (1925), No. 2, p. 52.

[13] *Loc. cit.*

[14] Bull, p. 53.

[15] *Loc. cit.*

[16] Bull, p. 54.

[17] *Loc. cit.*

[18] Teruya Yoshihiko, *Bettelheim: A Study of the First Protestant Missionary to the Island Kingdom, 1846-1854,* (Unpublished Ph.D. Thesis, University of Colorado, 1969), p. 1.

[19] Bull, p. 55.

[20] Teruya, p. 14.

[21] *Ibid.,* p. 17.

[22]"Letter from Dr. Bettelheim," *Chinese Repository,* Vol. XIX, No. 1, January, 1850, p. 19.

[23]*Ibid.,* p. 20.

[24]*Chinese Repository,* Vol. XIX, No. 1, P. 22.

[25]*Ibid.,* p. 23.

[26]Teruya, p. 36.

[27]*Chinese Repository,* Vol. XIX, No. 1, p. 28.

[28]*Chinese Repository,* Vol. XIX, No. 1, pp. 31, 32.

[29]Teruya, p. 23.

[30]*Ibid.,* p. 27.

[31]*Chinese Repository,* Vol. XIX, No. 1, p. 36.

[32]*Op. Cit.,* p. 37.

[33]*Chinese Repository,* Vol. XIX, No. 1, p. 37.

[34]Teruya, pp. 74, 75.

[35]*Chinese Repository,* Vol. XIX, No. 1, p. 38.

[36]*Loc. cit.*

[37]*Chinese Repository,* Vol. XIX, No. 1, p. 39.

[38]Kerr, p. 291.

[39]W. G. Beasley, *Great Britain and the Opening of Japan, 1843-1858,* (London: Luzac and Co, Ltd., 1951), p. 82.

[40]Quoted from official government correspondence in Teruya, p. 42.

[41]Teruya, p. 83.

[42]*Loc. cit.*

[43]*Ibid.,* p. 98.

[44]*Chinese Repository,* Vol. XIX, No. 1, p. 40.

[45]Teruya, p. 120.

[46]*Ibid.,* p. 122.

[47]*Loc. cit.*

[48]Kerr, p. 285.

[49]Otis Carey, *A History of Christianity in Japan,* (Charles E. Tuttle, Tokyo, 1976), pp. 267, 268, 276-278.

[50] *Ibid.*, p. 260.
[51] Carey, p. 267.
[52] *Ibid.*, pp. 267, 268.
[53] Carey, pp. 270, 271.
[54] *Chinese Repository,* Vol. XIX, No. 1, p. 41.
[55] Teruya, p. 143.
[56] Hattori, p. 37.
[57] *Chinese Repository,* Vol XIX, No. 1, p. 41.
[58] *Ibid.*, p. 43.
[59] Teruya, p. 146.
[60] *Loc. cit.*
[61] *Chinese Repository,* Vol. XIX, No. 1, p. 46.
[62] *Ibid.*, p. 47.
[63] *The Report of the Loochoo Naval Mission for 1848*, p. 6, quoted in Teruya, p. 161.
[64] Teruya, p. 162.
[65] *Ibid.*, p. 164.
[66] *Chinese Repository,* Vol. XIX, No. 1, p. 48.
[67] Teruya, pp. 148, 149.
[68] *Ibid.*, p. 149.
[69] *Chinese Repository,* Vol. XIX, No. 2, p. 60.
[70] *Ibid.*, p. 58.
[71] *Chinese Repository,* Vol. XIX, No. 2, p. 60.
[72] *Ibid.*, pp. 61, 62.
[73] *Chinese Repository,* Vol. XIX, No. 2, p. 63.
[74] Beasley, p. 78.
[75] *Chinese Repository,* Vol. XIX, No. 2, p. 65.
[76] Beasley, p. 79.
[77] *Chinese Repository,* Vol. XIX, No. 2, p. 67.
[78] Teruya, pp. 155, 156.

[79]*Loc. cit.*
[80]Carey, pp. 266-70.
[81]Teruya, pp. 218-20.
[82]*Chinese Repository,* Vol. XXI, No. 1, January, 1852, pp. 30, 31.
[83]Teruya, pp. 250, 251.
[84]Beasley, p. 81.
[85]Teruya, p. 252.
[86]*Ibid.,* p. 253
[87]Teruya, p. 255.
[88]Kerr, p. 286.
[89]Teruya, p. 277.
[90]*Ibid.,* p. 280.
[91]Kerr, p. 288.
[92]Teruya, p. 387.
[93]*Ibid.,* p. 299.
[94]*Chinese Repository,* Vol. XXI, No. 1, p. 36.
[95]Teruya, p. 270.
[96]*Chinese Repository,* Vol. XXI, No. 1, p. 31.
[97]*Ibid.,* p. 32.
[98]Teruya, p. 271.
[99]*Ibid.,* p. 273.
[100]Beasley, pp. 81, 82.
[101]Teruya, p. 307.
[102]Beasley, pp. 80-82.
[103]Teruya, p. 312.
[104]Hattori, p. 37.
[105]Teruya, p. 317.
[106]*Loc. cit.*
[107]*Chinese Repository,* Vol. XIX, No. 2 (Feb., 1850), p. 82.
[108]*Loc. cit.*

[109]*Ibid.,* p. 83.
[110]*Chinese Repository,* Vol. XIX, No. 2, p. 83.
[111]Quoted in Teruya, p. 320.
[112]Hattori, pp. 29, 30.
[113]Teruya, p. 322.
[114]*Ibid.,* p. 323.
[115]*Chinese Repository,* Vol. XIX, No. 2, pp. 75, 76.
[116]Teruya, p. 325.
[117]Bull, "Trials," p. 58.
[118]Teruya, p. 328.
[119]*Ibid.,* pp. 329, 330.
[120]Teruya, p. 335.
[121]*Ibid.,* p. 341.
[122]Carey, Vol. 2, p. 29.
[123]*Ibid.,* pp. 85, 86.
[124]Teruya, p. 345.
[125]Kerr, p. 295.
[126]Hattori, p. 62.
[127]*Ibid.,* p. 63.
[128]Kerr, p. 305.
[129]*Ibid.,* p. 306.
[130]Teruya, p. 349.

[131]*Commodore Perry's Visit to Okinawa: Selections from "Narrative of the Expedition of an American Squadron to the China Seas and Japan,"* ed. Seisho Hokama, (Tokyo: Kenkyusha, 1975), p. 166.

[132]*Ibid.,* p. 170.
[133]Hattori, p. 66.
[134]Kerr, p. 322.
[135]Teruya, p. 369.
[136]*Ibid.,* p. 377.

[137] Teruya, p. 371.

[138] *Ibid.*, p. 378.

[139] Hattori, p. 56.

[140] *Loc. cit.*

[141] Hattori, p. 56.

[142] Kerr, pp. 279-341.

[143] *Op. cit.*, p. 313.

[144] Teruya, p. 361.

[145] *Ibid.*, p. 389.

[146] Hattori, p. 52.

[147] Quoted in Teruya, p. 359.

[148] Hattori, p. 76.

[149] Bull, "Trials," p. 91.

[150] *Loc. cit.*

[151] Bull, p. 92.

CONCLUSION

[1] "The Cross and the Floating Dragon," pp. 1-16.

[2] *Habataki* (Sound of Wings), (Naha: Twenty-Fifth Anniversary Executive Committee, Naha Diocese, 1974), p. 4.

[3] *Op. Cit.*

[4] Robert Thomson, "Christian Work in the Liu-Chiu Islands," *The Christian Movement in Japan, 1909*, (Tokyo: Methodist Publishing House, 1909), p. 204.

[5] Robert Thomson, "Glimpses of the Liu-Chiu Islands," *Gleanings*, Vol. 5, No. 4, March, 1899, p. 6.

[6] Yoshio Nakadomari, *Dr. Kijin Nakachi*, (Minamihara, Okinawa: Daido Printing Co., Ltd., pp. 19-23.

Bibliography

Bettelheim, Bernard Jean. "Letter from Dr. Bettelheim." *Chinese Repository,* Vol. XIX, No. 1, January, 1850, pp. 17-49.

Bettelheim, Bernard Jean. "Letter from Dr. Bettelheim." *Chinese Repository,* Vol. XIX, No. 2, February, 1850, pp. 57-90.

Bettelheim, Bernard Jean. "Letter from Dr. Bettelheim." *Chinese Repository,* Vol. XXI, No. 1, January, 1852, pp. 8-42.

Beasley, William G. *Great Britain and the Opening of Japan, 1834-1858.* London: Luzac and Co., Ltd., 1951, pp. 71-82.

Bollinger, Edward E. *The Cross and the Floating Dragon.* Pasadena: The William Carey Library, 1983. 284 pp.

Bull, Earl R. "Trials of the Trail-Blazer, Bettelheim." *The Japan Evangelist.* Vol. XXXII, No. 2, February, 1925, pp. 51-59.

Carey, Otis. *History of Christianity in Japan* (Two Volumes in One). Tokyo: Charles E. Tuttle, 1976. Vol. I, 423 pp. Vol. II, 355 pp.

Forcade, Theodore-Augustine. *Le Premiere Missionaire Catholique du Japon au XIX siecle* (The First Catholic Missionary to Japan of the 19th Century). Lyon: Bureau of Catholic Missions, 1885. 201 pp.

Habataki (Sound of Wings). Naha: Twenty-Fifth Anniversary Executive Committee, Naha Diocese, 1974. Roman Catholic Church. 154 pp.

Hattori, Danjiro. *Okinawa Kiristokyoo Shiwa.* (Talks on Okinawa Christian History). Tokyo: Mishusha Printing, 1968. 209 pp.

Hokama, Seisho, ed. *Commodore Perry's Visit to Okinawa: Selections from "Narrative of the Expedition of an American Squadron to the China Seas and Japan."* Tokyo: Kenkyusha, 1975. 428 pp.

Kerr, George H. *Okinawa: The History of an Island People.* Tokyo: Charles E. Tuttle Co, 1960. 472 pp.

Marnas, F. *La Religion de Jesus Christ Ressuscitee au Japan* (The Religion of Jesus Christ Revived in Japan). Paris: Lyon: Delhomme et Briquet, ed., 1896. 432 pp.

Nakadomari, Yoshio. *Dr. Kijin Nakachi.* Minamihara,Okinawa: Daido Printing Co., Ltd., 1968. 92 pp.

Reischauer, Edwin O. and Fairbanks, John K. *East Asia: The Great Tradition.* Boston: Houghton Mifflin Co., 1960. 674 pp.

Teruya, Yoshihiko. *Bettelheim: A Study of the First Protestant Missionary to the Island Kingdom, 1846-1854.* Unpublished Ph.D. Thesis, University of Colorado, 1969. 389 pp.

Thompson, Robert. "Christian Work in the Liu-Chiu Islands," *The Christian Movement in Japan, 1909.* Tokyo: Methodist Publishing House, 1909, pp. 204-207.

Thomson, Robert A. "Glimpses of the Liu-Chiu Islands," *Gleanings,* Vol 5, No. 4, March, 1899, pp. 2-11.

About the Author

EDWARD E. BOLLINGER is a retired American Baptist missionary who came to Japan in 1951, serving first in the Osaka area until 1955, and then in Okinawa from 1955 to 1985. His ministry has been evangelism and church planting. He is a native of Kingman, Arizona, and received his B.A. degree from the University of Arizona in Classical Literature. He earned the Bachelor of Divinity degree from Northern Baptist Seminary of Chicago in 1943. He served for three years, 1943-46, as a U.S. Navy chaplain in the Pacific theatre. From 1946 to 1950 he was pastor of the Harvard Park Baptist Church of Springfield, Illinois.

The author was awarded the Master of Arts degree by the American Baptist Seminary of the West and the Graduate Theological Union in 1971, for his original work on Saion, Okinawa's foremost philosopher and statesman of the pre-modern period. He is the author of *Saion: Okinawa's Sage Reformer* (1975), *Reflections East and West* (1978) (both published overseas) and *The Cross and the Floating Dragon* (1983) published by William Carey Library.

Judson College of Elgin, Illinois, conferred upon the author the honorary degree of Doctor of Divinity in 1973.

Since retirement in 1985, the author has served as an interim pastor at the First Baptist Church, Santa Clara, California, as Regional Evangelist for the American Baptist Churches of the West, and as Minister of Visitation for the First Baptist Church of Sacramento, California.